NIGHT TRAIN
TO ODESA

COVERING THE HUMAN
COST OF RUSSIA'S WAR

Jen Stout

First published in hardback in Great Britain in 2024
by Polygon, an imprint of Birlinn Ltd

Birlinn Ltd
West Newington House
10 Newington Road
Edinburgh
EH9 1QS

9 8 7 6 5 4 3 2

www.polygonbooks.co.uk

ISBN 978 1 84697 647 6
EBOOK ISBN 978 1 78885 638 6

British Library Cataloguing-in-Publication Data
A catalogue record for this book is available on
request from the British Library.

Typeset in Bembo Book MT Pro by The Foundry, Edinburgh
Printed and bound in Great Britain by Clays Ltd, Elcograf S.p.A.

CONTENTS

Author's note | vi
Map | viii

PART ONE

Russia to Romania

November 2021–March 2022 | 1

PART TWO

Odesa, Kharkiv, Dnipro

April–June 2022 | 57

PART THREE

Lviv, Kyiv, Frontlines

October–November 2022 | 145

PART FOUR

Donbas

February–April 2023 | 223

Epilogue | 275
Acknowledgements | 277

AUTHOR'S NOTE

In Ukraine I spoke with people in Russian, English, and occasionally in Surzhyk, a dialect which combines Ukrainian and Russian. In this book I use Ukrainian toponyms and names, except when people preferred to be known by the Russian version of their name. I've used Russian transliteration when describing text or words that were in Russian.

For all those fighting so hard to make things better.

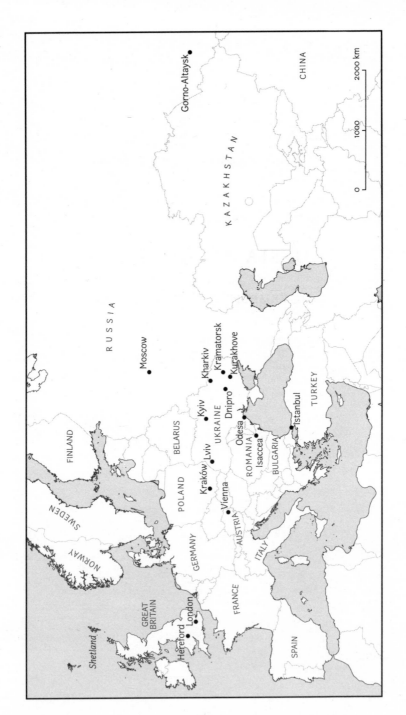

VIII

PART ONE

RUSSIA TO ROMANIA

NOVEMBER 2021–MARCH 2022

CHAPTER ONE

I CRANED MY NECK to see the news programme playing on the TV at the end of the bar. It was the same fever-pitch propaganda they'd been churning out for weeks now. On every state-controlled channel, claims of 'genocide' in Donbas, claims that Ukraine was full of Nazis, ran incessantly.

And there were no other news channels in Russia now.

On my phone screen, though, I could follow, through Western outlets, the massive troop build-up, Russia's vast army moving into position on Ukraine's border. I could read the warnings of an imminent invasion. But here in Moscow, these were dismissed as hysterical Western hype.

Next to me sat Andrei, a regular at the bar. He travelled for work, and I liked to hear his stories about distant parts of Russia I hoped to see. An easy-going, quiet type.

'You know I might have to leave,' I said, still looking at the TV.

'Why would you leave?' he shot back. His voice was suddenly clipped, angry. 'Russia's not doing anything. It's all Ukraine, ramping things up, Ukrainian *Nazis*.'

I looked at him, astonished, as he went on about how terrible Ukraine was, what a badly run and corrupt country. I eventually interrupted to ask when he'd been there.

'Well, shit. Why would I go there?' he muttered.

'You've never *been* to Ukraine?'

He stared at me. 'So what? Have you?'

'Yes,' I said, wishing at this point that I *was* in Ukraine. 'It's beautiful. Nice people.'

'It's a regime,' he snapped. 'Fascists.'

It was so out of character I thought he might just be winding me up.

'Come on,' I said. 'Are you serious? That's just propaganda – you're repeating what the TV says!'

And his retort, spoken into his pint glass as he avoided my eyes, summed everything up.

'Yeah, well. Your side is propaganda too.'

It had been a rough sea crossing when I left Shetland for Russia a few months earlier. Force six southwesterly, driving rain and poor visibility. A *day o' dirt*, we'd say.

From the ferry, the lights of Lerwick, blurry through the rain-streaked porthole, glimmered and danced, then faded into the darkness. I'd waited what felt like all my adult life for this. Not leaving Shetland; I'd done that enough times. But moving to Russia.

It began as an escape, at fifteen: a high-school class I actually wanted to attend, a whole new alphabet and syntax I couldn't get enough of, a teacher who encouraged me.

Russian snared me. I'd say later that I must have spoken it in a past life; I couldn't find any other way to explain it. With a huge fundraising effort, our teacher took the small class to St Petersburg for a week, and my mind was blown. I watched the ice floes moving down the Neva, felt a fizzle of satisfaction pronouncing the instrumental case correctly to get lemon in my tea; I was fleetingly so *happy*. I decided, on that trip, that I'd come back to this place. I'd sit exams, go to university, become fluent, become a correspondent.

It was a nice dream. I did get a place in a Russian Studies

department, but the £1,500 fee for the year abroad was well beyond my means, and in our third year my classmates set off for Perm without me. I switched to Sociology, graduated, and found a job teaching English in the Ural Mountains. But weeks before I was due to leave, my mother fell ill. A year of hospitals and hospices and fading hope followed. I made many more plans to get to Russia, but they always required at least some money, and I didn't have any of that. It wasn't until my late twenties that I got into journalism, with a bursary for training in Liverpool, a local newspaper job in a small Scottish town, and a slew of credit cards to keep my head above water.

I wanted, most of all, to learn things. To learn everything. I wanted to live in other countries, especially eastern European countries, and study languages – Polish, Ukrainian, Czech – I wanted to learn about the history and culture, the art and politics of other countries – I wanted all of it, desperately.

What I did not want was to spend my days producing TV news, which is what I'd ended up doing, and which was driving me slowly and completely insane. I went to Ukraine for a week in 2018 and loved it – I'd have moved there in a flash. In 2019 I was offered a bursary for a two-year Erasmus MSc that would take me to Estonia, Ukraine, Russia and Glasgow. I was over the moon until I read the small print. The bursary had been cut back, and for nine months I'd have no income at all. I'd come across this so many times that it was hard not to be bitter about these 'opportunities' that actually required the cushion of parental cash. A little golden carrot dangled then yanked away. I had also listened to too many interviews with people who invariably spoke in the same middle-class accent and who'd made it as foreign correspondents. 'Oh, I just went,' they'd say, the sheer grating insouciance of it setting my teeth on edge.

Shortly after the Erasmus setback another chink of light

appeared. The Alfa Fellowship in Moscow was nine months long and fully-funded, and it was open to Brits, Americans and Germans who spoke Russian, early in their careers in business or journalism. It felt too good to be true when I was accepted. Things were finally, finally falling into place. Covid descended and our departure was delayed for more than a year but I waited patiently, moving up to Shetland to work on the BBC radio station. I'd waited fifteen years; this was nothing.

'Moscow? That'll be . . . *interesting*,' almost everybody said, with a raised eyebrow, when I announced the news. Or more bluntly, 'You won't do any journalism there, will you?'

We knew it might be tricky, the dozen or so who'd made it this far on the fellowship. As our departure date approached and preparatory meetings increased, we were issued with strict instructions not to get involved in politics, not to attend demonstrations or cover them; there was training in digital security and recognising surveillance. But despite the Kremlin's paranoid turn and the crackdown on dissent, there were still many foreigners working in Russia. We would simply have to tread carefully. As for the war, I don't think any of us really believed it would happen. It seemed too absurd.

It was late November 2021 when I left Shetland. It felt good to go by sea, at least the first leg. You feel the departure, the break from a very certain world, when you sail away from it slowly. The islands are, to an extent, their own world, a close-knit community of 22,000. When I was growing up on Fair Isle, the little island between Orkney and Shetland, it really was my whole world, a place where I felt deeply known and rooted — but living on mainland Shetland had come to feel like that too, in part due to working for the local BBC station, broadcasting to all those kitchens and living rooms at teatime every day. To some newcomers Shetland feels stifling, and certainly during the pandemic we'd been more cut off than usual, but it's not insular. The long history of islanders travelling far and wide stretches back many centuries – a seafaring place with connections all over the world. Almost everyone goes away. Most return in the end. So my going to Moscow was not particularly unusual, except perhaps for the timing.

Moscow was slushy with grey ice when I arrived a few days later, the temperature just starting to drop below zero. Soon it would plummet, lacing my eyelashes with frost and sending me skidding across the black ice.

I tried to find my bearings, to understand the mood of Moscow. Other cities have a character, as if trying to communicate something. I came to feel that Moscow is indifferent. It is a machine, too vast to comprehend, on a scale which long ago exceeded the human. Not only because of its sprawling size – a veritable super-city – but the size of everything *within* it, the sense that much of its cityscape is the fevered dream of an insane tyrant, a man who thought he was creating the world anew, starting on the Moskva River. Stalinism seems here more vivid and grotesque, more pompous and enormous, than anywhere else in the dictator's former empire. It is exemplified in that strange combination of prissy grandeur and overbearing cruelty of the famous Seven Sisters, those hulking, wedding-cake skyscrapers. And yet I'd stand transfixed below them, hating them, unable to tear my eyes away.

I felt like a speck. The traffic, thundering across six lanes, would slow reluctantly to a halt, and I'd watch old ladies hobble fast to reach the other side of this chasm before the green light started to flash and the cars revved harshly across the striped lines. My bus would hurtle down to the vast expanse of Lubyanka Square, flanked by the hulking headquarters of the security services which have terrorised the population in various guises for more than a century.

The scale of Moscow can of course be beautiful, if unsettling. From the Sparrow Hills, with the towering sci-fi symmetry of the state university behind and the city spread out icy below, it is a pinch-yourself wonder. But traces of an older city, one of people-sized streets and charm, are hard to find. Eroded by the bombast of Soviet planning and hubris, old Moscow was then further butchered by the unfettered gangster capitalism that followed the fall of the Soviet Union, a period of terrible poverty, corruption, and architectural crimes which made the city uglier and harsher; gave parts of it a kind of *Bladerunner* aesthetic. Grey and forbidding tall buildings were inserted onto the cityscape, with glass-fronted American sports bars at the bottom and old people in rags begging outside.

All the talk when I arrived was of 'foreign agents' – *inoagenty*. The Kremlin published a weekly blacklist of the people it had deemed as being under foreign influence, often journalists and activists. Those listed would have to include a long screed of text in screaming capital letters on every public statement they made, even personal comments on Facebook. You would see little notes of congratulations on a friend's wedding accompanied by a block of ridiculous text: 'THIS MATERIAL WAS CREATED OR DISTRIBUTED BY A FOREIGN MEDIA PERFORMING THE FUNCTIONS OF A FOREIGN AGENT.'

It was farcical, but everyone affected knew this was no joke; things were only moving in one direction. One morning, riot police lined the streets, rows and rows of them silent behind metal shields. Down in the metro, dark-uniformed policemen with their cartoonish peaked caps scanned the faces and phones of likely suspects. Commuters reacted as though nothing was happening, as if they literally could not see the police. I walked to the other end of the platform, out of their sight, and asked someone what was going on. He just stared at me and edged away.

I recalled something a young man said to me on a short visit in 2016, about the uneasy and unspoken pact made after the huge 2011-12 protests were crushed by police. Mass rallies were over, protest criminalised – but Moscow was made more pleasant, with art galleries and amenities, and rising living standards for the middle classes. 'Now we just get on with things,' my acquaintance, who'd taken part in the protests, had muttered. 'Maybe it's fine.'

Few would be so cynically explicit: for wealthy Muscovites life was good, the city centre sparkling, champagne flowing freely. And this was true not only for native Russians but also for the (admittedly now diminished) contingent of foreigners. They could live like little kings here. With some honourable exceptions I found the expats pretty unpleasant: arrogant, rude about Russians, and used to getting everything they wanted. The city's massive underclass of migrants from central Asia, crisscrossing the icy streets day and night on delivery bikes, could bring them anything – 'Anything', a young American man stressed to me, eyes wide.

The kindness and sincerity I'd known in Russia before were there, though, if you dug a bit. An old friend, a brilliant artist, was still in Moscow, trying to use art to force society to reflect on its darkness, trying to build hope and decency. She was a conscientious and sweet person who felt powerless to stop what was happening in her country, and she wasn't alone. There was the wry affection of my Russian teachers, proud Muscovite women in their fifties, who helped us settle in. And at the Anglican church one evening, as I drank tea after the service, two women swooped in: one towering over me, the other no taller than a child. They introduced themselves as Nina and

Tanya, and we talked for a long time, about poetry and God and nature. They sparkled with that Slavic combination of humour, intellect and disarming warmth.

Nina took my face in both her hands as we said goodbye: 'Zhenya, Zhenya! How glad we are to meet you!'

It was the most intense little moment of love in an otherwise trying week, and I walked through the slush back to my solitary room, glowing. But I must have taken the number down wrong. I never managed to find them again.

I so often thought, during these strange months in Moscow, of Peter Pomerantsev's phrase, 'Nothing is true and everything is possible.' Although the book of this title was written about the more hedonistic, oil-boom years in Russia, it still perfectly captured what I kept coming up against: a seemingly infinite cynicism. While in 2016 we had thrown around the term 'post-truth' as we grappled with Trump and Brexit and armchair conspiracy theorists, here in Moscow it seemed deeply ingrained. In a lecture on Russian history – our fellowship began with three months of studying – one afternoon in a hot airless room, a former minister turned professor provided a real insight into the mindset of those in charge of Russia today. The wild fantasy, the twisting of history, the paranoia and insecurity; it was all there.

The picture he painted was of a uniquely cohesive and harmonious society in which not a single ethnic or religious minority had ever been mistreated. I heard this claim all the time, and it was extraordinary and ridiculous given that both the Russian Empire and the Soviet Union were deeply expansionist, ruling territories that covered nearly a sixth of the world's surface, won through centuries of violence and annexation.

But we were being corrected.

'No religious wars were ever unleashed on Russian territory!' he said, jabbing a finger for emphasis. 'Russia has *never* implemented a forceful assimilation policy, never destroyed the ethnic and cultural identities of peoples whose territories became part of the Russian state.'

There were, he conceded briefly, deportations of minorities like the Crimean Tatars, under Stalin. 'Deportations aren't an honourable part of our history.' We moved swiftly on.

It was the touchiness of people who put forward these arguments that struck me most. They'd lash back against criticism of Russia *before you even made it*; you could sit there silently, raise one eyebrow, and let it unfold. 'You say we had no referendum in Crimea,' the professor blustered later, as the daylight faded outside and the stifling classroom air got that bit more tense, 'but what did *you* do in Kosovo? There was no referendum there, whereas we had 97 per cent in favour!'

This is rubbish, but it didn't matter – he knew it was rubbish. It was a game: someone lies to your face, knowingly, with a smirk, and waits for you to take the bait.

'*You* invaded Iraq!' he crowed, looking triumphantly around the room, arms folded. I knew we'd get to this trump card sooner or later.

'Who, me? What, personally?' I quipped, an attempt to lighten the mood, but the truth was this stuff really annoyed me: I'd marched against the Iraq war; I wasn't a champion of the British state by any stretch of the imagination. Christ, I wasn't even that keen on my own country being *part* of the British state. But it was pointless. Never argue with a finger-jabber, I remembered, too late.

Meanwhile, the professor was ending with a 'topical' point. 'The Ukrainian government talks of colonisation,' he said, contemptuously, 'but Krushchev was Ukrainian!' He looked pleased with this. (It is also not true.)

'Anyway,' he finished lamely, suddenly bored, 'but what happened, happened.' And that was that.

Crimea, colonialism, the Russian empire – the list of topics that couldn't be discussed without a defensive, furious argument was long. Another was 'those so-called LGBTs, of whom we have none in Russia', as one of my teachers put it. Also off the table was anything to do with the Second World War, linked inextricably to the next looming war, which was simply another noble fight against fascism. That didn't make any logical sense, and it didn't have to; only the emotional resonance mattered. And there were bucketloads of that.

My naive and wildly optimistic plan on arrival in Moscow had been to persuade the editor of a famous investigative newspaper to let me join their staff for the six-month internship period of my programme, which would start in March 2022. In high school I'd followed the work of *Novaya Gazeta*'s correspondent Anna Politkovskaya. She was murdered in 2006 but the independent newspaper was still going somehow. Working there, even briefly as an intern, was my longest-held dream.

But I'd waited too long to get here. You could feel the last gasp of anything independent, a slow strangulation. People were becoming wary of Western journalists. Even writing something as innocuous as a good-news story about a foster village I'd always wanted to visit was now impossible; initially keen, the charity changed their minds. They wrote to me, stiffly formal. 'In the current political situation, we don't want any articles from you.' I tried not to hear the 'you' being stressed, but I could understand why it would be. Especially for charities with ties to the West, staying off the 'foreign agent' list was the main priority.

The danger of surveillance, as well as the unspoken rules and limits we shouldn't cross, were constant topics among foreigners at least. Russians, though, didn't want to talk about any of this. Just as people pointedly didn't look up at the looming Lubyanka building; just as shoppers ignored the policemen in balaclavas surrounding some minor protest.

At a party, after a fair amount of whisky, my neighbour at the table jerked his head to indicate a sullen, strange man who'd been sitting alone throughout the festivities, eyeballing everyone and sipping sparkling water. 'His dad was KGB,' my new friend whispered, 'and he didn't fall far from the tree.'

It was hard to distinguish paranoia from reality. Not because, as an older woman asserted one day, I was brainwashed into believing bad things about Russia, but because of the small, throwaway comments, the little gestures, the conversations that abruptly ended when the wrong topic came up.

A gregarious Muscovite I knew, who vehemently opposed the government, was holding forth in his flat one afternoon about the corruption surrounding him, the death of civic society and the looming war with Ukraine.

'I'll go and fight,' he insisted, eyes alight, 'on the Ukrainian side.'

I hesitated for a minute, wondering how, and whether, to phrase what I wanted to say.

'Look – you have a lot of Western visitors, you say all this stuff . . . Aren't you worried they're listening to you?'

It was a selfish question, in part; I was worried I was in a bugged flat, talking about opposition politics, which I was absolutely not allowed to be doing.

He paused for a moment and then made this small gesture I'd seen others do: a little flick of the eye, a backwards glance to a corner of the room.

'I don't care any more,' he spat.

A few weeks later, when I was no longer in the country, I heard he'd been arrested at a protest against the war, and later released. Writing to me afterwards, he gleefully related how he'd sung the Ukrainian national anthem in the police wagon that conveyed him to the station. Nothing has changed since Soviet times, my wayward friend was always saying, 'except now it's worse'.

Late February 2022. The snow had started to melt. I walked a small, flatulent dog around the half-frozen slosh covering Petrovsky Park. I was house-sitting, happy to escape the four blank walls of my bedsit. It was a strange limbo: no point in planning anything, no idea what the next day would bring, but at the same time, I was in a sort of idiotic denial. There couldn't possibly be a war. Could there?

The state TV channels were showing footage of 'grateful' refugees – confused and terrified Ukrainians – disembarking from trains in Russia, being handed soup and tea, little children and old women from Donetsk, escaping what the anchors said was shelling by the Ukrainian side. The *casus belli* on repeat: *genocide, genocide, genocide.*

'I feel sick, all the time,' a friend said, as we messaged late at night. It wasn't just us; I saw, online, the posts of many anti-war Russians I'd met, all talking about this lingering nausea. We all watched the maps and diagrams of the troops' build-up along the border, so close to Kharkiv. I checked in with a journalist I knew there. 'We're doing as well as can be expected,' he replied, tersely. 'Forty kilometres away from all that.'

Two days later the bizarre spectacle of Putin's security-council meeting aired on TV. The small dog and I watched from the sofa. When Valentina Matviyenko, the sole woman on the council, made a tearful and nonsensical speech about genocide in Ukraine, I realised she might actually believe it. And somehow that was scarier. Bottomless cynicism is one thing, lies to suit any occasion, but this teary woman seemed genuinely to think the claims were true.

There was no genocide; it was a lie. But that didn't matter; as someone had said to me, sniffily, that same week, 'You have your truth, we have ours.' Where can you possibly go from there?

CHAPTER TWO

THE OVERNIGHT PLANE FROM Moscow descended over a mountainous landscape as the morning light was breaking through the clouds. I looked out at the white peaks and tracts of forest, at the town of Gorno-Altaysk coming into view, rubbing my blurry eyes. I hadn't slept all night. I hadn't really slept for weeks.

It was the morning of 24 February. Over two thousand miles and four time zones away in Kyiv, the first explosions had already sounded.

We stepped onto the runway in breathtaking cold, digging around for our phones as we walked towards the small airport building. White-fringed forest and mountains on all sides, the sky a blank white; the world felt silenced, shrouded somehow. As we got closer to the building and signal appeared on mobiles, our chatter died. Some people gasped. I came to a halt and stood still on the tarmac, oblivious to my surroundings, reading the messages and news updates, my heart in a painful vice. 'They're bombing us from planes,' a Kharkiv friend had written, and it took me long, stupid seconds to understand the message.

Despite the volatile situation, it had been decided that this trip, part of our fellowship programme, would go ahead. Four days in Siberia, down where the Russian, Chinese, Kazakhstani and Mongolian borders converge. We'd be going to natural wonders and monasteries and ancient sites, and normally I'd have been thrilled. All I wanted to do now, as I stood on the tarmac trying to figure out which streets in Kharkiv were already rubble, was get back on the plane and leave Russia for good. I wasn't alone in this view, among our group. But for now we had no choice but to follow the itinerary.

The time in Siberia was surreal. My skin prickled as we sat down to yet another sumptuous meal in opulent surroundings. Luxury hotels are not my cup of tea anyway, but in the context of what was happening in Ukraine it all felt utterly wrong. At meal times, we would greet each other holding up our phones – 'Have you seen?' – another atrocity, another shelling of residential blocks in Kyiv, in Kharkiv – 'Yes, we've seen.'

The two young Russian women who'd organised the trip and ran the programme were trying to put a brave face on it but I could see they, too, had been crying sometimes. But the wealthy holiday-makers around us seemed unconcerned. A woman at the next table one morning looked at us contemptuously as we discussed the war, and flicked back her long, perfect black hair.

'It's a targeted special operation,' she said, practically rolling her eyes. 'Soon it will all be over.'

I stared at her, wondering if she could possibly be seeing what we were seeing on our media feeds. I was trying hard not to hate her, too. Failing.

All over Europe airspace was closing to Russian planes. We started to discuss land routes: Estonia, Georgia, Finland. On the last night of the trip the missive finally arrived by email. The fellowship was suspended with immediate effect, and we'd leave as soon as possible.

But before the early flight to Moscow the next morning, things had changed again. 'As you'll have seen in the news, flight options out of Moscow are rapidly decreasing,' they wrote. The New York team was moving heaven and earth to get us on the next available flight – we'd have to go via Istanbul, but there was a chance Turkey would close down that option, too.

There was a long delay at Gorno-Altaysk airport. I stood in the queue to board, watching a game show play on the TV fixed to the wall. It showed a stage with a row of people, hands raised in salute, cosplaying Second World War soldiers in khaki uniforms, red stars pinned to their berets, standing proud and erect. A big kitschy red star was suspended above them. Former glories re-enacted, the cult of victory and strength, and everywhere that appalling phrase: 'We can repeat!' All that sad, twisted anti-history, taking over the country like mass hysteria. It felt fitting this was playing as we shuffled out into the snow.

The nine-hour flight lasted forever, but then the final hours in Moscow seemed to speed by in a confusion of packing and goodbyes. By 1 March I was in Istanbul airport. It was six days into Russia's full-scale invasion and I was waiting to fly on to Vienna, leaning against my over-stuffed suitcase and scanning the departure boards wearily. A hand-painted t-shirt caught my eye. The young woman stood in the queue a few feet away, the queue I couldn't be bothered joining yet though we were both boarding the same plane. She had long blonde hair and was gripping a blue Ukrainian passport tightly, her small frame swamped in a man's white t-shirt. On it she'd painted, in shaky blue and yellow letters, 'STOP PUTIN NOW'.

People were giving her sympathetic nods and grimaces. One even stopped to give her a hug. I stood up, went over and said hello in Russian. She looked surprised.

'*Otkuda vy?*' I asked quietly – Where are you from?

She held my gaze, sombre, and there was a long pause. Then, 'Kharkiv,' with heavy significance, as though willing me to understand.

'You're serious?' I said. 'You're really from Kharkiv?'

She nodded slowly, and I explained how I'd been there a few

years ago, how I had friends in the city, was trying to keep in contact with them. How I hadn't thought of anything but Kharkiv for six days. And now – meeting her. I couldn't believe it.

Her name was Yana. She gripped my hands, almost imploring. 'They're bombing the city! Bombing it from planes!'

Yana and her boyfriend had been on a skiing holiday when the invasion began. He stood silently by her side as we talked about Kharkiv, that big industrial university city a stone's throw from the Russian border. And then I asked where she was going, after Vienna.

'Home,' she said defiantly, as though daring me to challenge her.

'How?'

'We'll get straight on a train in Vienna, to the Hungarian border. Then cross into Ukraine, and I guess just . . . get a taxi to Kharkiv.'

She knew, I think, that she wouldn't make it. But I understood why she was so adamant.

I found myself standing behind Yana in the passport control queue a few hours later. I tapped her on the shoulder, putting on what I hoped was an encouraging smile. She turned round, and I faltered. Yana was crying, great shuddering sobs; the tears running down her face and onto the white t-shirt. 'What?' I asked, shocked. She couldn't speak but motioned towards her boyfriend, who was stony-faced.

He held up his phone, turning it sideways. A video flickered, a CCTV quality, and I instantly recognised the tall, splendid facade of the regional council headquarters on Kharkiv's vast Freedom Square. The hazy image shook and then in a fraction of a second a little shard of something seemed to fall from the sky. The entire building blew up, a ball of white fire and then red dusty smoke engulfing it, and I flinched, inadvertently disturbing the quiet Viennese order around us by swearing loudly. Cold dread and shock flooded my body. He played it again. In case I hadn't understood. In the aftermath of the rocket strike the smoke billowed black over the square and a car emerged, skidding and weaving to a halt.

Yana's boyfriend put the phone away. I hugged her, hoping I could calm her down. We had to wait long agonising minutes to pass through the passport booth. 'Stop it,' he hissed at her. 'What can you do from here? Nothing!'

But she kept sobbing, leaning heavily on him, fellow passengers casting curious or worried glances in the shuffling silence of the border queue. 'We'll make it,' he was saying now, sounding unconvinced himself. 'We'll get home.'

In the sedate surroundings of Vienna I felt I was going slightly mad. Immersed in all that horror and worry, I looked up from the phone's screen to find myself on tree-lined streets, already sweet with blossom. I watched contented people stroll and shop in the sunshine, and I wanted to shout at them. It was like that strange period after a death when it feels offensive that the world is carrying on as normal.

My first stop was a research institute on the canal, where a Ukrainian friend Lidiia worked and where, by coincidence, Harvard historian Serhii Plokhy was giving a talk that same night. I arrived with all my luggage, exhausted. The atmosphere was grave, Plokhy's usual affability subdued, and Lidiia was holding back tears when I found her.

Lidiia is a force of nature: a tall, striking, dark-haired woman with an uncanny ability to look elegantly poised in any situation, while at the same time being constantly on the verge of some outpouring of emotion – joy, sorrow, deep empathy, hilarity.

She'd been working non-stop the past week, staying up late into the night trying to source bulletproof vests, night-vision goggles and all the other things Ukraine didn't have, throwing herself into a frantic pace of activity to keep the panic at bay. The equipment she wanted to buy had sold out overnight and prices were astronomical.

'Whatever you get, I can take it to the border at least,' I promised that evening, somewhat rashly. I didn't have a firm plan yet, but I would soon, and I knew it wouldn't involve going home.

Despite the heavy atmosphere at Plokhy's talk, I could relax a little there. The institute always felt like a haven: the book-lined rooms, dark wood and hushed atmosphere; the steep winding staircase up to a warren of offices where visiting fellows of the institute – journalists and researchers working on central and east European topics – spend their lucky months. I associate it, from previous visits, with bottles of pear brandy and dusty foreign books; with the view from office windows of old-fashioned trams scraping along the bridge in the evening light.

I woke early the next morning with not the faintest idea what country I was in, whose sofa this was, and why I felt so anxious. I let the jigsaw pieces descend one by one and realised, after a minute, that it was Lidiia's voice that had woken me, through the crack under the bathroom door: urgent, low conversation, anguished. I saw my stuff piled near the kitchen table and finally noticed her partner, still asleep, on the bed nearby.

Lidiia was, of course, speaking to her family in Ukraine in the bathroom, trying not to wake us. When she emerged she looked distraught, and I tried to comfort her, but there was nothing to say. I'd already read the news: planes had bombed the centre of Kharkiv; footage showed the national university on fire. Borodianka, near Kyiv, had been pummelled by artillery. High-rise flats blackened and smoking, at least forty killed. 'Kharkiv may fall,' anchors intoned grimly at the end of newsreels showing appalling devastation. Lidiia's family were in the west of Ukraine, which was slightly safer, but of course nowhere was safe from this onslaught.

I spent three days in Vienna, whittling down what belongings I still had until they fitted into a hiking rucksack, and made a plan. I wanted to start working. The flood of messages expressing sympathy made me feel a fraud: our hurried departure hadn't exactly been a hardship compared to what others were going through. Yes, I'd had to pack quickly and leave some things behind. So what?

But people knew, I suppose, how desperately I'd wanted that chance to be a correspondent in Moscow. I kept responding, trying not to sound tetchy, telling them that none of that really mattered now. I wouldn't have stayed in that country. With every piece of awful news that filtered through I hated the Russian regime more, and I was happy to be out. I just didn't intend to go home.

In a spare room kindly offered up by a couple through a Shetland connection, I scrolled compulsively late into the night, absorbing the images of tank convoys, rocket strikes and night-time skies above the cities lit up orange. I read about thermobaric bombs. These explode twice – the first strike dispersing a cloud of high-explosive fuel, the second creating a fireball, destroying bunkers and buildings. I read about what this does to the human body. The oxygen is sucked from the air; eardrums burst, lungs rupture. Within the blast, people are vaporised. The day before I'd left Russia, CNN reporters had spotted the rocket launchers creeping over the border south of Belgorod. Towards Kharkiv.

I couldn't stop worrying about people I knew there. One I'd met in Prague five years earlier, on a journalism training programme with Lidiia. Roman had co-founded an independent media company, providing important coverage of the unrest stirred up by the Kremlin in 2014. He was idealistic and stubborn, but mischievous under his serious facade. Last time I'd seen him, at his cosy house in the city, he and his wife Viktoria had plied me with homemade cherry liqueur and *salo* – delectable cured pork fat – before I took the night train to Kyiv. That had been in 2018, an impromptu holiday during a cold winter: I remembered the snow falling as I got on the train, settling on the paving stones of the platform, and the cold air full of coal smoke. That nostalgic smell. Admittedly, I could be a little romantic about Kharkiv. But it was easy to be so; an actor, Bohdan, had shown me around, painting a picture of a city layered with history, full of ideas and art.

Then there was Ivanna. In 2018 I'd been keen to meet activists and journalists, to learn more about Ukraine, and had found Ivanna, a cultural project manager and activist who took me to meet the Kharkiv LGBTQ+ group. It was an eye-opening and humbling discussion. It was still too dangerous, at that time, to stage a Pride march in the city; far-right groups could attack them with relative impunity.

I tried not to pester them all with worried messages, instead using Facebook's 'last active' status to reassure myself. Bohdan, somehow, was finding time to compose poems in between the bombardments and the mad dashes to deliver bread. But this is the thing with Kharkiv – when the volunteers keeping people alive also happen to be the writers, the poets and the playwrights, the descriptions they produce will be powerful.

By now our group from Moscow had scattered far and wide, most going back to Germany, the UK and the US. But Bennett, my big American buddy, had now reached Warsaw, where he was buying a sleeping bag and other kit he needed to cover the war. We chatted long into the evening, sharing what information we'd gleaned from colleagues and online channels about how to proceed, where to go first. I decided to try one of the border points, in Poland or Romania, and report on the refugee exodus.

Sitting on the floor surrounded by half-packed bags, I read reports from the big crossing points: Siret in Romania, Medyka in Poland. Thousands were crossing every hour – by car and train, but so many on foot, dragging suitcases behind them in the snow. There was very little time to decide where to go, and I needed local knowledge. By amazing coincidence the former Fair Isle nurse Elena now lived in Romania with her husband. We talked online, and I was unsurprised to hear that she'd thrown herself into the voluntary efforts to help Ukrainians escape the war.

Elena was a godsend, full of ideas and advice. It was she who suggested the southeast – Isaccea, in the Dobrogea region. Way down near the Black Sea, this small river port formed a border crossing and the closest point of exit for the thousands fleeing cities in the south of Ukraine. It seemed to have little news coverage. I pored over the map, trying to familiarise myself with this part of southeast Europe.

The network of people was so extensive by now that cars and trucks were taking aid and people to the border day and night, and Elena quickly found me a lift from Bucharest airport the next day. I booked a flight I could barely afford, and started sounding out acquaintances at BBC outlets. They were keen – they knew me, I spoke Russian, and I was going to be in a place none of their correspondents had covered yet. At the last minute, a TV producer, another freelancer who'd left Moscow too, decided to join me.

On the last night in Vienna I met Lidiia in a bar on a cobbled street for an emotional goodbye, and a handover of the flak jackets she wanted to send into Ukraine. God knows how she'd managed to find them, or how much they cost, but back at the flat my host – ex-army – prodded them and declared them incapable of stopping a sniper's bullet. My heart sank. But we parcelled them up in a big blue Ikea holdall, bound the whole thing up in tape, and propped it in the hallway next to my equally tatty rucksack. I had absolutely no idea what was ahead.

CHAPTER THREE

HALF A MILLION PEOPLE had fled Ukraine by 1 March, an extraordinary flood of human beings moving west. By the time I arrived in Isaccea, the UN put it at more than a million. At each big transit point I passed through – Vienna train station, Bucharest airport – there were boxes of sandwiches and piles of nappies, signs offering help in Ukrainian and Russian, volunteers with name badges greeting the new arrivals. The magnitude was hard to comprehend. Where would all these people go? How would they manage?

Heading in the other direction – *towards* Ukraine – were the aid workers and reporters, the volunteers and evangelists, the cat-rescuers and the mercenaries, and I was in this counter-flow, though taking a slightly circuitous route. In Bucharest airport I dragged the unwieldy bag of body armour through to arrivals, where a Romanian volunteer almost wordlessly greeted me and took the big parcel. It was destined for people Lidiia knew, but would pass through the hands of many volunteers first – all these informal networks helping to provide Ukrainian troops with equipment.

It felt so paltry, such a small offering. A few flak jackets with plates of questionable quality, being physically carried like pass-the-parcel through Europe, to people facing real shells, real bullets. I was thinking, too, about my own options if I did go to Ukraine: if this was all Lidiia and her networks had been able to muster up, how on earth would I get body armour? I'd done a cursory search in Vienna and found that, as she'd said, this stuff was like gold dust now.

Isaccea is a small town, ramshackle, and dwarfed by the tall electricity pylons assembled on its outskirts. To get there we drove for twenty minutes from our B&B in Somova, through a landscape of vineyards and villages. The Măcin Mountains were still covered with snow, while on the other side of the road, the great Danube ran somewhere behind the haze of tall, yellow reeds. The river here is half a mile wide; Orlivka, the Ukrainian border post on the other side, was faintly visible.

We hit the ground running in Isaccea. It was 5 March, just over a week since the invasion, and more than a thousand people had arrived each day since then, through this one small crossing. Marian, a local businessman, was part of the team organising volunteers at the port, and from our first meeting he helped us in every way he could. A sincere and seemingly inexhaustible man, humorous and diplomatic, he was a central figure in all this, and I decided almost at once to trust him. It was a very good move.

The fact that it wasn't total chaos at the port was down to locals like Marian as much as the authorities. The place was heaving. Normally a handful of lorries and cars would be queuing for this ferry, which crossed the river every couple of hours. Now, the boat was packed with people every time it arrived; in the middle of the night, early in the morning, still they came, the firemen told us.

Lined up alongside the hot-dog stand and the municipal bins were people holding pieces of paper and cardboard with Ukrainian names written shakily in biro or felt-tip. 'Ania', one said simply, held by a stocky young man in a puffer jacket. I talked to Adela, a retired chemistry teacher in her seventies. She had the collar of her sheepskin coat turned up, trying to keep out the cold, and in her gloved hands were a single red rose and a shaker of salt, a symbol of welcome. Her son held up a sheet of paper: 'Maria Gladysheva'. They'd got the woman's name from an NGO and hoped to find this Maria and take her back to the capital to stay with them.

Adela talked about this as if it were entirely normal, a twelve-hour round trip to find a total stranger. Certainly she felt it was the *right* thing to do.

There were a lot of stories like this at the port, I'd find – good people doing the right thing without thinking twice – but there were also rumours of trafficking taking place in the chaos of border posts. That this was a problem was evident from the signs taped to the railings near the tea tent. In Russian, they read, 'Be careful who you get in a car with.'

My TV friend had a small camera set up for filming, and we moved through the throng – aid-agency workers in tabards, volunteer translators in hi vis vests and Ukrainians waiting to hear where they'd be sent. Everyone bundled up in winter coats, holding paper cups of tea. There was a bitter wind – worse out on the water, of course, and when the ferry arrived, the crowd of people packed on to the open deck looked freezing.

The *Noviodunum*, a big, slow barge with only a small Portakabin for shelter, slid alongside the pontoon, and the ramp clanked into place. Ferry workers slid the blue railing back, and people began to pour off, squeezing between the articulated lorries and cars and onto the ramp. One worker in a bobble hat helped to lift children over the gap between barge and ramp. There were almost no men: under martial law, only women, children and the elderly could leave Ukraine now. Old women had blankets wrapped tightly around their shoulders; children were walking stiffly in many layers of clothing. And such meagre luggage

– little cabin suitcases, canvas holdalls, even plastic shopping bags hinting at a hurried, last-minute departure.

Firefighters walked into the crowd, smiling and offering to take heavier bags or carry babies, and medics hovered near their ambulances up on the pier, ready to jump into action. As the boatload of people trudged up the concrete slope to the welcome tent, I filmed from the railings above, feeling uncomfortably voyeuristic. They looked scared, stressed, unsure what to expect.

Queues of people and cars formed quickly and volunteers moved around handing out soup, sandwiches and SIM cards. We crouched at car windows to talk to people, and I began by apologising for speaking Russian and not Ukrainian, but nobody minded. Almost all were Russian speakers from Mykolaiv or Odesa. This, of course, does not mean they had any affinity with Russia – it's just the language many speak in southern and eastern Ukraine. A nuance many Russian chauvinists seemed unable to grasp.

People were, by and large, keen to speak – and to show me what they'd escaped. One woman pulled up a photo on her phone: a grey sky, choppy sea, and on the horizon the faint outlines of ships. Russian warships. 'Five of them appeared the other day,' she said, still sounding stunned. We talked to resolute old sailors railing against their old 'comrades'; young mums with crying, clinging babies; harassed port officials and firemen. It was getting dark when we left, and 2,000 people had come through Isaccea since daybreak – but still the *Noviodunum* chugged across the river, still people came, the lights of the river port providing their first view of the Romanian shore.

The B&B in Somova was perched high above the reed beds that stretched nearly three miles out to the Danube itself. Down a steep slope at the end of the garden, another little river snaked along – one of the countless tributaries, streams, and backwaters that made up the delta. In the distance, on the far shore of the Danube, was Ukraine.

Marian, the local organiser, messaged first thing in the morning: Would I like to come on a trip, talk to some refugees? Marian's group of volunteers was heading down to Sarichioi, a village on the edge of a large Black Sea lagoon where many families had been billeted. 'It's the biggest Lipovan village,' he said. 'Old Believers from Russia.'

Leaving behind the hills and the river delta, we drove south: flat fields as far as the eye could see, interrupted only by clusters of wind turbines and the steady march of pylons. Underneath the thawing snow, green grass poked through hopefully, though it was still barely above zero. I was given a brief history lesson as we went.

The past is not simple in Dobrogea. All those empires that came, ruled and fell: Roman, Byzantine, Bulgarian, Ottoman; all those waves of migrants, exiles and settlers. Particularly out on the marshes, it's the Lipovans that made their mark. Descendants of seventeenth-century Old Believers who fled persecution under Tsar Nicholas I, they maintained distinct and self-contained communities. Marian pointed out the houses as we entered Sarichioi: the pretty carved woodwork framing doors and windows was painted the same sky-blue, the walls fresh and white.

Casa Filip may have been new, but it too was in this Lipovan style: thatched reed roofs, neatly trimmed, and delicately carved gables and fencework with lovely blue shutters on every window. The guesthouse, explained owner Alex Filip, was now housing sixteen refugees, and today there was a fundraiser, a community meal they were cooking. A further seventy Ukrainians were housed in the village and many more in the settlements scattered around the lagoon. They were surprised to find these 'Russians' welcoming them, Alex said with amusement. 'Maybe we can show the world it's OK to live together,' he said, optimistically.

I was recording, holding up a lapel mic attached to my phone, having suddenly thought what a nice radio piece this would make. In the communal kitchen I interviewed Alyona – 'our Masterchef!' – and the other women preparing Ukrainian food: borscht, beetroot *shuba* salad, *deruny* – fried potato pancakes – and *varenyky*, sweet and savoury little dumplings. The women were all from Odesa Oblast[1] which stretches from the big port city itself, west through Bessarabia to the Danube river. One woman, Angela, was on the verge of tears as she spoke, talking about all the help Romanians had given them, how overwhelming it was.

'But we really hope we can go back to our homes –' and her voice failed. She looked down at the worktop, blinking, and began rolling balls of soft cheese in herbs. 'It will all work out,' she muttered, as though talking to herself. 'Everything's going to be good. We will return. Everything will be OK.'

They all had to keep talking about the future instead of the present situation. 'When we can go home, we'll invite these people to *our* homes, so they can see our country, our Ukraine,' another woman said.

Kids ran in and out, pinching things to eat, and the women went back and forth to the big dining room with plates of food, receiving bursts of applause from the Romanian guests seated at the long tables. I got a bowl of soup and sat down next to Florin Sava, a larger-than-life character in a bright striped jumper. We'd

---

1   Ukraine has twenty-four regions, called oblasts, most named for their capitals, which sometimes causes confusion – for instance, it was often reported that Kharkiv was liberated, but the city of Kharkiv never fell under occupation, only parts of the oblast surrounding it.

met at the port the day before, where he was volunteering with Marian's group. Fizzing with energy, he talked with a sense of awe about the sheer scale of the cross-border solidarity of the past eleven days.

'We are in touch with people from Braşov, from Constanţa – from Arad! Can you imagine! The other side of the country! People write to us: "I have a house, how can we help?"'

'Yesterday I drove a family to Varna [in Bulgaria], got back last night, and in Varna people were collecting donations, providing shelter, food, cash for gas. . .' He shook his head in wonder. 'This . . . *guy*,' he said contemptuously, meaning Putin, 'I don't know what's in his mind, but look, people have united in such a way, *in such a way,* that nothing can damage or affect this kind of unity. People get together with open minds, open hearts, contributing as best they can.'

Florin repeated what I'd heard many times since arriving here: that Dobrogea and the delta have at least fourteen nationalities – actually Florin increased this to eighteen – from Crimean Tatars, German colonists and Bulgarian settlers to Turks, Roma, Greeks and many more. (Sarichioi's name comes from the Turkish Sarıköy).

Florin's point was that this cash-strapped and overlooked corner of Romania was actually a place from which the rest of the continent could learn something. 'My neighbours are Turkish, Ukrainian, Italian, Macedonian: we join together and share a meal, talk politics, talk football of course, and share *feelings* – genuine feelings!'

And food helps, I suggested. 'Ah! Food!' he exclaimed happily, almost shouting. 'Food connects people! On an empty stomach you can say crazy things, but when you're full, happy, fed, you're relaxed, you feel open-minded.'

The EU here is a distant entity, Florin reminded me, delivering his verdict on Brussels: 'Tight shirts, fancy people, uptight asses.'

'But *this*!' He swept his hand out to encompass the room and its happy buzz of diners. 'This is the ground floor, the genuine reactions, open-minded people; this is the *real heart of Europe*, 100 per cent EU!'

He was almost bouncing up and down while delivering this impassioned speech, which ended with a call for all the EU offices to be relocated to Dobrogea – 'No, *really*,' he insisted – before pausing to reflect on how this society was changing as a result of the demands placed on it in recent days. This crisis, the flood of refugees and the war next door had brought unexpected benefits, Florin thought. The pandemic had done great damage to society here, as elsewhere. Fragmentation, isolation. 'In recent years people were moving against each other. Educated against uneducated, vaccinated against unvaccinated.'

He looked around with satisfaction at the strangers talking to each other over plates of Ukrainian food. 'But here we are,' he said, smiling broadly. 'Here we are!'

After a while Florin and the others began a meeting, so I walked down to the shore of the lagoon. After the manic pace of the last couple of weeks – indeed, after months of Moscow city life – I was struck by the peace of Sarichioi. The water's edge was only a few dusty streets away, past picturesque, decorated facades. I stood still in the road and listened to the blessed silence. I could only hear the wind, which blew stronger down on the shore of the lagoon – northerly still, it formed little crests to break on the gravelly sand. Lake Razim is so big I nearly mistook it for the sea, till I spotted the little plumes of smoke on the horizon. Spring-time fires to clear vegetation. The freshwater lagoon had once been a vast estuary, fed by canals and by the Sfântu Gheorghe, a distributary which splits from the Danube just east of Somova. Razim became a lagoon after it was dammed in the late 1970s as part of the regime's insane attempt to drain the whole delta for 'productive' agrarian land, the effects of which are still evident today.

More hints of Sarichioi's Lipovan identity were evident by the water: the side of a well was decorated with a picture of warriors in a boat, the words '*ATAMAN STEPAN RAZ*' written above. Undoubtedly this referred to the Russian Cossack rebel leader Stepan Razin, who challenged the Tsarist empire and was executed – dismembered, in fact – in Moscow in 1671.

That night more volunteers turned up at the Somova house: a Dutch-Romanian couple who, like so many, felt compelled to drive here and try to be useful, their car packed with humanitarian supplies. Much of my evening was spent crouched in the wardrobe with a duvet over my head as we recorded voiceover for the TV package. To our enormous relief, a contact at a big broadcaster had agreed to take the piece and pay a reasonable fee. Our plan, incredibly, was working.

From all over Europe the donations were arriving at border posts like Isaccea: an unpredictable, random flow of items, both useful and less so, which someone had to deal with. In the town on the morning of 7 March, that person was Mihaela Dan. I found her sitting at a trestle table in a marquee, surrounded by Post-it notes and bits of paper and empty coffee cups. I tried to interview her, with another volunteer translating, but she really didn't have time for journalists, understandably: her mobile phone rang incessantly. Chain-smoking and rubbing her tired eyes, Mihaela told me she had barely slept in days, and I believed her. The strain on everyone was tangible.

In a tent stacked with clothes and shoes, Adriana Susma, a young volunteer from Bucharest, attempted to maintain order. 'We're trying to sort them out into different categories,' she

said. 'So that we can identify what's in every box, because . . .
Well. . .' She made a slightly despairing gesture at the stack of
unmarked cardboard boxes, which only grew with every truck
arrival.

This critical flow of humanitarian supplies was entirely
contingent on people like Adriana, Mihaela and the many others
here unpacking and repacking trucks by hand late into the night.

One of the problems, Adriana said, was lack of communication
from donors: people just packed up a van or truck, drove
staggering distances, and arrived without warning in the middle
of the night. No wonder these women weren't able to go to bed.

I could see on social media that small vans were being sent,
mostly full of clothes, from as far as northern Scotland. It was
well-intentioned, but not efficient.

Over the next few days I worked at Isaccea's port, talking to
Ukrainians, taking photos, and reporting live over the phone
for BBC radio outlets. Our TV package had suddenly been
dropped – their own correspondent was 'doing the same story',
I read with incredulity – and we had to flog it to another outlet,
for a much lower rate that didn't begin to cover costs. Luckily I
much prefer writing for newspapers to the endless, grinding faff
of TV, and an email arrived from a Scottish Sunday paper which
wanted in-depth, on-the-ground reporting. It was the biggest
stroke of luck I had all year.

Thanks to Marian and his family, I was able to report from
Isaccea and the region for most of March, staying in his boat
repair workshop in the regional capital of Tulcea — they even
lent me a car to get back and forth to the port. It was ridiculously
kind.

I got to know the people working at the border. The cheery
couple running the hot-dog truck, my favourite Russian-
speaking translator Valentina, who'd touch my cheek, all

grandmotherly solicitude, always worried I'd catch a chill – while she herself stood for long hours in temperatures near freezing, without complaint. And Red Cross volunteers like Jacob, a firefighter who was so affected by the children coming across – 'they're scared of the unknown' – and the Adventist charity workers who'd approach with their giant trays of hot tea and sandwiches, insistent that journalists get a hot drink too.

One thing stands out in almost every interview I did with the new refugees coming across at Isaccea: their fury. While the paper wanted heart-rending stories of escape and despair, my interviewees wanted to tell me what a bastard Putin was, what a madman, what a piece of shit. It was the kind of eloquent rage I'd encounter all over Ukraine in the year to come: laced with sarcasm and swearing.

But of course they did have terrible stories. It's bad enough to pack overnight after the air-raid sirens and fear and frayed nerves got too much. But women from Mykolaiv had experienced a real hell, unimaginable to me. One, named Katya, described it as we talked outside the welfare tent. 'Every day we'd hear rockets, something blowing up, someone shooting, tanks. People were dying, homes burning.'

A city of ship-building and industry on the Southern Buh River on Ukraine's Black Sea coast, Mykolaiv was still holding out. From the first minutes of the invasion, 4 a.m. on 24 February, missiles and bombs rained down on this city of nearly half a million people, as troops approached from the east. But they hadn't managed to take it, which was the main reason Odesa had not fallen, either. Mykolaiv was the bulwark.

Katya's four-year-old son Maksym was playing with a toy train the Red Cross had given him. I asked how she explained it all to him.

'I don't,' she said sharply. 'I don't want my child to know about this.'

She'd told Maksym they were on a trip. But he was always asking questions, she said: unanswerable questions like 'Why is Mama crying?' or 'What was that bang?' or 'Where's Papa?'

They'd had to leave Maksym's dad behind. He was thirty-two and had joined the territorial defence.

Katya's sister had come along to help on the journey, though with clear reluctance: when I asked how she was feeling, Iryna, jaw set, said she felt 'militant', and guilty for 'abandoning' her country in its time of need.

In another car, Maryna was waiting, eating the hot sandwich she'd just been handed, a little dog nestled on her lap. She was thirty-six, with white-blond dreads and a little nose ring in the shape of a Playboy bunny.

The strikes, she said, had been close enough for the house to shake and the windows to ring on each impact, and it amused her how quickly she'd got used to it: '*Oh, explosions again, but at least they're in the sky . . .*' she laughed, bitterly.

'But then you understand it's coming closer, closer to your town, your home. Much scarier. You realise that to sit and wait to get blown up, to wait until your house is blown up . . .' She shrugged. 'You master your fear, gather up a few things. I took my one and only relative, my little dog.'

She had no family to travel with – 'I'm alone, an orphan, never had anyone,' she added, defiantly – and was going to a town near Bucharest where volunteers had accommodation for her.

The queue wasn't moving. We talked about Russians, those who refused to believe what was happening. Maryna watched their channels – 'monitoring', she called it – so she knew they weren't being shown the attacks on residential areas, the explosions in cities. 'But now Ukrainians are sending them stuff, over and over, so they can see. And bit by bit they understand.'

She'd seen the demonstrations being held in Moscow and had sympathy for those being sent to prison for their opposition to the war.

'In general, everyone is suffering, and we – ordinary people – what can we do? Nothing. We can only run away, become refugees asking our neighbours to take us in.'

Oleksandr, a retired sailor, stood by his big black Land Rover and told me he'd had tears in his eyes when he heard, that morning, from children who'd hidden under tables as bombs fell around them in Mykolaiv. What really set him off was a little boy saying, on reaching Romania, 'Mum, now nobody will bomb us!'

'Just awful,' said Oleksandr, gravely.

He was born in Crimea but moved to Odesa at fourteen. 'I've been to Russia many times, with relatives, for work, and it's like Kuchma said: Ukrainians and Russians are different. Nobody understood him then, but we *are* different: by mind, by understanding. By heart.'

The younger generation, he explained, choosing words carefully in his formal English, were also different to those who, like him, had been Soviet people. Oleksandr, now sixty-six, would have been in his thirties when Ukraine became independent. You could see the splits within families: while the older ones might be more equivocal about the fighting in the east of the country, more amenable to the Russian version of events, the younger ones had no such illusions.

'They say no, we are united, we're with Europe, we want a new life,' he said, smiling wryly.

'They don't want to go back to what you had?' I asked.

'Never!' he said, adamant. 'Never.'

Putin, he laughed, had 'united all Ukraine' – achieved what successive politicians and presidents had failed to do. At that moment in Odesa people were building the city's defences by hand – forming chains to pile sandbags high on the waterfront and around the city's statues and famous buildings. 'They are preparing the city,' said Oleksandr. 'They're saying, "We will not leave our place."'

It was a sentiment he shared. Firmly with his children's generation now, this former Soviet sailor was heading straight back to Odesa once he'd taken his grandson to Germany for medical treatment.

'It's my land,' he said, standing up slightly straighter. 'If *he* wants to bomb me, OK, I'll die in my house, but I won't leave.'

A Romanian customs official appeared with a declaration to fill in, and I thanked Oleksandr and wished him luck. It was sleeting again, and the ferry was moving back across the Danube towards us, lined with little figures pressed against the railings. The bitter cold, the Romanians kept saying, was unusual for this time of year. Early spring on the Black Sea coast should be much warmer, up in the high teens, not this miserable biting wind and snow.

Watching the barge approach, looking at the faces of kids cold and scared, wrapped in coats and blankets, I suddenly felt furiously angry, unable to do anything to really help, unable to control any element of this situation. I kicked the metal railing, stupidly, only achieving a bruised toe, and as I stood and rubbed it I thought how idiotic it was to be raging against the weather – the *weather*, which was indifferent to all this.

Boxes of gloves, hats and scarves ran along the blue railings that funnelled people towards the passport control booths, and there were toys too: one little girl was clutching a giant stuffed strawberry. She was laughing out loud because her mum, Nastya, was jumping up and down with her, singing a song. I stopped to speak to them. They'd packed and left in a matter of hours, she told me. They had hardly any luggage. 'But we're really sure we'll go home soon,' Nastya said brightly, looking at her beaming daughter. 'Right, *zayka*?'

It's a sweet, affectionate nickname – 'little hare'. *Mishka*, little mouse, she called her too. I asked Nastya a bit more about the situation in Odesa, but she was vague, and it was so clear she was trying to keep it together, not cry in front of her four-year-old. Ahead of us, a young woman with a tiny baby in a sling was trying to hold the fleecy blanket in place around her child and not drop her documents, while also dragging a big suitcase. A volunteer in hi-vis rushed to help her, and they moved off towards the tents. I wondered how she'd made it this far on her own. I went back to Marian's workshop, driving warily on the 'wrong' side of the road, and began a long evening of work: translating interviews, writing, pitching, and processing the hundreds of photos I'd taken.

On one of these long chilly days in Isaccea I'd eventually taken refuge in the volunteers' caravan, warming my frozen hands by its little heater. I started to transcribe interviews on my laptop but fell asleep, done in. Ten minutes later I was woken by the door bursting open, and in a flurry of wind and snow and chatter three women appeared, dragging bags behind them. Kateryna, her mother Maryna, and their neighbour Liudmyla, from Odesa, had been on that morning's ferry and had just made it through customs. They had nowhere to go, but volunteers had promised to find them temporary accommodation, so here they were, waiting.

We talked for an hour; they were surprised to find me there, a Russian-speaking Scot. All three were constantly on the verge of tears or laughter, or both at the same time: the sheer giddy relief of making it here, of being met with kindness and help instead of hostility. I liked them immediately, especially Liudmyla, who was so very Odesan with her gold-and-black beret and her wicked sense of humour. I offered to help in any way I could. For their part, they wanted to give me contacts in Odesa, if I did end up going there, though they were horrified by the idea.

CHAPTER FOUR

BY 12 MARCH THE flow of people at Isaccea had lessened to a steady trickle. Eighty-four thousand had crossed since the full-scale invasion began, most going on to other countries, but some remained in the local area, or went to the coastal city of Constanţa. The authorities, it was rumoured, wanted to open camps. Local volunteers like Marian were vehemently opposed to this. It was inhuman, a recipe for disaster, they thought. Much better for people to stay with locals, even if the arrangements were sometimes a little ad hoc.

One morning, with a radio report out of the way, I left Isaccea and drove inland, through the forested hills and towards the ancient Măcin Mountains, their still-snowy peaks soft, sunk under the weight of millions of years – these are the oldest mountains in Romania. I followed straight, dusty roads through grasslands to a small town called Jijila, where the Odesan women had been staying for a week.

In the kitchen, we talked as Liudmyla cooked borshch; talked about the war, of course. Russia had been attacking deep into western Ukraine, hitting Ivano-Frankivsk and Lutsk with missiles, and heavy fighting around Kyiv was continuing, the capital half-besieged. The world-famous Sviatohirsk Lavra monastery had been bombed. The news was relentless, and horrifying, and I could never figure out if hashing over it endlessly was cathartic or perhaps quite the opposite.

We sat down to eat with Lena, their Romanian host, getting by in a mix of English and Russian. The borshch was the best I'd ever eaten, full of chicken and cabbage and swirls of sour cream, and Liudmyla tried to give me second and third helpings as we spoke about how they might get to Germany.

Lena, who had two young children, explained that she had hosted several families already. I asked why. She was washing up, looking out the window at the yard where chickens were pecking about under the tree: a picture of quiet rural life.

'Because we might be next,' she said, so quietly I nearly missed it, and I realised she was crying. She wasn't the first person to voice this fear. Here, they really understood the danger Russia posed.

I drove home to Tulcea the long way, south around the mountains, making a detour to a monastery. It was a sunny day at last, and I wanted to be out in the hills, to be up high.

Izvorul Tămăduirii monastery is at the end of a gravel road, the scree slopes and peaks looming behind the whitewashed walls. I walked through the monastery grounds and up into the hills, through a grove of trees all dappled sunlight and birdsong, feeling peace settle in me quietly. The 'healing spring' after which the monastery is named was enclosed in a little house, and the late-afternoon sun lit up the paintings on the walls inside: vivid, colourful depictions of the saints, bearing scrolls of script. Shadows moved slowly across the pictures. The path became harder to follow as it climbed higher, and I scrambled the last stretch. A metal cross and a torn Romanian flag tied to a long stick marked the peak. The views were extraordinary: a chessboard of fields, brown, green and straw yellow, stretching off to another peak, much higher than this and white with snow. Looking west, past terraced brown hills, a towering, alien shape dominated the skyline: three great vertical legs surrounded by an intricate lattice of scaffolding and cranes. A new bridge was being built across the

Danube, to Brăila. From where I sat, through the long lens of my camera, it really did look like the structure had only recently landed on earth.

Below the rough rock of the Țuțuiatu peak I found a spot to lie down, took my heavy boots off, and stared up at the vivid blue sky. There is always a day in early spring when the sun seems brand new, seems to warm your skin in a way you'd forgotten, and in a way that feels so good, so *benevolent*. I closed my eyes and thought only of how that sunlight felt on my face, the sheer joy of it. And I thought of the joy and privilege of scrambling up a hill fast, of aching legs, of being high up, of being here. Here in this corner of Romania, where I never expected to end up, and which I now loved so much.

The sun was setting when I got back to the car, casting the softest light over the landscape: tall, pale grass and the wind shushing through it, a line of old wooden telegraph poles of uneven heights tapering off ahead. The brown bracken of the foothills was shaded deep purple in the sunset, and beyond it all such a perfect little mountain, gently rounded, its slopes and gullies picked out in snow which glowed in the last of the day's light.

My temporary home of Tulcea was a town of 73,000 people and many identities. It is, for the tourists who flock to the delta each year, the gateway to the fabled nature reserve located on a bend of the river where the Danube begins to branch out and split, where the marshes begin. The waterfront had a shabby, relaxed Black Sea feel to it, little leisure boats tied up alongside the fish restaurants and hotels. But when coming in by road, the impression was industrial: giant cooling towers of an alumina refinery belched greasy white clouds, and the port's big blue and yellow cranes loomed beyond. Harbours, ports, big infrastructure – these are some of my favourite things, and I'd watched it all whizz by from the passenger seat, wide-eyed, on my first day there.

But this little city, I found, had layers, contradictions. Up the steep hills Tulcea's streets wound, cobbled and charming, all the way to the grand Independence monument, a hundred limestone-clad steps leading to a seventy-foot granite obelisk, flanked by statues of a soldier and an eagle. From up here, behind the colossal 'TULCEA' letters hammered, Hollywood-style, into the slope, you could see it all: the sinuous curve of the river, a heavily laden barge moving slowly; a jumble of red-tiled rooftops, among them the golden domes of churches and the pale minaret of the Ottoman-era Azizyie Mosque. Tulcea may not be known as a tourist destination other than as jumping-off point for boat trips to the delta, but I thought it was truly beautiful, all the more so for being such a jumble of architectural styles, history and stories.

That same hilltop is home to a Roman fortress, too. This place has seen a lot of civilisation, and a lot of its opposite: war, massacres and siege. And now war had returned to this region. Standing up here I could look east, across the meandering river, towards Ukraine. The NATO bases nearby made people I'd been speaking to feel a little safer, but not entirely. They balked when I said I might leave this safe haven, might cross that border and cover the war. But I couldn't pretend that wasn't my plan.

At the port, someone had come up with the idea of tying cuddly toys to the railings of the ramp, so that when children disembarked they could take one, but unfortunately they'd been attached with cable ties, and I watched a Python-esque scene one morning as a well-meaning and increasingly desperate fireman hunched over a fluffy blue elephant, hacking at the plastic tie with a knife. A small child watched him, wide-eyed and holding her mother's hand tightly as floods of people tried to get past them with their luggage.

The cars coming off the ferry now had signs taped to them, usually printed or felt-tipped A4 sheets with the word *dety* – 'children'. We'd all heard the reports of Russian troops firing on civilian cars as they tried to flee. The signs were little white flags, requests for decency. But just a few days ago the Mariupol theatre had been deliberately targeted and half-destroyed, despite the tall letters painted on the ground outside, that same word. *DETY*.

What a desperate step to take, I thought as I took photos in the customs queue. A flimsy bit of paper taped to the rear windscreen, in the hope it might stay the hand of a soldier with an automatic rifle, or halt a tank lowering the barrel of its gun to aim. It's strange what gets you, and when. These little sheets of paper suddenly had me in tears, and I stalked off to the deserted end of the pier, embarrassed.

'Take some time off,' Marian and his wife Mihaela insisted – they who never seemed to stop working, neither at the boat business nor on the refugee effort. But one day they took me out on a boat Marian needed to test-run, with their son Costi, and I finally saw the delta. The waterways and lakes were still iced over in parts, that unseasonable cold clinging on, and the boat broke through with a strenuous cracking, creaking effort. There was no wind, the sky heavy and layered with clouds, and when the boat stopped I could hear my own breathing, the reeds rustling, and the strange calls of birds I'd never encountered before. Coming up to the village of Mila 23, I had to blink and blink before I could believe it – pelicans. Great rafts of pelicans, hanging out with the cormorants, heads tucked low and long orange bills reaching the water. To me they were fantastical, incredibly exotic; I took a thousand blurred pictures. To my Romanian friends they were just pelicans and I was losing the plot.

All that pleasant day in the delta, though, I struggled to relax. Without work as distraction all the worries came pouring in. I did finally check my phone after lunch and I read a news alert that made the floor lurch under my feet – a *New York Times* journalist had been shot near Kyiv. I excused myself, went outside to read further, thumb faltering over the screen, sure I was about to read the name of my friend Valerie. But it wasn't her. Brent Renaud, a filmmaker, had been shot by Russian forces in Irpin. He'd been carrying a *NYT* press card from an old assignment. Brent was one of the first journalists to be killed in this invasion; the next day, another team came under fire, and two more lost their lives.

Kharkiv was always in the news, and it was always awful, though of course the bigger picture – that the city, despite its proximity to Russia, remained in Ukrainian hands – was remarkable. So I worried about my friends there, but worried about them being hit by rockets rather than tortured under occupation.

From the office above the boat shop I rang Ivanna, the activist I'd met back in 2018 in Kharkiv. Her smiling face popped up, blurry on my laptop screen. She'd agreed to be interviewed for the newspaper. If I couldn't be there, I could at least report on the situation second-hand.

Ivanna is someone I consider heroic and someone who hates being called heroic. The things she had done in the last four weeks were extraordinary, but she told it all casually, with light irony.

On the night before the invasion, 23 February, she'd stayed up with a friend, drinking wine in the kitchen – an all-nighter, nearly – as they tried to reassure each other that it would be OK. She'd only been asleep an hour when it started: bombs, rockets, the early-morning invasion. Ivanna had bundled relatives into the car and drove, joining thousands of others trying to flee the city. She drove for thirteen hours, stopped for two, and then did another twenty-one hours on the road.

For a few weeks in western Ukraine, pitching in with the aid efforts, she shared a flat with seven other people. And then Ivanna drove all the way back, into a city under daily bombardment.

'I understand it seems a bit crazy,' she said, 'but this is my home. My friends, volunteers, they're tired, they need more help.'

I wasn't remotely surprised she'd done this. She confessed that her mother didn't actually know she'd returned to Kharkiv yet. 'She'd go crazy. I called her today, while I was walking down the street, and I prayed for it to be calm, because if she heard some explosions . . . Well, lucky me, it was ten minutes of calm, and she didn't realise!'

We were laughing together – *laughing* – at the absurdity. But she knew perfectly well what the stakes were. One of the first tasks had been supplying a neonatal unit, in a hospital hit heavily by the strikes. Women were giving birth in the basements.

'For me, the doctors, the medical workers, they're the most heroic people – the hospitals get bombed but they can't leave, they stay and help people. I thought, how can I just sit in a shelter being afraid? I have to do something.'

The postal service was still functioning, and it was a vital link for volunteers sending supplies around the country. She was often waiting in line there. Earlier that day, a postal centre was hit. Six people in the queue were killed.

I asked how she was coping with risks like this.

'I can't say I'm not worried about being shot. Being wounded. Of course. But it's like – this is our life now. You can die at any time. And you know. You know it.'

She lived close to Freedom Square and had watched, from western Ukraine, just as I had watched in Vienna airport, that footage of the regional headquarters being blown up. She'd burst into tears, but then almost immediately the phone rang – someone needing something, another urgent request – and she got on with it. There was no time for crying, for any despair.

But I was thinking of that place now, of Freedom Square, of the fantastical 1920s Derzhprom building I loved so much there, of Kharkiv. It was mad, but I wished I was there. Ivanna had told me about visiting a friend the other day, on the eighteenth storey of a high-rise, of going out onto the balcony to smoke. She could see the city, spread out before her.

'It was sunset, and at first glance everything's calm,' she said. 'But then you see the smoke, where a district has been bombed. It's this . . . mix of beauty and pain. Every moment.'

The following morning I heard from the Odesans I'd met in the caravan – they'd reached Berlin. It had been a group effort, with Romanian volunteers buying flights, a lift to Bucharest with English volunteers, and accommodation through a university friend of mine. It was a small triumph. They put me in touch with their neighbour so I'd have somewhere to stay if I did end up going to Odesa. I still wasn't sure. I didn't want to be the idiot journalist who walks unprepared into a war zone, a burden on others, getting in the way.

I went over and over it in my head, though. I could speak reasonable Russian, I'd been working as a journalist for seven years, desperate always to do precisely this kind of reporting. I knew Ukraine and had contacts all over the country. I wasn't going to sit on the border forever, and I absolutely wasn't going to go home. So in spare minutes upstairs in Marian's boat workshop, I was making enquiries – about flak jackets, about hostile environment training, about *funding* to do the training, which costs around £1,500. I joined Reporters Without Borders for their discounted insurance, got letters of commission and reference from editors and the NUJ and accreditation from the Ukrainian military. The obstacles seemed endless, but by late March I was making headway. Marian reckoned he could find a flak jacket despite the continent-wide shortage, and given his skill in procuring the impossible, I believed him.

But the biggest obstacle was my own doubt, which was echoed by some people I looked to for advice. 'Absolutely stupid idea,' said one. 'Reckless and selfish. Do not go,' warned another. They thought I didn't have enough experience of conflict reporting, that I was rushing into things.

One night I had a dream in which rockets rained down on a city, and I was hiding in a basement, wondering when they would ever stop, cursing my stupidity and the relentless nature of the explosions. I never dreamt about strikes later, when they were real and close; only this one nightmare, like a warning shot from my subconscious. 'Good,' I thought, when I woke up sweating. 'Pay attention.'

It wasn't long before Marian and I did go to Ukraine. Just for a day at first, just to Orlivka, directly across the river from Isaccea. Stuart, a businessman from York who'd been working hard on aid efforts, came too, the three of us squashed in to the cab of a delivery van. It was early in the morning and we were all a little apprehensive. Waiting to get through passport control, I had a stomach-churning moment as I remembered my own passport was full of Moscow stamps, Russian visas, and even a slip of paper with Moscow phone numbers on it. An emergency list I'd forgotten to throw away.

But the officials didn't seem to care, or perhaps didn't see. Marian's contact in Orlivka, Hennadiy, took us to warm up in a green canvas tent, something straight from the Second World War. There was a faded white and red cross painted on top, pallets over the mud floor inside, and a pot-bellied stove, which we crowded around, chilled from the long wait in the dawn air. A stark contrast with the well-funded infrastructure on the Romanian side, where it was all pub-garden-space-heaters and shiny orange UN tents.

The nervousness subsided with all the normality of potato soup, laughter, kids running around. In the village nearby we visited some young women who'd come here with their children – this was a safe place, with no real threat of strikes and certainly not of imminent invasion. Or so Hennadiy reckoned. A big cheery man, he was banking on the fact that one of Russia's major gas lines ran underground a few kilometres away. 'He wouldn't bomb his own pipeline!' he laughed.

This side of the river, a different kind of emotional scene was taking place – the awful goodbyes between husbands and wives, fathers and children. Men in fatigues hugged their young families tightly, down on their knees at the big port gates.

Among the refugees leaving Ukraine that day was a Roma family, the kids bright as buttons, playing and swinging on the barge's rails as they watched Isaccea come into focus. From the water, the substation behind the town is most visible, making it look grimy, industrial. We were making the crossing back to Isaccea, late afternoon, and I stuck my head in the Portakabin, where some of the family were huddled in its relative warmth, including a granny wrapped in shawls and leaning heavily on a wooden stick. One little girl, thin and walking with a limp, began chatting to me, introducing herself as Regina Petrivna. I nipped back to the van to see if Stuart had any chocolate. He didn't, but he started rooting around in a bag and pulled out a homemade card and a little toy rabbit, slightly embarrassed. 'Do you think she'd like this?'

His granddaughter back in England had made the card, covering it with rainbow stickers and shakily drawn hearts. It was the sweetest thing I could imagine. It's perfect, I said. He walked over, smiling sheepishly, and gave Regina the cuddly toy and folded paper. She beamed at him.

Even her grandmother smiled for a minute. But when the kids went to play this smile fell away. 'Where are you from?' I asked, and she looked at me, anguished, and said in a whisper, '*Mariupol.*' You couldn't have uttered a word with more horrible significance at this time; the coastal city was being bombed to rubble. The few photos reaching us looked like Grozny in the nineties. Makeshift graves in courtyards, bodies on the streets. Hell. She had no idea where they were going, how they'd manage. Getting out was enough.

In late March, Marian and I crossed the river to Ukraine once more. This time we'd drive through Bessarabia as far as Bilhorod-Dnistrovskyi, an ancient fortress town, taking supplies to a home for children with disabilities.

A spectacular sunrise, deep purple and bright pink, greeted us as we drove to the port, Marian offensively cheery for such an early hour. The deck of the *Noviodunum* was empty but for one couple, Elena and Mihail, instantly recognisable as Odesans with their almost Parisian dress sense and air of pride. The couple were standing, her arm in his, looking back at the Romanian safe haven as the barge slipped through the still waters of the Danube. These were the first returnees I'd met – already sick of refugee life, they felt the risk in Odesa was manageable.

In Ukraine, the blue road signs on the highway had been scrubbed out, some ingeniously re-worded. At a roundabout, next to a large stone cross, arrows pointed in various directions, telling potential invaders in which direction to 'fuck off', including 'all the way back to Russia'. Crude but effective humour – or at least, it made me laugh – if a little incongruous alongside the sombre Christian memorial.

Billboards, too, were requisitioned for war purposes. On one, a picture of a tilting Kremlin, echoing the recently sunk *Moskva* warship, disappeared into a pool of blood. The *Moskva* had been the flagship cruiser of the Russian fleet, a looming threat to Odesa, guns bristling on the horizon since the invasion, and had been recently sunk by Ukrainian forces to much rejoicing. 'Russian warship, fuck off!' the sign exclaimed. Others exhorted belief in the armed forces – the ZSU, *Zbroini Syly Ukrayini*. 'God protect us,' another said simply.

Several stark red-and-white signs drew comparisons between Russia's invasion of Ukraine and Hitler's invasion of the Soviet Union: '1941 Fascist occupiers. 2022 Russian occupiers.' I took a photo from the van as we sped past, the flat rich farmland of southern Bessarabia stretching out behind the hoarding. History is complicated here. The sign didn't mention that this territory was invaded by the Soviet Union first – in 1940, when Stalin and Hitler were allies. Before that, it had been Romanian.

Soldiers waiting at the concrete-block checkpoints searched our van but quickly waved us through on seeing the medical supplies. Some of the lads looked so young, but their guns were old, wooden handles polished with use. A female soldier, with carefully applied makeup and neatly set hair, waved cheerily at a passing petrol tanker. Despite the situation, the mood at checkpoints was cheery, resolute.

At the children's home the staff had laid on a spread, and we all sat down to eat. Fruit juice and potato croquettes, cheese and salami and devilled eggs, and sweet sticky baklava. It was a nice place, old but well cared for, with bright classrooms. The residents ranged from four years old to thirty-five. They often stayed on as adults, the director explained. Around them, she was cheery, but once out of earshot, in her office, she was incandescent with rage describing their situation.

'Don't they have enough to deal with?' she demanded. The sirens sounded most nights, and she said the children often became hysterical, understanding nothing as they were hurried into the cold basement.

'Some of them have no parents,' the director went on. 'They all have to cope with illnesses.' It was pointless trying to keep the kids in the dark about the war – 'We don't isolate them,' she insisted, and the older ones had mobile phones anyway. 'We try to focus on positive things, find things to take joy in. Flowers, the sunshine.'

The biggest worry for her was the medication running out, especially for those with epilepsy. I could see as she talked, her pale eyes teary, that she was actually very scared. 'It's the difference between them having fits and not having fits,' she was saying. Everything depended on the cobbled-together efforts of volunteers like Marian and Hennadiy, and whatever they could pack into a little Citroën dispatch van.

I'd seen the list the head nurse had sent them, blurry and handwritten, and forwarded on messaging apps to doctors and volunteers on the Romanian side. It was long: analgesics, anticonvulsants, antibiotics, magnesium sulphate. Obtaining the prescription items had been extremely challenging, Marian told me on the return route.

I wrote up the story for the *Sunday Post*, and as a radio essay for Irish broadcaster RTE, while wedged into the corner of an old couchette on a sleeper train to Budapest a few days later. I barely slept, the train lurching and rattling over the tracks. Around

2 a.m. I felt the familiar sensation of a chest infection settling into bronchitis, a sharp pain when I breathed in. Then came a bout of food poisoning. In the morning I staggered into Budapest, grey and sweat-sheened, and tried to record the radio piece at a friend's flat in between coughing fits.

Once back in the UK, I had a few days' rest at a cousin's house, an oasis of toddlers and normality, then went to London for a short conflict-zone training course. We learned how to apply a tourniquet and what a sniper's bullet does to the human head (illustrated with a slow-motion film of imploding tinned tomatoes). A day later I was back in Tulcea with a bad cough and a blurry printout of my Ukrainian military accreditation. I'd decided, perhaps predictably, to go as far as Odesa.

PART TWO

ODESA, KHARKIV, DNIPRO

APRIL–JUNE 2022

CHAPTER FIVE

THE BARGE MOVED SLOWLY towards the black sliver of land on the other side of the Danube. All around us the deep ink blue of the fading night became a soft sunrise gold as it met the land, almost perfectly reflected in the river's still waters. I shivered, leaning on the low metal railing and watching Ukraine come into view. Fireflies darted about, their strange halting dashes leaving an imprint on my tired eyes when I rubbed them. Swallows and swifts greeted the boat as we approached the shore.

To the starboard side, a small fishing boat slipped past, prow high as the outboard motor churned the water, and the wake it made swirled the vivid hues of the sky like paints mixing.

Two Red Cross workers were watching the shore too, smoking roll-ups. We talked for a minute, about the unseasonable cold we'd not prepared for (they were in shorts, I had on a flimsy child's raincoat), about the beauty of the delta region, and where they were heading. These young men from Greece had never been to Ukraine – they had barely given it a thought before the war – and the apprehension was written all over their faces.

The huge lorries which crammed the deck, gleaming new and emblazoned with logos of humanitarian organisations, roared one by one into life, the cacophony breaking the near-peace of this Danube sunrise hour. I found our little red van and hopped in, blowing on my frozen hands. Valerii greeted me, ticking me off for getting so cold. He was a retired doctor who'd been working with Marian and others to get medical supplies for this run. We talked in Russian, but like many people in this border region he could speak Romanian and Ukrainian too.

In the long Orlivka queue, I sat in the chilly cab while Valerii disappeared into the port buildings with our paperwork, and by mid-morning we were allowed through. Despite having set off five hours earlier, we'd barely travelled twenty miles and had a long way to go, through innumerable checkpoints and, briefly, Moldova.

It could have taken a day or more, but we had a golden ticket – Anya, our military escort, who met us an hour into the journey, turning up at a roadside coffee shop in an ancient little car. Because Valerii's supplies were going to Odesa's military hospital, Anya would escort us all the way. This was a godsend.

Anya was a young woman of stony determination and appalling driving style. She jumped in to the van, stuck on some patriotic tunes and put her foot down. It remained there. As we approached the queues of cars waiting at a checkpoint, she'd drive, skidding, down the dusty edge of the road – or simply head straight into oncoming traffic, honking the horn. I thought this was fantastic, having grown up with island driving, but poor Valerii, wedged in alongside me in the van's small cab, was gripping the seat and pleading with Anya to slow down. 'This woman!' he kept exclaiming. 'Going to get us killed! Oi, what a girl!'

She laughed. Thrusting her military credentials out of the window to flash at the outraged drivers and bewildered young soldiers, she was a force of nature nobody would stop, and we reached Odesa by lunchtime, somehow still in one piece.

The military hospital in central Odesa is a sprawling complex of buildings and tree-lined courtyards. It was also, at this point, a massive target. Russian forces had shown a marked enthusiasm for blowing up hospitals across Ukraine, and everybody knew there were missiles on those Black Sea ships, and on the Crimean bases, aimed squarely at this city.

But it was hard to feel fear on this glorious spring day as the men unpacked the boxes. As ever, my attempts to help with anything physical had been rebuked with bemused, slightly offended looks. Walking round the grounds with one of the volunteers, shirt sleeves rolled up and birdsong loud in the cherry-blossom trees, I could only feel a real joy that I was finally here, in this city, at this time. While there were terrible things happening here, there was also a tangible feeling of solidarity and purpose, nowhere more so than with these volunteers attached to the military hospital. For a while they all stood on the pavement talking, laughing, joking around – then someone would begin to cry quietly as they recounted some loss or grief, or the latest awful news from the east – Mariupol, Kherson. Then, laughter again. The atmosphere was highly charged with emotion, but not in an unpleasant way, not with that energy that makes you tense up. No, this was a sincerity and emotional honesty that seemed to infuse every conversation and interaction.

Upstairs in a ward, two young men were propped up on pillows. Artur was missing a leg; his comrade, an arm. From his bed he described what had happened.

'We went out, got hit with a drone, a Grad [missile] flew in and I –' and he actually laughed – 'I ended up in a tree!'

Artur's tone was carefully casual, but on the recording I made you can hear him relentlessly rubbing his thigh, like a nervous tic.

The story was not really funny, of course. Left leg amputated, right leg injured. 'Twenty-two years old and no leg,' he said, his face belying the indifferent tone he was trying for. He looked at me, suddenly angry, as though daring me to pity him as he lay in that hospital bed. 'But we fulfilled our mission. Everything was OK.'

His parents were in a safer part of Ukraine, his girlfriend too. Artur told me he wanted to get married, have kids. Most of all though, he wanted a prosthetic limb, so he could go back to fight.

'To defend Ukraine – but understand,' he said, fixing me with a fierce stare, 'we're defending all of Europe.'

In a dark tone he warned that the West would be next if Ukraine fell. 'They'll capture *your* cities, rape *your* women, shoot *your* children.' He spat out the bitter words. 'He [Putin] fancies himself an emperor, a Napoleon, a Hitler. If you don't help us, there'll be no more peace in your homes.

'I sacrificed my health, at twenty-two years old. I gave it to protect the whole of Europe, the whole of *civilisation* from Russian madness,' he finished in a rush, and slumped back down onto the pillow.

On that very first day in the city, talking to that group of volunteers outside on the pavement, I met Oleh. He was wearing a red polo shirt and shorts, and his eyes were constantly creasing with laughter as he cracked jokes and winked extravagantly. 'Take my number, I'll help you with train tickets,' he offered gallantly, when I explained I'd only be in Odesa for a week or two. How kind, I thought, with utter innocence.

In a tall block of flats overlooking the Black Sea a birthday party was in full swing. I'd landed here by way of my Odesan women, now in Berlin; they'd given me a contact – Larysa – and when I rang that afternoon, she was already expecting me. 'Hurry over!' she'd said impatiently, giving me the address, and when I arrived, she ushered me in, beaming. There was a huge spread of food – every conceivable pickle, fried meat patties, potato salad liberally layered with dill. A glass of vodka appeared, another of wine, and I was placed at the head of the table, a crowd of expectant faces peering at me. I explained who

I was and everyone said hello, and then several conversations resumed at once.

A small child was bashing something noisily in the corner, prompting occasional mild rebuke; from somewhere else a bird squawked. Kindly women were insisting I sample every single thing on the table, in particular the pickled tomatoes – '*Domashnye!* Homemade!'

It felt surreal to be in such a domestic setting as a birthday meal. For weeks I'd been preparing to go to Odesa – a war zone, technically; for weeks I'd been fretting about body armour, insurance and contingency plans. Now I was eating *zakusky* and chatting at a party to a backdrop of toddlers' shrieks and the chatter of a caged parrot.

I was overwhelmed by Larysa's hospitality. She'd never even met me before but was soon suggesting she introduce me to the mayor, after I said I'd like to interview him for the newspaper. I readily agreed.

The table chat turned from reminiscing to the inevitable topic of the war. The older women were trying to keep a lid on this, deploying pleas and eventually tears. 'Let's not, guys, please, let's not talk of bad things,' Larysa implored. But five minutes later it was back. Could Odesa be encircled? Could the territorial army defend the city, thrown together as it was and barely armed? And these fucking Russians, huh. These fucking Russians.

This was the young men talking. Angry, animated, they had no good words for the bastards attacking their country. But the scene around this table was a microcosm of the wider tensions and conflicting loyalties simmering in Odesa. It's not that the older generation was pro-Russian. They knew who the aggressor was. It's that some were, emotionally, still quite *Soviet*. Russian-speaking, and with no high opinion of the government in Kyiv and its 'decommunisation' policy, under which streets had been renamed, statues removed. In recent years, anything glorifying, celebrating, or even marking the Soviet Union was no longer safe. And for this older generation, that felt threatening. The big lettering on Odesa's palatial train station no longer read in Russian but in Ukrainian. It wasn't a practical problem for them; they understood both languages. But it struck some deep emotional chord.

Now this generation was watching the last links to Moscow quite literally blow up, watching hatred build against a country with which they had once been tightly bound up.

Then there was the difficult question of all their Russian relatives – often close family.

'You have to try to talk to them,' Larysa was saying, clasping her hands to her chest, almost in a plea.

The men were unmoved. 'They're zombies,' one said. 'They think we're fascists, they're brainwashed.'

'And after Bucha?' another interjected, angrily. 'After Mariupol, we should talk nicely with them?'

But she insisted. She'd rung friends and relatives in Russia, explained what was really going on. Told them Russia was really bombing its own neighbours. And it was a hard conversation, she added, but worth it. 'Please!' she said, tears in her eyes. 'Just try!'

It seemed to fall on deaf ears, and soon she was urging them again to talk of something, *anything*, else.

After a couple of hours I pleaded total exhaustion and was let go; Larysa took me down to the taxi.

'I don't know how to explain it any more,' she said, miserable. We walked with her little dog past the neat flowerbeds to the main road. She turned to me, throwing her hands up in exasperation.

'I'm against war! *Against* war! Ugh! You should have seen it here when they sunk the *Moskva*! People were clapping,' she said bitterly. 'But there were boys on that ship!'

Gesturing to the nine-storey block, a typical apartment building, she sighed, trying to explain the complicated tangle she found herself in. 'It's fifty-fifty here,' she said. This didn't mean that her half was 'pro-Russian'. That would be absurd. But they were conflicted, certainly, still clinging to the idea of the *bratskiy narod*, 'brotherly nation', that still held so much sway among this generation. Even as the bigger brother was firing rockets from the Black Sea.

The muted wail of sirens woke me up several times that night, but I was too tired to do anything more than note the time and go back to sleep. There was a basement, my host had explained, but on another street. Absolutely nobody seemed to be going there. It was barely 6 a.m. when I had to leave for the strangely covert rendezvous with Trukhanov, the mayor, in Victory Park. It was his morning walk and he'd agreed that I could join him for a few minutes. It was a sort of vetting, I gathered, after which – if approved – I could do a sit-down interview with him.

The taxi ride there was surreal – another air-raid alert formed the backdrop to a normal, bustling morning, street traders setting up on pavements, crowds of people already gathered with shopping bags. Around half of the population had left the city by now, but you wouldn't have known it.

Rumours swirl about Trukhanov and his loyalties, or they did then – he was too close to the Russians, it was suggested, or at least too close to the mafia which held such sway in this port city. This wasn't just gossip; he'd been arrested in 2018 on suspicion of embezzling state property, in a dramatic airport snatch. Younger people I knew in the city hated him and pointed to his public appearances, in 2014 and 2015, with a St George's ribbon pinned proudly to his black suit. This orange-

and-black anachronism had been revamped in Russia as a symbol of support for its annexation of Crimea and, by extension, of Putin. That the city's mayor had proudly sported such a symbol even *after* Russia invaded both Crimea and Donbas in 2014 spoke volumes about Odesa's messy loyalties and mistrust of Kyiv. Or perhaps just about Trukhanov's.

Outwardly though, he had taken a side since the full-scale invasion, railing against Russia and promising fierce resistance if Odesa was touched.

Trukhanov's walking route changed frequently for security reasons, Larysa told me as we marched around Victory Park. Finally a phalanx of hard-set men appeared, rounding a corner, a big dog bounding alongside.

Flanked by the burly men, who muttered into walkie-talkies, we walked round the park, and Trukhanov made clipped, cautious statements about the position of Odesa, the expected Russian attack and the strengthening of the city defences. I tried, mostly in vain, to soften him up, walking at a trot to keep up. After twenty minutes I was told I could call a certain number and was dispatched in the direction of a bus. I later realised all this was fairly unnecessary, as the mayor's office was granting interviews to most of the accredited journalists who applied. Trukhanov had a message and was happy for it to be amplified; that message was, broadly, 'Don't you dare touch Odesa'.

The transformation of the city into a fortress ready for Russian attack had been documented almost daily in the international press, images of the grand and iconic landmarks lined with sandbags and patrolled by soldiers. At the famous opera house, the sentries quickly accosted any photographers – you had to be sneaky or, preferably, get special permission. I didn't feel the need to add to the pool of similar images already available.

It had all happened before, of course – Odesa, during the Second World War, had prepared for invasion. The black-and-white pictures were jarring in their similarity to what we could see now, 80 years later. The same hulking steel shapes of anti-tank obstacles scattered down the cobbled streets; the same sandbags heaped up around the Opera Theatre and the statues of Catherine the Great and Duke of Richelieu. On street corners, makeshift ramparts bristled. Odesa held out for two months in 1941, before Romanian and German troops broke through. Under the Nazi occupation 25,000 people, mostly Jews, were murdered, tens of thousands more deported.

I stood staring at the streets I'd dreamed of seeing for so many years. Tree-lined avenues dug up for barricades against an imminent invasion. How could this possibly be happening again?

Walking one evening with an old friend who grew up in the city, we stopped to look down Derybasivska Street. Spiky anti-tank obstacles, like giant rusting scatter-jack pieces, littered the graceful boulevard and cast long shadows. 'It has a different kind of beauty like this,' she mused, and I was glad she'd been the one to say it.

Getting anywhere near the iconic Potemkin Stairs which stretch down to the shore proved impossible. Stopped at a checkpoint, I was told sternly to come back with an escort and written permission. It was 7 a.m., a few days into my spell in the city, and I'd gone out with my camera. Not for a job, not to document the sandbags and barbed wire, but for the simple pleasure of photographing an extraordinary city I'd always wanted to see. The wary soldier wanted to check my photos, and I flicked through them on the camera's display: architecture, flowers, statues, and early-morning light falling on the towering columns of the Transfiguration Cathedral. He thought I was an idiot but let me go. Perhaps I was, but to spend an hour or two doing something purely creative, purely for myself, felt like a pressure valve amidst the articles, radio scripts and safety worries.

I didn't realise at the time how much stricter the martial law was in Odesa compared to other Ukrainian cities at this point in the war. In April the threat of invasion here was high. The authorities warned of possible encirclement if – however unlikely – the Russian-controlled troops stationed in Transnistria, the breakaway splinter of Moldova to the north, were mobilised. The Black Sea bristled with warships, and only the fortitude of Mykolaiv, the port city to the east, was holding back the Russian land army.

Adding to this obvious threat was the invisible activity of saboteurs and FSB operatives. This was nothing new; the Russian intelligence service has long enjoyed deep infiltration of Ukrainian society and local government, but now it was feared sleeper cells and agents would be preparing the ground for the coming invasion.

Territorial defence soldiers – some of whom had never held a gun until early March – manned checkpoints on every other corner, and the Telegram channels were filled with daily news of captured 'saboteurs' – men acting strangely, men with Russian ID cards hidden in their socks; men whose mobile phones revealed too many recent calls from Moscow, the giveaway +7 code. There was a strong sense of paranoia in the city, of vigilance by citizens and soldiers alike.

But in one of the real hearts of old Odesa, the open-air market Pryvoz, normality and humour prevailed. I went there to chat to shoppers and traders for a feature, to get a feel for the mood here, and, naturally, to do some shopping.

Pryvoz is a giant maze. I entered through a crumbling archway and adjusted my eyes to the gloom. The stalls seemed to stretch on forever. A vast metal roof, like an aircraft hangar, covered the open market area, while substantial older buildings housed the fish, meat and dairy sections.

I had never in my life seen such a variety of food. And this in wartime, with many supply routes cut off. Many of the traders I spoke to had brought the produce from their country gardens. Life was going on, because it must.

There were berries of every colour and shape, buckets of bobbing fermented apples that fizzed on the tongue, hand-pressed oils made from nuts and seeds. Gleaming honey like I'd never tasted, giant scaled fish that I couldn't put a name to. Whole plucked birds dangled from the stalls, and great spreads of fresh vegetables and dried fruits dazzled me. I hadn't really shopped for ages, and it felt like a strange treat, to be picking out food.

It was a din of voices, jokes and conversations, haggling and shouting, traders calling to each other and porters pushing tall trolleys, trying to part the crowds. Tables with the little painted Easter eggs and sweet *paska* cakes (like iced brioche) drew crowds – Orthodox Easter was approaching. This was mentioned by almost everyone I interviewed. You have to keep the spirits up, many said. Celebrate life no matter what.

At the back of the market in a quieter spot, I spoke to a seller who was more subdued. The tall, red-headed woman held my gaze steadily from the other side of her stall, across the rows of homemade *pastyla* sweets wrapped in paper and string. 'I want people to know what's happening here, because it's terrible. And yes, we need help' – she sounded irritated now – 'but only because we didn't expect that our neighbours – I won't say brothers, I won't use that word – that our neighbours would attack us.'

Are you scared, I asked rather stupidly, of further attacks? From the sea, from the air? She gave me a slightly withering look. 'Yes, of course. We know rockets can fall anywhere, any day. You go out and you don't know if you'll ever come home again.'

It was Pryvoz life that was keeping her spirits up. 'You wake up in the morning and scroll through the news, the Telegram channels, and you're just inundated with it. But come here and people are joking and smiling – well, how can you live without that?'

She looked exhausted, ground down by worry, but had an almost haughty pride which I admired, her chin jutting slightly, the queen of her small stall. Without doubt this pride was an Odesan characteristic too, one I'd seen every day at that freezing border crossing in Romania.

Others in the market put on a happier face, none more so than Olya and Tolya, a couple selling fermented foods in the middle of the vegetable section. In their fifties, both twinkly with mischief, they bustled around as they spoke to me, packing sauerkraut into tubs for customers, fishing out the pale apples and dill-soaked gherkins from big plastic tubs. They both talked over each other constantly, without the other seeming to notice, as though finishing each other's thoughts.

'We'll never give up Odesa,' said Tolya.

'Never give up our *Ukrainian* Odesa,' added Olya. 'It's Ukrainian,' she repeated with a glint in her eye, making sure I understood. 'Odesa is always Ukrainian.'

They may have already had their fill of foreign journalists asking about the city's loyalties, because when Olya told me they believed in victory, she quickly added, 'Ukrainian victory. *Our* victory.'

And what of Russia? 'Well, we think he [Putin] simply went insane,' they both concluded.

'Russians don't know what's happening, they don't have information. They think we're all Nazis. But we aren't. We're hardworking, we're friendly people. That's why it's so painful that they're trying to smash us up.'

When I told Tolya and Olya that at home I made my own sauerkraut and fermented vegetables, they were delighted, opening every tub for me to sample, and we talked about cabbage for quite a while. I left Pryvoz laden with fermented goods, with chewy apple *pastyla* sweets, a little bottle of flax oil, and a bag of tomatoes so ripe and perfect I ate the whole lot before I got home.

Everyone spoke, with trepidation, about the 'relative calm' in Odesa, the long weeks that had passed since the fuel depots had been blown up. That morning, the sky had burned red, my neighbour told me. We were chatting in the courtyard I'd moved to on Nizhynska Street. Her little boy was playing on a trike, zooming between the bedsheets strung up across the yard.

'It was absolutely terrifying.' The smoke had hung thick over the city – this block was quite close to the port where the fuel tanks were located – and she'd tried to stop it seeping into the apartment.

'You don't want to leave?' I asked, curious. She shook her head, vehement. I looked around the pretty little courtyard and could understand – the cherry blossom, the cats lounging in the sun, the ramshackle, faded grandeur. I had loved it from the minute I arrived. The Transfiguration Cathedral was a few minutes' walk away, and when the air-raid sirens started up, its bells would also start to chime. It was hauntingly beautiful, the eeriest music.

The courtyard, and the bedsit, became my temporary home, and Oleh from the military hospital became a frequent visitor. It is not really possible to go on dates under conditions of strict martial law with early curfew, and we were both too busy in any case. He would just appear late at night, back from whatever the day's mission was. Sometimes he'd been through Mykolaiv, a short drive to the east, a city I was desperate to get to, if just for a day. Oleh wouldn't countenance the idea of my coming along; he said it was too dangerous. Instead, I pestered every journalist and fixer I knew, asking to tag along if they were going, and crossed my fingers.

CHAPTER SIX

HENNADIY TRUKHANOV GLARED AT me across the black plastic table in what he called his 'Information Defence Centre'. It was the press centre of the city administration, and behind him, slightly incongruous, were brightly coloured satirical cartoons about the war, fixed by clothes pegs to twine strung between coat stands.

One showed a fearsome Russian tank, guns bristling. '*Achoo!*' the speech bubble said, and the next frame showed it disintegrating into rusted pieces. Another featured schoolboy-Putin crossing out the names of major planets on a blackboard. ~~Sun~~ *Russia* ~~Venus~~ *Russia* ~~Earth~~ *Russia*. They'd made me laugh as I waited for the mayor, but I quickly realised I'd been right to be apprehensive about this interview.

'Tell me how I'm pro-Russian,' he demanded, interrupting my careful attempts at phrasing the question. We'd started talking through a translator, which I didn't really need, and she'd used the Russian term *pro-Russkiy*. It wasn't what I'd said. I wanted to know, thinking of Larysa and her friends, about the complicated relationship Odesans had towards Russia, and how this had changed since the February invasion. But 'pro-Russian' appeared, and he'd pounced.

'In Odesa we have a speciality. Answering a question with a question,' he said, talking quickly and angrily. 'Many journalists say, "Oh, in Odesa they sympathise with Russia," but what is it we sympathise with? As a foreigner, what do you actually understand this so-called *Russkiy Mir*[2] to be?'

I said I wanted to understand, beyond the stereotypes sometimes printed about Odesa, but he'd already begun again.

'I'll tell you, so you don't have to bother answering. Foreigners see it as support for Russia's politics, for its vision for Odesa – together with Russia.'

In fact, he said the vast majority of people branded with such 'sympathy' were simply products of a city which had been bound up with Russia for a long time. Poets, composers and writers working in Russian, most people still speaking Russian, an economy of trade and shipping tied up inextricably with Russia. Cargo flows. The exchange of ideas and information.

'So that's why people have feelings,' he concluded. 'But in terms of ideology, in my opinion, Odesans have always had Odesan views.'

None of this I disagreed with. 'Odesa thinks firstly and almost only of Odesa,' a friend here had said to me, and that made sense. It ran by its own rules, slightly separate. But not *separatist*.

Echoing what I'd heard already, Trukhanov said that the older generation in particular had a hard time imagining that Russian soldiers 'could so ruthlessly kill our people and chuck missiles at residential areas', but 'with each passing day' the realisation was growing. 'People understand this is a fact.'

We moved on to the military situation in the city, the possibility of invasion from sea or land.

'There's a saying,' he said, reflective now. 'If you want peace,

---

2   *Russkiy Mir* is an ideological concept of a civilisation beyond Russia's political borders, encompassing those places where Russian was or is still spoken. Very bound up with the resurgent Russian imperialism, and with the Russian Orthodox Church, it translates as 'Russian world' but also, deeply ironically, as 'Russian peace'.

prepare for war.' The threat to the city was not imminent, but nothing could be ruled out.

Trukhanov projected a calm sense of purpose – almost dismissive of the risks. Transnistrian troops? Too few, ill-equipped. Russia was focusing on the east, on Kharkiv. But yes, of course, firepower wasn't equal; Russia dominated the sea and the air, so more weapons were essential. Anyway, everyone knew that. He wanted to get back to the thornier issues – what tied people, still, to Russia. Not just language or affiliation with the (Moscow-tied) Ukrainian Orthodox Church; it was also understandings of the Second World War which determined the feelings of Odesans, Trukhanov explained. My ears pricked up. Thorny indeed.

In the west of the country, he said, religious adherence was different, and views on the war were different.

'There they treat [Roman] Shukhevych and [Stepan] Bandera as heroes. Here in the southeast, these men are not perceived in that way.'

That was putting it mildly. In Soviet history books, in Soviet ideology, which once ruled absolute here, these two men were painted as bloodthirsty and degenerate fascists, Nazi collaborators. The truth, as usual, is complicated, and few aspects of the Second World War are quite as complicated as what went on in western Ukraine when Soviet, then Nazi, troops stormed through it.

But whatever divisions over history and identity lingered, Trukhanov argued, now it was very straightforward. 'Life today shows we are Ukrainian, we are ready to defend *Ukrainian* Odesa, we are Russian-speaking patriots of Ukraine.'

He added that even a decade ago he'd criticised Russia's portrayal of Ukrainians in films – they were always either traitors or goofs – while on an inter-parliamentary group trip to Moscow.

'I said, that's not very fraternal, is it? But then it was all still . . . under the table, so to speak. Now it's all come out in the open.'

Links between Russians and Ukrainians would be broken for a long time, he predicted. Russians were incapable of looking in the mirror and admitting what they'd done.

'They won't say, "Ah yes, we're fascists, we're murderers." They'll find 150 excuses for themselves. They'll talk about some nationalist movement, about Azov. Riots, whatever. Well, you can walk around Odesa and look at the monuments to the soldiers of the Great Patriotic War. No one tears them down!'

What *had* been torn down was Odesa's Lenin statue, seven years prior as part of the 'decommunisation' enforced by law across Ukraine – to the delight of some, to the horror of others and to the sheer glee of Russia's propagandists, who cast the toppling of all those Lenins as an attack on the very memory of those killed in the Second World War – here called the 'Great Patriotic War', the most sacred thing in Soviet, and Russian, collective memory.

In Odesa, the statue of Lenin was replaced by one of Darth Vader. The city of dry humour.

Trukhanov's point about the unblemished war monuments was that the Russian propaganda about 'Ukrainian Nazis' tearing everything down was nonsense. Walking home after the interview, I came across an example – the weathered bronze bust of Malinovsky, Soviet war hero, one of the few who avoided being summarily shot in the Stalinist purges. An Odesan boy who rose to the highest ranks, Malinovsky died in Moscow. Both his bust and plinth were covered in hammer-and-sickles, Soviet stars and medals, and even a little bony-headed Lenin badge – the lot. Someone had laid daffodils at the general's feet, but no red paint or vandalism marred Malinovsky.

As expected, it was Easter weekend when the Russians struck. I had walked through the long Oleksandrivskyi Prospect, a pretty green boulevard stretching several blocks, with stalls lining the central walkway.

Reflecting the national mood, they were selling mugs printed with Zelenskyy's face and t-shirts emblazoned with the popular postage stamp showing a soldier giving the finger to a sinking *Moskva* battleship. There was even a mug depicting Boris Johnson as a Cossack hero, to my faint horror.

Each Saturday a crowd gathered to listen to live music, sitting on benches and cross-legged on the ground around some young, energetic guys and their amps. Today things had moved up a gear and a group of musicians was playing lively jazz from a balcony.

The place was packed. It was the first day that felt really warm, a taste of the hot summer to come. In the UK, I thought, such a Saturday afternoon gathering would be the occasion, or excuse, for copious amounts of booze, but here only coffee was being sold, from one of the market stalls. I ducked into the cafe underneath the balcony to send some emails. The windows were boarded up completely to prevent the glass shattering, and I stepped into the gloom with a shiver. Not quite 3 p.m. yet – the cut-off for alcohol sales – so some customers were enjoying a Saturday afternoon tipple, but the atmosphere was hushed.

I worked for a while on my laptop. The sirens had sounded earlier, but there was no warning before the first explosion hit. In the cafe we all felt the blast, strangers staring at each other as if for an explanation. Then another huge boom, and another. I jumped up and started to pack my things away. The man across from my table made a wry expression which made me laugh, and as I got up to leave he wished me luck with that awkward sincerity of people who would otherwise have no reason to speak.

The atmosphere on the street had changed – children were being hurried home, the balcony had emptied.

Racing back to my bedsit, I messaged contacts for information about the strike – it was forbidden to post information about locations before the authorities did, but there were always rumours. Within an hour I was at the site. Black smoke was still hanging over the block of flats – a fairly new, swish apartment complex south of the centre.

I stood there on the tram tracks that ran alongside the block, feet sodden in the flood from the fire engines' hoses. I watched as emergency workers carried out a body in a black bag and helped survivors into ambulances, their faces covered in blood. 'There are absolutely no military sites here,' people said to me, again and again. Old couples stood staring up in shock at what had been their flats. A woman told me she'd been painting traditional Easter eggs when it happened. A quiet Saturday afternoon at home, getting ready for the grandchildren coming for the holiday. Painting eggs.

'I ran out into the corridor. There was already smoke in the entrance,' she said. 'It was too late to run to the basement.' Somehow they'd made it down and into the courtyard of the sixteen-storey building. 'Everything was burning.' Their car was one of those parked outside, a row of them all gutted by fire, tyres melted, paintwork seared by the heat so the shells were all a lumpy gunmetal grey. In one of these shells, they were saying, a man had burnt to death.

The explosions had ripped a hole right through the centre of the block, and I watched as firemen somehow moved around *inside* this shattered space, across partially collapsed slabs of concrete, picking their way around the dangling rods of rebar.

It was late in the evening when I sent the last updates to the Scottish newspaper – it would make the front page, a big foreign news story told first-hand – and by nightfall the death toll was five, including a baby.

The temperature had plummeted and my fingers had stopped working; I was grateful when Oleh appeared in his van, insisting I go home. We hurtled through the pre-curfew, tense city centre, and he muttered about leaving for Mykolaiv shortly. I knew the shelling was heavy there, from Telegram channels we all followed, but it was his choice. We each had our work.

'Emotions?' he asked simply, as we stood in the dark courtyard on Nizhynska, noses touching.

I shook my head. '*Spokoino.*' Calm. It was the truth. Busy with a job to do, I'd avoided absorbing the pain and shock of those I'd interviewed, avoided also feeling my own racing heart at the first big explosions that afternoon.

'Good,' he replied, kissing me on the forehead as he left. 'Sweet dreams.'

But I did not sleep that night. That fragile bit of peace in Odesa had been broken, forcefully reminding the hundreds of thousands of people in the city just what a terrifying situation they were really in. The authorities had warned of a pre-Easter strike, and they'd been right. I lay in the bed alcove, heavy curtains drawn across it, as the sirens began again, and again, at 1 a.m., 4 a.m., the bells of the great church joining in so sonorous and strange, and I thought about the large windows and French door which made up the outside wall of the bedsit, I thought about glass exploding in slow motion, slicing through the heavy curtains and into a soft body. Then I got up and made coffee, because the sun was shining. It was Easter Sunday.

'The second phase of the war is beginning and you should get out of Odesa.'

I read the message on my phone, sent from a friend in Romania, and groaned. I was getting many others. A pincer movement could happen at any moment, went the theory. Amphibious landings from the sea, Transnistrian mobilisation, a breakthrough at Mykolaiv. Odesa, so it was said, was the jewel in the crown for Putin; Odesa was next. There had been explosions in the Russian-controlled enclave of Transnistria to the north – confusion reigned over what had actually happened. A provocation. Murky KGB stuff. Who knew. But the air was thick with theories and dark speculation. You could go mad trying to find any fact amongst it all, or trying to decide which threat to really pay attention to. Personally I was more worried about the ammonia stored in tanks east of Odesa. I did some doom-Googling. The cloud would be orange if the storage facility were blown up. It would burn the eyes, the skin, airways. I put the phone aside and made lunch, adding ammonia clouds to the 'things you can't do anything about' list.

'The second phase of the war has begun, and it's going to be very heavy,' Oleh said, lying on his back and staring up at the ceiling. The bed alcove was dark, the curtains drawn against the early light. It was just after 6 a.m., and he was needed at the hospital. But he seemed, suddenly, frozen.

Two days ago he'd been joking around as usual, a winking, laughing, caricature of Odesan levity. 'Everything will be OK' was the mantra, day and night. *Everything will be OK*. It wasn't just him; people said it almost reflexively.

But when he'd appeared from the darkened courtyard the night before, whispering greetings and setting a plastic bottle of sweet monastery wine on the little table, something had changed. I brought glasses, and we sat close, knees touching. His expression was awful.

'What happened in Mykolaiv?' I asked eventually, quietly, and he wouldn't say. Only, 'It was heavy.'

He didn't like to tell me about his work. Neither about where he was going, nor where he'd been. I didn't push it, and we just sat, holding hands, taking solace in each other, and soon went to bed.

But now it was morning, and the sirens were on again. I'd heard them before he did, the first faint wail, more and more of them cranking up, atop the buildings around us. It took a couple of minutes for the cathedral to join in.

Oleh sighed, finally acknowledging the air-raid alert. 'The bells,' he said sadly, noting the cathedral's arpeggio warning. The cacophony built around us, so utterly at odds with the peace of a shared warm bed on a sunny spring morning. We got up.

The flak jacket my magician friend Marian had sent came down to my knees. This was one of the big problems for female reporters, I was learning. He expressed disbelief – it had fitted his wife Mihaela! I reminded him that Mihaela is quite a tall woman, and I am barely five foot. I thought perhaps I was being fussy until I tried to run in it and couldn't bend my knees.

Somehow he found another one, a neat little stab vest for female police officers, made in a now-defunct Warrington factory. He sent it over from Romania in a supply convoy, and I slotted the ceramic plates of the big UN jacket into this new one, delighted. And just in time; I'd found a ride to Mykolaiv.

On a quiet, pleasant city square, the intense green of southern Ukraine's warm spring all around, stone lions on little pedestals gazed out, protectively, at the street. The main drag was lined with the usual shops – the jewellery chain Zolotyi Vik, sushi and espresso bars, the excellent Marmalade Jack sweetie shop. A gentle pop ballad played from loudspeakers. Pigeons fluttered around the unimposing statue of the saint who gave the city its name, and two old men stared at a chessboard on the bench between them, oblivious to their surroundings.

This was Mykolaiv, ship-building industrial hub on the Southern Buh River, bang in the path of the Russian onslaught from Crimea – that onslaught which had swallowed Kherson, an hour's drive away, in the first days of the invasion. After fierce fighting in and around the city, the Russians were pushed back, though they'd continued to lob rockets and artillery from their positions. Two days before I arrived, multiple rocket launchers were used to fire cluster munitions at the city, hitting shops and flats.

And yet the main square felt like an oasis of calm on this last day of April, 2022.

It was this strange, sometimes absurd, paradox that I was finding so hard to explain to people at home. But more and more, it made sense to me. No one can spend all their time underground in a dank cellar, paralysed with fear. The spring sunshine beckons, the next strike could be anywhere, or nowhere, and you want to play chess with your old friend in the park. You shrug, and head out.

I'd wheedled a lift here with journalists Glib, Vitalii and Misha. In Chestnut Square we spread out to do the thing journalists must do – annoy people having a quiet afternoon.

The men playing chess, Ivan and Oleksandr, laughed away my questions.

'What? Life's fine!' Ivan chuckled in a hoarse voice. 'Still alive!' Shaking their heads, they returned to the game.

A family passed by, and I chatted to them about the water shortages. When Russians blew up a pipeline two weeks ago, the taps ran dry. Not far away a queue had formed around an old water truck, people clutching battered plastic bottles.

The teenagers in the family admitted it was hard, always going back and forth with the bottles, washing from a bucket. But in the grand scheme of things, they added, it was 'nothing'.

Nearby a young woman in cycling gear – full Lycra, fingerless gloves – sat next to an older guy on a bench, her bike propped up behind them.

'It's quieter already,' beamed the woman, Olya. 'We're waiting for these weapons from the west, then we'll kick that lot off our land. Just as quick as they came, they'll have to run away.'

Despite strikes in their suburb – 'They bombed a summer cafe, nobody was standing outside,' Olya said casually – and despite the lack of running water, the two felt lucky. In the places the Russians had taken over, not so far to the east, horrifying stories were emerging.

'Terrible. Terrible. They're not letting people leave. They torture men – yes, and women, and not only those with a link to the army, but people connected to the police too.'

Olya said she'd even read of farmers being tortured. The grain requisitions in occupied Kherson were big news at that time and echoed the terrible stories from the famine-terror of the 1930s. We all knew about the houses picked clean by marauding Russian troops in Bucha, in Irpin, Olya said – 'But the same is happening in Kherson Oblast.'

They wanted, she said, to fill the car with supplies and drive to Mariupol – 'But obviously Russians wouldn't show restraint.' Olya had heard of civilian convoys coming under fire on leaving the city.

'They shot at them,' said her friend Vadym, in quiet disbelief.

We sat for a while, birdsong loud in the trees around us. Their talk of Russian relatives – who, of course, did not believe them, and told them Ukrainians were 'bombing themselves' – led them to the issue of locals also sympathetic to Russia.

'We had these people, yes, trying to talk about *Russkiy Mir*, but now they've all shut up. Some left – some simply disappeared,' Olya said.

She'd mentioned the events of eight years ago, and I told her of my friends' fears back then, that an Odesan People's Republic loyal to Russia was possible. They hadn't trusted Trukhanov to stick with Ukraine if push came to shove.

Olya shook her head. 'It doesn't matter what the mayor says. A mayor can cross over if he wants. The people would never give up Odesa.'

'But don't those in authority have power?'

Both interrupted me, slightly exasperated with this clueless foreigner. 'It doesn't work like that in Ukraine,' Vadym said firmly.

'They can come and go, it doesn't matter,' his friend added. 'It's not like there's one guy who speaks and everyone listens. Perhaps what he says is in accordance with popular opinion. Perhaps not – then, goodbye.'

After ten minutes I got up to leave. 'People seem in a resilient mood,' I remarked to the pair.

'What choice do we have?' Vadym laughed, genuinely amused. They waved cheerily as I walked away, self-conscious as the only one in a flak jacket.

Suddenly the piped street music, which was getting a little grating, was drowned out by a loud air-raid siren; after a few seconds a loudspeaker voice boomed out over the intersection, ordering citizens to turn off the lights and mains gas and take shelter.

Nobody paid the slightest bit of attention. A man on a bicycle swerved politely around a group of pedestrians crossing the road;

two soldiers in bucket hats sauntered, smiling, into a coffee shop. After a while the sirens stopped – the threat, whether it had been a Russian plane launch, or a rocket in whose trajectory we sat, had passed.

For the next six hours Glib, Vitalii, Misha and I moved around the city, documenting the destruction, often in shocked silence. We saw the spot where rockets had landed two days earlier, a handful of bright tulips tied to the railing where a woman buying groceries had been killed.

In a nearby courtyard Glib pointed out evidence of cluster bombs, the odd spatter-shaped explosion marks on brickwork and pavements, so different to the big craters and blasted facades. There were plenty of these too, though. In the Korabel'nyi district we walked into what had been a well-tended homestead. Spring onions were growing in the veg patch, but their orderly rows fell away into a steep-sided crater, at least the width of a bus. Apparently here aerial bombs had fallen on 7 March, killing one woman and destroying everything in their path.

But the pear, apple and peach trees were coming into blossom in the abandoned gardens, bricks and debris strewn around their trunks. I was struck by how lovely it had been here once, on Pshenychna Street.

Across the road a little blue-painted house was boarded up, the roof just a nest of broken beams. The cherry tree outside was splintered and snapped, but tulips, neatly set in rows of scarlet and sunburst yellow, had appeared since the explosions, whoever planted them no longer here to see. A single, straight-stemmed, near-black tulip had bloomed. Twisted wrecks of cars littered the road; the almost-intact steering wheel of a Mini stood on its own on the sandy ground.

The strange and guilty sensation that accompanies poking around in the ruins of other people's lives made us say little in

NIGHT TRAIN TO ODESA

Korabel'nyi. There was more of this to come – back in the city centre the army liaison allowed us inside the destroyed headquarters of the regional council. Nine storeys tall, and flanked by conifers and birch trees, the building had a hole ripped right through the middle. High up, the wall of an office was still intact. Files were stacked on a shelf, open to the elements. A desktop computer dangled by its extension lead right in the centre of the big hole, swaying in the wind. A concrete floor hung by a thread, bits of parquet flooring still stuck to it.

Upstairs, crunching tentatively through the unsteady floors, I photographed the remnants of office workers' lives. Smears of blood were left on a corridor wall, as though someone had slumped there, trying to escape.

The rockets had hit one day at the end of March as people were arriving for work, milling around in the foyer, getting a coffee to start the day. The foyer now was a shell, heaped with debris, open to the elements. Thirty-seven people had been killed here.

Outside in the grass I nearly tripped on something as I poked among the smashed concrete and twisted metal rods. It was something solid, a massive piece of burnished metal. I had to take a step back to see what it was – the Ukrainian state symbol, the trident.

In pre-war pictures you can see how it sat in pride of place atop the imposing council building. Somehow it had survived the blast – perhaps landing here forty yards away, or placed here after it came loose, but an extraordinary sight either way. A journalist next to me prodded it with his foot. 'Symbolic, no?'

We drove back to Odesa as the sun set; a splinter of rays over the vast horizon of the region's flat, fertile farmland. And suddenly smoke appeared on the horizon; suddenly phones were pinging; the Telegram channels we relied on for instant news were all lighting up.

Odesa's international airport had been the target. After driving away from the supposedly more dangerous Mykolaiv, we were now heading straight towards the plumes of black smoke, towards a city under attack. Not a little ironic, one of the men pointed out. He was pissed off. 'We only just built that bloody airport.'

It was a lesson – there's always a 'more dangerous place', but when you get there, your risk level shifts again. To those in Tulcea (or, of course, those anywhere west of the Danube), going to Odesa had seemed crazy. To those in Odesa, a trip to Mykolaiv was absurdly reckless. As for going to Kharkiv? For many in Ukraine, let alone in the West, that was completely out of the question – if it was even possible.

Kharkiv had become one of those heavy, sombre names: a byword for aerial terror. In those two months since the 24th, Russia had managed to change the face of that northeastern city, obliterating parts of its historic old centre and whole districts of high-rise flats on the northern edge. But I knew from keeping in touch with friends that it was entirely possible to go there, to work for a week or two, as I had done in Odesa. A train departed every night.

Sitting in the courtyard that evening with Oleh, watching the cats curl up on a bit of old blanket under the drooping cherry blossom, I was about to tell him this when he guessed.

'Promise me you won't go to Kharkiv,' he said suddenly. I said nothing. 'It's too hot there,' he kept saying. 'Please, don't.'

I tried to defend my decision as work, as my job. I knew Kharkiv, I knew people there, I could tell stories from there. He understood, eventually – or perhaps understood that I'd go anyway.

Odesa's railway station was in total blackout, the hulking shape of the main building looming over the concourse. We groped our way along, trying to find the right train – Oleh would have to leave soon as curfew was imminent. David, a British journalist I'd met on the London training course was coming to Kharkiv too, but he wasn't here yet. Dark figures stood around, waiting for the Kyiv and Kharkiv trains. I approached a woman with a large long-haired dog and asked if she knew which platform the Kharkiv train left from.

She stared at me, horrified. 'No. Why on earth would you want to go to Kharkiv?'

From the darkness behind me came a snort.

We finally reached the right platform and stopped outside the sixth carriage. Oleh put the big rucksack on my shoulders, the heavy ballistics helmet swinging from a strap. I was already wearing the flak jacket; it was easier than carrying it. The smaller day pack sagged with the weight of my camera and lenses and laptop and, admittedly, several books. He looked at it all, crestfallen.

'How can you possibly carry this weight?' he asked, pointlessly.

I shrugged. We stood together for long minutes in the dark, me smoking a last cigarette and him worrying aloud, before he really had to run or risk breaking curfew. To avoid having to watch him leave, I turned and swung myself and what must have been about twenty kilos of stuff into the cramped carriage and sank onto the narrow bunk. David arrived just before the whistle blew and slowly, haltingly, the train shunted north, taking me away from Odesa.

CHAPTER SEVEN

THICK STRIPS OF TRANSPARENT tape across the train windows smudged the passing countryside into a blur of vivid green and birch-tree sunlight. It was a bright, beautiful morning in northeast Ukraine.

The tape was supposed to stop the window splintering if something blew up nearby. And there had in fact been some shelling, we were told, requiring the train to divert. We'd be a little late into Kharkiv. Artem the conductor was apologetic, and I wanted to laugh, thinking of the contrast with delays on British railways.

David was in our compartment working on his laptop. We were the only passengers in the carriage, it turned out. He seemed to have rested well during the night, chuckling and shouting incoherently in his sleep. I, obviously, had not slept much.

I stood with Artem and watched the villages and gardens pass by. Smart in the company's navy-blue uniform, Artem was a serious young man, dedicated to the job – it was his part in the war effort, he said.

The ability of the state railway company, Ukrzaliznytsia, to keep running against all the odds was proving critical for the country's survival – moving soldiers, supplies and refugees across the vast territory – and it was fast becoming a cause célèbre far beyond Ukraine. Photos of the packed evacuation trains, the weary soldiers in bunks and tracks being hastily repaired encapsulated Ukraine's resilience. Of course, less discussed, the railway's success also owed something to the Soviet legacy of state-run infrastructure and a heavy industry which provided a dense network of tracks.

The night train had taken us 500 miles from the southern coast of Ukraine to its northeastern border, crossing the Dnipro River in the small hours. I felt nervous as we creaked towards Kharkiv. Not so much because of the danger – strikes had eased a bit lately – but simply because, having heard so much about the damage done to the place, I didn't know what I might find. What the Russians had done to Kharkiv was so extreme that it had taken up a lot of my thoughts for two months now.

Perhaps unsurprisingly, the hotel David had booked online turned out to be completely closed. They hadn't thought anyone would come so didn't bother removing the online listing. The confused manager, in slippers and shorts, emerged blinking in the sun, and I spent a while persuading him to take us for one night. He finally agreed but said there was no food, so we'd better go and find a shop.

'Are there any open?' I asked in surprise, thinking of the scene outside, all the shop-fronts smashed and boarded up. He shrugged and shuffled off down the corridor to find sheets.

David and I picked our way down Sums'ka Street, which leads down into the historic centre, widening out abruptly to become the massive Constitution Square. I remembered it well. Here were cathedrals and theatres, monuments and statues, a glass-fronted modern museum . . . Here, traffic would flow constantly across many lanes. But now, almost nothing moved.

The horrible silence was broken only by the crunch of broken glass under our feet and by the occasional military vehicle screaming down the big avenue. It was unreal, like a bad dream.

Where the square meets Moscow Prospect (an arterial street soon to be renamed) the buildings once made up a long, stunning neo-classical frontage with fluted columns, shining gilt and sea-green paint. Right behind was the Dormition Cathedral, a cluster of cupolas and golden domes and a tall bell tower.

The architecture of this place was dizzying, eclectic, slightly insane, a mix of the rare Ukrainian modernism of the 1920s, exquisite Art Nouveau, red-brick workshops of early industry, outrageous Soviet pomp and its heavy Brutalist successors. All this, Russia had bombed – in places, down to rubble.

The sea-green facade at the top of the prospect was blasted off, and the windows hung empty and black, daylight showing through on the upper storeys as the roof was entirely gone, the brickwork crumbling. The Orthodox church had fared better, windows replaced with bin bags but otherwise intact. We eventually found a cafe open, catering to soldiers and journalists, piles of body armour under all the tables. I'd barely sat down when I got a call from Vitalii, who'd been on the Mykolaiv trip. He and Misha were in Kharkiv too. Did I want to come to Saltivka?

A taxi wouldn't take me all the way into this northern district – too dangerous, too many checkpoints – so I was on foot when I found the two men, round the back of what had been a supermarket. It was wrecked, incinerated. A stack of yellow shopping baskets caught my eye, melted down one side.

Saltivka is vast, a mega-district of high- and low-rise blocks with several large metro stations, tramlines, and parks. Hundreds of thousands of people used to live here.

Russian forces, pushed back from their positions on the outskirts a few weeks earlier, still weren't far away. As we walked through the twisted metal structures of what had been an open-air market, a regular rhythm of explosions seemed to follow behind, some distant and rumbling, some sharper, closer.

A woman with a blonde ponytail stood smoking a cigarette round the back of a tall apartment block on Heroes of Labour

Avenue. We talked to her, surprised she was still here. 'Oh, my son's with me too,' she said, quite casually. 'We're living in the basement.'

So down we went. It was dank and dark, a confusing warren. They were living as deep as possible, in the boiler room. Here, Yulia's little boy, impish and blond, was curled up on a camping bed watching videos. Thick metal pipes criss-crossed the walls, and propped up on one was a drawing he'd made. It showed their nine-storey block surrounded by a shaky rainbow, an angel hovering above. 'God save and protect us,' he'd written, in felt-tip. He was eight.

Yulia had set up a study desk for him with an angle-poise lamp and school books. A makeshift bench along one wall was a kitchen – kettle, bottled water, bananas, tea and sweets.

Above, the booms hadn't stopped. They were, we guessed, bombing North Saltivka. Yulia sighed, exasperated. It had been quiet for a week, she said. 'Until today.'

The whole block was empty except for three women, one of them bed-bound. Volunteers brought food and water. Initially Yulia and Misha had decamped to a quieter part of the city, but it 'didn't work out'. As for going abroad, she didn't see the point.

'You can go away from the war, but then a time will come when you have to return and set everything up again,' she shrugged.

Those who left were always telling her on the phone how difficult it was, their new lives as refugees.

'It's better like this,' she gestured around at the basement. 'Our own walls.'

I asked how she coped with fear.

'Fear? Oh, well . . . At first, sure, there were hysterics. Terror. But you get used to it.

'Anyway,' she concluded, 'there's nothing to fear.' I looked at her quizzically.

'We're in God's hands!' she replied, a little ironically. But I could see she really meant it. There was very little about this situation she could control. Life and death would be decided by bigger forces.

We walked back upstairs, and I commented on how cosy she'd made their boiler-room home. She brightened. 'Yeah! It's warm, while the heating's on. And you know, if you want to create cosiness, you can create it anywhere. Look, we're trying our best, we aren't letting it get to us. We pray! And we hope.'

Misha, Vitalii and I left and walked towards the wide avenue, silence all around except the near-constant thuds to the north. The light was fading slowly, casting long shadows down the asphalt, which was marred by the telltale starbursts of cluster bombs. These were everywhere. In the burnt-out market, around Yulia's doorway, on pavements and around bus stops.

'Let's go.' Vitalii was grinning, gesturing across the broad, empty road. The noise was getting louder, harder to ignore.

Misha was less sure. 'That's quite . . . er, that's quite close, don't you hear it?'

'Well,' Vitalii said lightly, 'we're not going *straight* in that direction, are we?'

It only got worse though, and as we reached the tram tracks in the middle of the avenue there were suddenly people running towards the underground station. Not with any massive urgency, more of a pissed-off half-jog, but it was persuasive, and we ducked inside the metro too.

Down in the tiled underpass people paced, tense, smoking cigarettes in the gloom and waiting for the thunder to stop. Stress was etched into their faces; they'd endured this for two months already. Someone had taken a dog with them, and it barked and barked, a frightened, abrasive yelp.

It was not a deep underground station. On the platforms there was a sea of people, stretched out on bedding and blankets, huddled in between the ticket barriers. There were cuddly toys, a row of them on a ledge like mascots watching over proceedings. Houseplants and vases of lilacs, jigsaws and toys, a giant inflatable pool lounger – people had dragged everything down here. A woman said she'd speak to me, and I crouched on the floor next to her.

I asked her what her life was like at the moment. She spoke in a flat, angry voice. 'I've lost my apartment and my pension and everything. No apartment! In my old age . . .'

She couldn't evacuate because her family was still in the city; her daughter, a doctor, was treating the wounded, there were grandchildren to help with.

Staying down here twenty-four hours a day was getting to her, though. 'The air is so damp,' she sighed. 'People are coughing. But then, at least they feed us four times a day, even fruit.'

Even more journalists had appeared now, little clusters of navy flak jackets and helmets stepping over people, setting up TV cameras. I got up to go.

But at the top of the wide steps leading to the ticket barriers, a bright tartan waistcoat caught my eye. The woman wearing it was seventy years old with a mischievous expression. She was delighted to hear I was from Scotland. 'Just for you!' she grinned, gesturing at the waistcoat and doing a little twirl.

I asked how things had been, how they were managing, but she brushed it all off. 'We're alive, we're alive.' Her neighbour on the blankets was a French teacher, who was continuing her classes online, using the excellent mobile signal. Life went on.

Their main concern, these older women sleeping on a stone floor in a war zone, seemed not to be for themselves. Their main concern was for me.

'Oy, *solnishka*[3],' the French teacher said sorrowfully, looking me up and down. 'Surely it's too heavy for you?' She meant the flak jacket, which admittedly was now rubbing welts into my skin.

'Doesn't your granny worry?' the other woman asked. 'It's too dangerous here, dear!'

She did worry, I agreed, and they both nodded sagely. I thanked them – very sincerely – and ventured back to the now-quiet surface.

I made it back to the shuttered hotel on Sums'ka later that evening, starving, and slumped on the bed with my laptop to start work. After a while the door opened and the manager appeared, holding in his arms a packet of nuts, Pringles and a bottle of white wine. 'This is all I can find,' he said, apologetically, and I could've kissed him.

The next day I really got to see what had been done to Kharkiv. For many hours we barrelled around in a VW saloon, being shown what felt like every single bomb site in the city. I was taking pictures, David reporting; our indefatigable guide was Nataliya Zubar. I will say many things about Nataliya, but the first is that her hatred of Russia exceeds that of anyone I've met.

Oleksiy, her colleague, drove fast over the cobbles of Freedom Square, one of the largest in Europe, and as the huge constructivist office block lurched into view, its strange white symmetry marking the distant edge of the square, I felt a surge of emotion. I loved this building. A photo I'd found, from 2018, showed me standing under one of its soaring archways years earlier, grinning, a tiny figure in an oversized woollen coat.

Derzhprom was light-years ahead of its time when

---

3   'Little sunshine', 'darling', 'sweetheart'

built in the 1920s. A 'miniature skyscraper city built from scratch'[4], a shining white showpiece of the Ukrainian avant-garde movement that briefly flourished in Kharkiv before the Terror.

If the sight moved me, a visitor, imagine how symbolic this building had become for the residents of this city, *Kharkivyany*. Its very construction method had become a slogan, a new moniker for the unbreakable city – *zalizobeton*. It translates poorly as 'iron-concrete', or more precisely, 'reinforced concrete', a phrase which brings to mind multi-storey car parks and drab post-war schemes. But in Ukrainian it sounds powerful.

I was told again and again that *zalizobeton* was why Derzhprom had withstood the bombs of the 'Rashysts' (a portmanteau of Russian and fascists) just as it had when Germany attacked in 1941. In the popular imagination this building had come to symbolise Kharkiv's steely strength.

As we bumped across the square I saw the windows had been blown out all down one facade of Derzhprom; not far away stood the blackened facade of the district council building – the one I'd watched engulfed by fire in that shaky video while standing in the Vienna airport queue. Incredibly, it was still standing. The heavy columns along the facade were scorched black in the corner where the rocket hit, the dark marbled stone scored by shrapnel. We got out to have a look and were able to clamber down, through the big hole the rocket had made, into the basement, which was full of debris, chunks of floor mixed with smashed crockery. Six storeys had collapsed onto this spot; above was a rectangle of bright sky.

We covered miles that day, Nataliya talking at a rate of knots. She knew all the locations because she'd been documenting each strike, forensically, obsessively, with her team at the NGO Maidan

---

4   Owen Hatherly's perfect description of Derzhprom, in 'Amerikanist Dreams', *London Review of Books*, 21 October 2021

Monitoring. Just as investigators and journalists were collecting testimonies of torture, rape and execution, they gathered the stories of Kharkiv's architecture, adamant that the relentless bombing, particularly of civilian infrastructure, constituted a war crime.

Their case was certainly illustrated by the grim procession of bombed-out nursery schools, universities, court buildings and flats we saw that day. It had to be deliberate; the Russians couldn't be *that* bad at aiming. And as the BBC correspondent Quentin Sommerville had pointed out, walking down a devastated Kharkiv street in early March, 'If these tactics are unfamiliar to you, you haven't been paying attention, because this is the Russian attack playbook, perfected in over ten years of war in Syria.'

The terror, in this strategy, is the *whole point*.

Going further this time into the high-rise maze of Saltivka, I photographed charred blocks still smoking from a direct hit an hour before and descended into more basements where a stubborn few residents were clinging on. At the entrance to one cellar a religious icon was held in place with a bit of wire: a prayer in the dark.

As I chatted to one of the last remaining occupants, a black cat jumped up and settled on her shoulder, nuzzling her face. She nuzzled back, eyes closed, half-ignoring me and my silly questions about refusing evacuation.

'I feed ten of them,' she said simply. The cat purred loudly. 'Anyway – where would we go? We've nowhere to go.'

Without money, unsure of what support they'd get further west, they were sticking it out.

But the entrance to the flats behind this woman was spattered with recent shrapnel marks; the vehicles parked nearby were burnt out. No gas, no electricity upstairs. And too lethal, upstairs. The cooking pot balanced on a makeshift fire on the asphalt had a shrapnel hole the size of a fifty-pence piece, seared through the side. Sticking it out – but for how long?

I'd moved to a hotel in the south of the city, one of the few still open. The streets all around were badly damaged, but it was a short walk to the river, so one morning I clambered down its steep grassy bank to the water's edge. It was like entering another world. The sun felt sweeter down here, the pace infinitely slower. On the mud flats, exposed by the unusually low level of the Kharkiv River, men were hunched over on camping chairs or milkboxes, still as herons, multiple fishing rods propped on struts in front of them. Across the river were the low red-brick buildings of Old Kharkiv, a district of merchants, traders and artisans in the eighteenth and nineteenth centuries.

The swaying veil of a tall willow tree cast a pool of shadow, its tips just touching the slow, slick surface of the river. I sat cross-legged on the ground, let my eyes follow the darting shapes of swallows around the struts of the bridge. They flew in dizzying patterns around each other, a dance I couldn't understand but would have watched for hours, little waves of happiness washing through me. In this river-world, even the siren, which had been the background track to my morning tasks, was muted and distant. That mournful noise didn't belong here, where downy seeds spun through the air, or floated on the surface of the slow-moving river.

Reluctantly leaving this world, I climbed up the embankment and followed a big street lined by modern glass facades which had all been destroyed in the March air raids. I'd been summoned by Nataliya that afternoon to a mysterious secret concert, and I was looking, optimistically, for a clothes shop. I had two pairs of trousers; old Levis, thick denim jeans that could withstand anything, were grimy with dirt and ash from the bomb sites in Saltivka yesterday, not helped by my habit of kneeling on the ground to take photos. The other pair, quick-dry hiking trousers, now hung too loosely around my waist.

I had no luck finding a shop so returned to the hotel, raced through a last-minute article for the paper and dashed out again, discreetly holding up my trousers.

A password took us through steel doors and into the courtyard of a shabby old brick building. As we went down echoing steps into the darkness, the sound of a guitar grew louder, and we emerged into a party in full swing. This was Selo i Ludy (Village and People) – half recording studio, half bomb shelter.

The low-ceilinged bunker was packed with amps and leads, pianos and guitars, drum kits and more than one accordion. On an assortment of twirling office chairs, sunken couches, and old sea chests, people were sitting in knots of intense and noisy conversation. The bricks of the vaulted roofs were whitewashed, old carpets overlapped on the floors, and makeshift walls of chipboard divided one room from another. It looked remarkably like the long-lost squats I used to visit in East London. I felt at home.

I wandered through the interlinked vaults, finding the recording studio where local band Papa Karlo was playing its folky pop songs. This was being broadcast live to a party in Berlin, to raise more donations for the army. A Ukrainian flag pinned to the wall at the back of the room was covered in scribbled words of thanks to members of the 302nd anti-aircraft missile regiment.

After a few songs I ducked out and found the owner of the studio, Oleksandr. Tall and quiet, wearing rimless glasses, he had a cat cradled in his arms and a cigarette tucked behind his ear. The cat lived down here, he explained.

The jumble of recording equipment and instruments was the result of a merger, said Oleksandr. 'We evacuated two studios of our friends, who were not so lucky – they were flooded after bombing. Everything was underwater.'

Some of the gear was wrecked, but they'd salvaged the rest and transported it – 'fortunately just a few kilometres' – to this bunker.

These are problems musicians elsewhere don't have to think about, I suggested.

He shrugged. 'Well, yes, it wasn't so easy, there was water about a metre high.'

Now, though, they had everything they needed down here. Even a cat.

About half the fifty or so people milling around were in military garb, a mishmash of styles and eras, a kind of wartime chic. Amidst all the khaki green fleeces and heavy boots, you couldn't always tell who was who, but some in the bunker had clearly come from active duty, bleary-eyed, with medkits and tourniquets strapped to their armoured vests, mud on their boots.

Yaroslav, a thirty-year-old soldier, blinked at me, trying to focus on my questions. Yes, he said, he was a volunteer, in the territorial defence. He had a day in the city then had to return to the fighting; he couldn't say where.

I asked him to describe the scene in Selo i Ludy this afternoon. He smiled, deep dimples appearing above his wiry beard.

'Some crazy people having some crazy fun,' he said. 'We're at war, but we can still have fun. I think it's good.'

He was so tired, sagging against the chipboard wall. 'It's hard to think like this,' he apologised. 'But one important thing to say is that our community is really strong, and we'll win because truth is on our side.'

The fundraising was crucial, he stressed. 'Everybody is trying to help the army, and it's so important for our independence. For democracy.'

Someone began playing an old song about a Cossack who falls in love with a girl. The wonderful Ukrainian word for love – *kokhannya* – repeated in the sad and melodic refrain. In a corner I found Oleh Fedorov and his teenage son Maksym – peas in a pod, both in fatigues.

Illustrative of the broad range of backgrounds in this section of Kharkiv's social scene, Fedorov turned out to be a senior judge in Kyiv. He spoke in deliberate, precise sentences. He'd been a volunteer soldier since the invasion of 2014 and belonged to a group which helped supply the army.

Like so many volunteers, Fedorov was part of the territorial defence – the army reserve – and his brigade's patch was sewn on to his high-collared jacket. 'MRIYA', it read, with a giant white plane over the blue and yellow background.

Mriya, which means 'dream' or 'vision', was the affectionate name for the world's largest plane, an Antonov cargo aircraft based near Kyiv which had carried absurdly heavy things around the world, such as power-plant components and battle tanks.

When Russia invaded in February 2022, the Hostomel airfield was one of the first targets; *Mriya* wasn't evacuated in time and was destroyed in its hangar. The hastily formed volunteer brigade in Kyiv was named in honour of the beloved plane, Fedorov explained – 'But also because the *Mriya* of all Ukrainians is to become strong, to stay here and struggle for our independence.'

Concerts had been a feature of the fight in the east since 2014, Fedorov said. Musicians performing for troops helped keep morale high, reminded them what they were fighting for.

Looking around at this close-knit group of musicians, poets and soldiers, I understood something – the military was not, here, some distant state organisation, something you supported out of patriotism or pragmatism. Both were factors, of course. But the men and women defending this city right now, not that far from this bunker, were not strangers – they were family members, close friends, bandmates of the people standing next to me. Like the man playing the guitar in the band, Vasyl – his brother was fighting. And every man in this bunker knew that he might be called up, or indeed might volunteer, sooner or later. Imagine, I thought, the tireless energy with which you'd fundraise if each new donation might mean your dad or brother would have night-vision goggles as Russians tried to shoot at them in the dark.

I'd grown up blissfully ignorant of such hard choices, far from war, where it had been easy to adopt a knee-jerk pacifism. As I learnt more about history, I understood the argument for self-defence; the 1930s in Spain grabbed my teenage imagination and never let go. But in my own time, my own country, war was something I associated with British colonialism – on the streets in Northern Ireland, with the Americans in Iraq. It was easy to be against it.

Here, in Ukraine, but most forcefully here in this bunker, any clear dichotomy between soldiers and society disintegrated. The atmosphere was a super-strength distillation of what you could find all over the country – solidarity, collective effort, a powerful sense of common purpose. And this feeling itself was keeping people going – everybody commented on it.

'It gives a lot of energy,' said a musician in pink-tinted shades and a camo bandana. He paused. 'It takes a lot too, though.'

I was commenting on the catchy and artistic designs of many of the patches sewn onto fatigues – the stylised posters for the event looked similar – when someone said I could speak to the designer himself. I found him out in the courtyard: thin and intense, blinking in the sunlight.

'You can call me Patrick,' he said, in rushed English. He had an Italian surname, an Italian patch on his baggy, 1990s army jacket. Long Italian lashes gave him a bashful air.

Patrick's designs – he showed me more on his phone – were fantastic. Futuristic, blocky and bold, evoking constructivism, Bauhaus, the radical 1920s which in Kharkiv have particular resonance. My favourite featured the angular symmetry of Derzhprom, symbol of the iron city.

It was a deeply personal project, he said. 'When you've seen Derzhprom and other constructivist buildings since you were two or three years old, and you live for decades in this city, you become part of it.'

The style, Patrick said, had come naturally – 'I just feel it, it's inside of me.' His role was vital, his remarkable abilities as a designer connecting him to the brigades, to the soldiers, to the wider activist movement. That Derzhprom design, with the 'iron concrete' slogan stamped beneath it, was being printed on hoodies and t-shirts and caps as we spoke, and from every one a little bit more cash went to the front.

As the afternoon wound on a bit of alcohol appeared – only a couple of bottles of wine, rare because boozing was frowned upon, particularly among soldiers – but enough to make the noise in the cramped space rise significantly, loud laughter and chat competing with an open mic, and I was fighting a losing battle to record the faint words of an absurdly young woman with long, braided red hair. She looked like some elvish queen swamped in an oversized army uniform.

The cacophony around us grew, and I abandoned recording and joined in with the merriment. Chatting with Hennadiy, a musician and army medic, and his friends, I explained where I was from, and they all looked at each other with devious grins.

'What?'

'Shhhcotland?' said Hennadiy, already giggling like a little boy. They all joined in – 'Shhcotland!? Shhcotland!?' – in what I realised were Sean Connery impersonations.

Then it got more surreal.

'What should we shay?' one of the soldiers said, still hamming it up. 'Oh yes. Eleven! *Ii-leeeh-ven!*'

All three began producing extraordinary versions of the word *eleven*. I was cracking up. How on earth the lift sketch from Scottish comedy show *Burnistoun* had made its way to Kharkiv, I couldn't begin to fathom. The Internet is an amazing thing.

Nothing went on late in Kharkiv because of curfew, so it was still light as I wandered home, mind racing, happy. The hotel, as was evident from the assortment of vehicles parked outside, was serving as a base for journalists. Hulking, polished black jeeps sat alongside crappy old Ladas with 'PRESS' taped to their windows, indicating the broad spectrum of budgets. Everyone, from the major TV channels to the shoestring freelancers, was here.

The atmosphere was comradely and cheery despite meagre rations of actual nutrition, and I talked to colleagues over my dinner of one meatball and a puddle of rice. To my total delight, Bennett, the American from the Moscow programme who'd been reporting in Ukraine since the invasion, turned up and we shared a beer on the balcony upstairs, smoking cigarettes and watching the swallows darting round the rooftops as the sun slowly set. We hashed over our plans for a long time that evening. He was off to Zaporizhzhia on the night train with some foreign freelancers; they'd pooled resources and would find a car, go further east. 'It's pretty risky,' I said, doubtful.

He made the same non-committal little *hmm* that he always did. Bennett was just as he had been in Moscow – unflappable and calm, impeccably courteous in that American way, a big solid rock of a guy. I thought about going to Zaporizhzhia with him. But there were so many things happening here that I wanted to learn more about, pieces I wanted to write, and old friends I still had to see. And I didn't think I knew enough to go to a 'real' frontline. Cities with a risk of shelling felt within my 'acceptable risk' zone, but without having done the real, hands-on hostile-environment training, I decided I shouldn't go near the front. It was a wrenching decision, though.

After he left, I stayed out on the balcony watching the darkening sky, lit occasionally with flashes of light from the fighting to the north. But the stars, when they came, took my whole attention.

The blackout created the extraordinary effect of a starlit city. I thought how absolutely strange it was, to sit in the centre of a big city home to more than a million people, and look up at a blanket of stars that you'd normally only find in the deepest countryside. Stars so bright you could see by them, a great sweep of light spread across the black night.

Oleh rang from Odesa, worrying, and I promised it was quiet here, a good day, no issues. No sooner had I hung up and gone to bed than explosions rang out, one after another, rhythmic and massive. Distant enough, though. I counted them, breathed in the silence that followed, until my heart had slowed and I could sleep.

The story Ivanna told me the next day convinced me I was right to stay. Right to try to understand this place. We met at Strilka, a park on the spit of land where the Lopan' and Kharkiv Rivers meet. It was hot – by my standards – and we drank lemonade in the shade, talking.

Four years had passed since we first met at the Pride centre. Once a cultural manager, working in the arts, she was now what was loosely termed a 'volunteer' – fundraising, finding supplies, getting whatever was needed to brigades and to civilians. It was her life. And, it turned out, she was very good at it.

What she told me, though, went deep into the thorny, complicated politics of Kharkiv, and by extension, of Ukraine.

Football ultras had long been a fixture here, the groups melding into militias when Russia first invaded in 2014. These ragtag battalions of self-organised fighters played a key role in fighting back then, because the 'real' army was too weak thanks to years of underfunding and corruption. The best-known of them all, the Azov battalion, had its roots in Kharkiv – and in the far-right. It was subsequently reformed and brought fully under the control of the Ukrainian army. But Azov was not alone in this.

The Freikorps group also originated in Kharkiv. It has insisted the name comes from the tendency of the Western press to dub all 2014 Ukrainian militias 'Freikorps' – a reference to the anti-communist, right-wing militias in Weimar Germany – and that the group simply took on this moniker. They also enthusiastically took up the battle against gays and 'liberals', and regularly disrupted or even attacked the nascent attempts to stage a Kharkiv Pride march.

I remembered all this from 2018, and remembered my shock when the LGBTQ+ activists, mostly young gay women, told me they'd chipped in to fund these militia battalions, the same groups who harassed them in public. 'We knew they'd come for us,' one had said. 'But what choice did we have?'

In 2014 Kharkiv was a key target in the Kremlin's campaign to stoke unrest and annex territory, and Russian-backed separatists worked hard to take over here, as they did in Donetsk. Russian invasion, for the LGBTQ+ activists, would be horrifying. They'd held their noses and supported the only people able to defend the country at that time.

Freikorps, like the other militias, professionalised and grew. Its commander had been Heorhii Tarasenko. Ivanna knew him. She'd tried hard to persuade him that Russia was the real, common enemy – not Kharkiv's leftists and queers.

'I told him, when the tanks roll in we'll be on the same side,' she said. It showed considerable foresight; not many believed that tanks would really roll across the border and attack Kharkiv and Kyiv – even as late as February 2022, when all signs pointed to invasion. She'd somehow seen it coming, years before, and recognised that Russia posed a greater threat – an existential threat, to people like her – than their own home-grown fascists.

Her network of volunteers, buying everything from tactical gloves to medical supplies, were too important to snub, and Tarasenko was persuaded. When the tanks did indeed roll in, and Kharkiv was nearly surrounded, he led his soldiers in the battles that raged on the outskirts. And then he was killed, near Mala Rohan', a few weeks into the war.

Ivanna, retelling this story, paused. Then she said something extraordinary.

'He was the first guy I cried for. He was my political opponent. But he did a great job as a young general.'

Political opponent made it sound like they were in divergent political parties, whereas this man virulently hated her, and her friends. He stood for the kind of mindless far-right nationalism that is on the rise everywhere, 'Christ and the family' stuff, with runes and wolves thrown in for extra testosterone. It's a phenomenon all over Europe, not least in Germany and the UK; its existence in Ukrainian society should never be glossed over, but it is wrong to pretend it only exists there.

Ivanna understood all this very well, better than any Western commentator making sweeping judgements about the situation. And yet she tried to help Tarasenko because it was pragmatic. It was necessary. And because she genuinely believed she could get through to him. After his death she had written, with real sincerity, on social media, describing her respect for him and the way he had defended the city. It had been met with a hail of abuse from his 'comrades', outraged that someone like her would so much as utter his name.

She'd shrugged it off, focused on the bigger picture. There was little time to dwell on things. Hospitals and schools needed supplies, soldiers all along the front needed tourniquets and blood-clotting powder and bullet-proof plates. And, somehow, she had to retain some semblance of order in her own life, resisting the urge to simply work every minute of the day.

We parted at the bridge, but a few days later met again at the city's main fire station – she'd managed to source an incredibly expensive bit of kit needed to find people buried under rubble. It had finally arrived, via Finland, and the firemen gathered in the courtyard for a celebratory photo around the new box, which they'd opened like a Christmas present. In the photo I took, one fireman is gazing, quite adoringly, at Ivanna, and she smiles confidently straight into the camera, the very picture of a woman with a mission: a bullet-proof vest under her black leather jacket, red lipstick and torn jeans; she looks pleased. She looks in her element.

CHAPTER EIGHT

'WE CAN GO TO Vilkhivka', a text from Nataliya announced. I'd been hoping she'd say this. With the Russian forces now pushed back north of Kharkiv – in some places nearly to their own border – more villages and towns had come back under Ukrainian control, and journalists were beginning to creep in, documenting the devastation, interviewing those who'd survived both the occupation and the fighting.

Her colleague Zhenya – short for Yevhenii – drove us, fast, bouncing over tram tracks and potholes. It was already twenty-four degrees at 9 a.m., and the sun beat down on the old car. We swerved to avoid being driven into a wall by a thundering truck; an angry horn blast trailed in its wake. Nataliya, practically swinging by the grab handle, turned round, grinning and joked, 'Welcome to Cairo!'.

The villages we were aiming for were usually a ten-minute drive from the city limits, but this eastern edge of the city was badly damaged, and soldiers were still twitchy on the checkpoints that blocked the roads.

We passed the tall and blackened menorah which marks Drobytsy Yar, the ravine where at least 15,000 Jews were killed by SS officers in 1941. For a strange second I thought the monument was perhaps deliberately scarred; twisted and ripped apart to reflect the horror that happened there. But no – it had apparently been hit by Russian shelling.

Off the highway and onto dirt tracks we made slow progress.

Burnt-out cars, vans, tanks, trucks, you name it – even a helicopter lay crumpled in a field. When the Russians had held this territory, they'd set up their heavy guns in the field and fired artillery almost relentlessly at the outskirts of Kharkiv, which lay a few miles west. Then the counter-attack came. Ukrainian forces took back the positions at the end of March, but at a heavy cost. The young general Ivanna had mourned was not the only one to die here. And the place was wrecked.

We were supposed to be interviewing people, but at first we could find none. The eerie silence of a ruined street and the thud of distant artillery was becoming a familiar soundtrack. On Peace Avenue, the Ukrainian flag flying at one gate was punctured by a row of bullet holes – deliberate, precise. Somehow I found this more chilling than the half-ruined house behind. Not a single vehicle was intact – though I did see a man driving a Hyundai completely riddled with bullet holes, the windscreen cracked and impenetrable. A 'Z' marked the vehicles the Russians had requisitioned.

The road and settlements followed the Rohan'ka River, which widened into a reservoir, and I caught glimpses of it, an intense blue visible through the broken fences of cottages and modest brick houses. What a lovely place this must have been, I thought, for the umpteenth time. Clearly Kharkiv's elite had thought so too – along the water's edge some enormous residences loomed, all turrets and crenellations. The shells hadn't differentiated, though, between the houses of the rich and the houses of the poor.

We found only a handful of people in Vilkhivka, and most had left before the occupation, coming back only now to salvage what was left. We spoke to those who were willing; most were not. Too scared, too traumatised. A man in his fifties, Valerii, was trying to patch up his house and stopped to talk. His elderly mother had been injured in a blast and she had to walk with sticks.

What Valerii really wanted to talk about was the harmony that had been here once. No one had cared, or even known, who was 'ethnically' Russian, and who Ukrainian.

A neighbour interrupted us, lurching up unsteadily. 'I'm a Ukrainian German,' he shouted, at no one and everyone. 'But I'm faithful to this land! See how they destroyed my home? I built it, built it with my own two hands!'

He was ashamed, brushing tears away, trying to explain that he wasn't usually drunk. 'Only *now*, only *now* I'm drinking,' he slurred. He wasn't the only one. There was a heavy reckoning in these villages, a terrible legacy the occupation had left behind. Rumours had been swirling of collaboration, and there were mutters of deportations, of family members still missing after the day in March, as the Ukrainian advance approached, when a whole group of people were taken 'to safety' by Russian troops – but never returned. But no one really wanted to talk about that.

'I'll speak to you, you use my name, and then the Russians come back, and what happens to me?' a man shouted from his gate.

That the territory might change hands again was a real fear for people in Vilkhivka, despite the assurances of the Ukrainian side.

On this day more than any other I felt the frustration of not-knowing, of picking over the ruins and trying to guess what had happened. In the burnt-out shell of the high school, Zhenya waved a metal soldier's helmet in the air. Bent out of shape, a bullet hole through one side, it looked like a relic from the Second World War. He laughed. 'Look at the shit the Russians use.' As we picked our way through the rubble, the gas masks and empty bottles of wine were further proof the Russians had indeed used this as a base. That's what Nataliya had been told. They'd holed up here until Ukrainian forces overwhelmed them.

But then I found the gym hall. Climbing frames, basketball hoops and a big hole in the roof. Next to a yellow tennis ball on the wooden floor lay the green fuse of a rocket, half the wings still intact. I trod extremely carefully, crouching down to take the photo which would end up printed in the paper, illustrating the piece. Dust and debris, ammo boxes, boots and clothes . . . but these uniforms weren't Russian. I looked closer. The jackets, the food rations, cigarettes and toiletries – they were all Ukrainian.

Had Ukrainian soldiers subsequently used this as a base? We had no idea. 'Maybe we don't have the correct information,' Nataliya admitted. Echoing what I was thinking, she continued, 'We only see the outcomes, the destruction . . . We don't know what happened, exactly.'

The next mystery was much worse. On the dirt road between two of the villages, the Toyota bumping along slowly, I saw a shape on the verge that didn't make sense. A person, prone, but somehow wrong, twisted out of shape. We stopped, and I made myself get out, knowing what this was, and not wanting to see it.

It seemed bleached of colour, the corpse. The shaggy hair was nearly white. A grey shapeless jumper was bunched up, the grey skin of the lower back punctured by a puckered hole. I thanked God, silently, that this man lay flat in the dirt, so I wouldn't have to see his face. The grass and weeds were already growing up around him; fat flies crawled across the mottled skin.

I wondered how long he had been there. I wondered, of course, why he had been left like this. Left on the side of the road to rot, left to the flies. Inexplicably, next to him, was a pair of boots, neatly placed side by side, something colourful inside, perhaps a tin of food . . . I was going to look closer, then recalled a warning someone had given me about booby traps. I edged away.

The contrast was the strangest thing. All around the scene was so idyllic. Small vegetable gardens on the gentle slope of a hill, fences painted bright colours, the sound of birds and the nearby river.

Nothing was clear, nothing was making sense. We drove on, but the smell was in our clothes now, in our hair; why, I thought angrily, why on earth was it so *sweet*? I kept getting new wafts of it through the open window as we wove around the country roads. Perhaps it was my imagination – Nataliya thought so. 'That's bodies,' I blurted out at one point, but she couldn't smell it. 'Perhaps dead cows or something,' she replied, uninterested.

There *had* been many bodies here – Russian soldiers, abandoned by their retreating comrades – but these had been removed weeks ago. Their stuff was still here, though. Not just the burnt-out tank, parked almost neatly outside a small brick house, but also random items of their clothing scattered around the dusty streets.

I filmed from the car window as Zhenya drove past a pair of Russian army trousers, he and Nataliya cheering at the sight. As explosions cracked sharply nearby, the two belted out a popular punk-folk song, 'Arta', about the legendary ability of Ukrainian artillery to blow up *Moskali*, or Russians.

'*No more* Moskali, *fuck all left at all!*' they sang gleefully as we rounded a corner, completely unperturbed by the very real artillery outside, which had left my ears ringing.

We'd run out of time, and there was the night train to Kyiv to catch. I hoped, as ever, that I had enough material, and I began writing up the day's events, trying to quell my clammy carsickness as we lurched around the craters on the road back to the city.

The problem with a late-night train during curfew and blackout is probably obvious; the trains leave well after curfew descends, so you have to arrive hours early. I'd enjoyed the sunset outside Kharkiv's magnificent train station, its two towers and tall columns the perfect stage for a flight of swallows playing in the evening light, but now it was dark, there was another hour to wait and I was slumped down under my flak jacket and rucksack, half-sitting against the wall of the dimly lit underpass. I looked around at my potential fellow passengers, hoping I wouldn't get stuck in the *kupe*, a four-person compartment, with a snoring bloke, and spotted two young women in uniform. I caught a few words of English from their murmured conversation. 'I bet I end up sharing with them,' I thought.

In the scrum down the tunnel I lost them, but sure enough, they reappeared in my compartment. Both quiet, thoughtful women. I had the last of a plastic bottle of cherry liqueur someone had given me, and shared out the dregs.

One was nick-named Kasya, and she revealed, cautiously, that she was Belarusian. The way she talked about her role in this fight was poignant. Freedom for Ukraine would hopefully lead to freedom for her own country too, an end to the tyranny of Putin's puppet, Lukashenko. Having joined the Ukrainian armed forces, she had essentially barred her own way home. Her mother was still there. She said all this in a matter-of-fact way: she was doing what was necessary. No need for emotions.

Lev, meanwhile, was Canadian. No one could mistake that accent. But I was staggered to hear how she'd got here.

A full ten years younger than me, she was already a seasoned army medic. At home in Canada years ago she'd read about the Kurdish fight in Rojava, northern Syria, and about the feminist, left-wing revolution taking place there, under threat from ISIS. 'It said you could donate, or better, you could go and help as a medic,' she recalled. 'And I was like, "That's great, because I don't have any money; I guess I'll just go there."' She laughed.

Lev had spent years in that grim fight against Islamic State. Years which I couldn't imagine, and which she didn't go into.

When the war in Ukraine really kicked off, she said, it was a natural choice to come and volunteer. She believed in the cause and had the skills they needed. The two women had been paired up because Kasya could translate, and you could tell they'd been spending all their time together, under intense pressure; there was an invisible piece of string between them. I watched them from the opposite bunk during a lull in conversation. They were communicating without words. That kind of bond, that kind of closeness, is hard-won.

Lev and I went to the end of the rocking carriage, to smoke cigarettes in the chilly air. This had been banned on Ukrainian trains, which was annoying, and at first the conductor had flatly refused our request. Ten minutes later she'd reappeared, whispered that we could smoke if no one saw us, and even winked.

I told Lev briefly about the last few months and the reporting I was doing now. I mentioned the long rambling diary I kept religiously, a compulsion to get everything down on paper before memory mushed it up or let it slip away.

'I kept a diary for a while,' she mused. 'But it got too dark.' She'd lost a lot of good people in Syria, good friends.

I looked at Lev, her face just visible. She dragged on her cigarette, and it flared briefly in the dark. She looked so, so young – rosy cheeks and a shy smile – but there was something about her, something I couldn't pin down, which was making a deep impression on me. A stillness at her centre. A quiet certainty.

I was thinking how embarrassingly awestruck I was by this person when she turned to me and said, 'It's so brave, what you're doing'.

I was completely taken aback. 'What *I'm* doing? Are you serious? You're a frontline medic! It's not even your own country.'

She just smiled back, Buddha-like, nodding slowly.

I'd come to Kyiv, in part, to hole up and write. I had several deadlines looming, including a long essay on Kharkiv for a literary journal, and I needed time, peace, and perhaps some distance.

Of course I'd also come to see it once more, to immerse myself in this endlessly surprising city. I went to the famous golden-domed monastery, St Michael's, and sat for a long time at the back as priests and parishioners came and went; as the choir assembled, sang, and left. Still I sat there, calm in the dark, cool peace of it all, undisturbed. I needed to let my brain race and ramble; it produced images and ideas and urgent tasks and phantom arguments, and I let it rage on like this until some quiet returned.

I saw old friends, went out for dinner, almost as though I were on a short break in any normal city. Some anti-tank obstacles remained on the streets, but not many; soldiers on rotation or recovering from injuries walked the streets but were outnumbered by couples with kids and dogs and groups of giggling teenagers. I talked to Marta, another journalist I'd met in Prague; she was pregnant with her first child and full of excitement and trepidation. She had left, she said, gone to Moldova, but it broke her heart to be apart from her husband, from her parents. They were her whole world. When her doctor's clinic reopened a few weeks ago, she'd taken it as a sign, and rushed back to Kyiv.

She was tripping over herself trying to explain it, and I tried to assure her that I completely understood. These agonising decisions so many were having to make: to have a baby far from your loved ones in some temporary exile or in your native city, your own doctor on call, in which you have a very slim chance of coming under attack. No one who hasn't had to contemplate such a decision can judge it.

After all this time on the road, I didn't find it easy to sit still and write for long hours. In fact, unless I did it early in the morning, I found it almost impossible. I wasn't sleeping much, though that was nothing new, but I knew I looked more exhausted than usual; I was getting dizzy at random points through the day, and sharp noises – a motorbike in traffic, high-pitched music in shops – were strangely painful. The pieces all got written – they always do –

but I started thinking about taking a break. The messages from Oleh in Odesa, and from friends back home, were increasingly worried, asking when, or if, I'd actually go home, and I reassured them – soon. Just not quite yet.

The train back to Kharkiv a few days later was stiflingly hot, packed with people returning home for the first time since the 24th. In our compartment the women told me they felt it was safe enough, *just about*. I said nothing; it would be unhelpful to point out that there were still people living in metro stations, still multiple air-raid alerts a day; still regular strikes.

But people long for home – that much I could understand. I was beginning to long for mine, secretly. Not least because it would be a sensible twelve degrees in Shetland right now. I sweltered on the top bunk in vest and pants, only occasionally falling into an uneasy half-sleep, as the train clunked and screeched over endless switches, diverting onto minor routes, lurching with enough force to throw you out of bed. It felt like the carriage was trying to violently leave itself behind.

A brief word about conductors. *Providnytsi*. There isn't really an English translation; *conductor* would suggest they're only going up and down the length of the train checking tickets. These women in the neat navy uniforms – and sometimes now men, too – are in charge of the self-contained world of their single carriage for as long as the journey lasts: reminding people to get off at their stop, resolving disputes, providing bedsheets and hot drinks. Or refusing them. In the past, it was one of those jobs that made evident the Soviet legacy of being inordinately rude to customers, but more and more often *providnytsi* were actually nice.

Not this morning.

'WAKE UP! STRIP YOUR BED!'

The door was wrenched open, and a head appeared, shouted the order again, then withdrew. The yelling and banging of sliding doors went on for several minutes. I dug around and found my watch. It was shortly after 5 a.m. I'd slept for about two hours.

As instructed we blearily stripped our bunks, and I walked down the corridor to hand in my bed linen. The *providnytsia* was gathering it into a sack.

'Where's your towel?' she demanded, outraged. I staggered back and retrieved it, grabbing my little bag of coffee in the hope I might be able to make some. Each carriage has a samovar supplying constant hot water, but I didn't have a cup. I asked, as politely as I could, if I could pay to use one of the many stacked up behind her, a little hoard in her dragon's lair.

Her lips curled. 'We do not give them out, and we do not sell them,' she pronounced, with enormous satisfaction.

It was 7 a.m. when we finally pulled in to Kharkiv, and I was feeling like shit. I had a strange booming echo in my head and felt I'd lost half my strength, the two rucksacks and helmet suddenly impossibly heavy. I was staying in a small hotel near the station for a few days, the Ryleev, and when I clumped in bleary from the train the kind women running the place made me breakfast before Nataliya and Zhenya arrived. And what a breakfast – *syrnyky*, little cakes of fluffy cottage cheese, crispy and light, hot from the pan, sour cream and jam melting in a swirl on top. The sugar, and caffeine, revived me, but so too did the warmth of the women who ran the place. The building was on a little hill, the kitchen where we ate giving on to a long garden, the city skyline beyond. I loved it from the first minute.

Kharkiv really was returning to life now, only three months into the war – a crowd outside the station, and traffic on the roads. It was another hot, sunny day, and we were going to pick through the ruins of Vilkhivka again, trying to piece together what had happened on that day in March when so many people disappeared.

In the village, a work team was repairing the sagging electricity lines along the lakeside road, and there were now slightly more people about. But these were still deeply scarred and barely habitable places; the people we spoke to frequently broke down in tears, or stared, numb, into the distance. Not only were they traumatised, they were scared of what might come next. Could the Russians return? Ukrainian authorities said not, but who really knew? And it might be twenty-five degrees now, the start of the hot summer, but what about the winter if the gas was still off?

This was the main concern of Zina, an old woman in a headscarf and cardigan, drying slices of bread on tea towels in her dark living room to make them last longer. The side of the house had been blown up, and the bath was full of rubble. Not that there had been water to fill a bath, not for months.

'How will I survive the winter if it's not fixed?' she asked, over and over, her bony hands twisting in worry. I wished I had an answer for her. Zhenya and Natalia made a note of what she needed; they'd pass it on to the volunteers coming this way.

On the same street a man in a plaid shirt with a sad weary face showed us the basement where his family had slept during the worst of the bombing in March. A nearby hit had cracked the ceiling.

It turned out Nikolai was exactly the person to talk to. He'd seen it all unfold – and narrowly avoided ending up in Russia himself.

It happened on 28 March, several weeks into the occupation. Nikolai had already experienced some run-ins with the soldiers. They'd asked him for a spade one day, to dig a trench. He had to give it to them, obviously, and the soldiers started talking to him, pleased to hear that he was originally from Kursk, a town across the border in Russia.

'Oh,' one of the soldiers, also from Kursk, had said, 'then

you're a *zemlyak*!' (It means 'fellow countryman', someone from the same land.)

When Nikolai told them how the family had had to hide in the cellar for a month, the man in command replied, 'Why were you hiding? We came to liberate you!'

And at that, Nikolai had snapped a little.

'I said, "Did I invite you here? Why would you liberate me?" And then he hit me, pulled his gun on me. He said, "You know, thirty of my men were killed in Vilkhivka."'

The others had grabbed their commander, prevented him from shooting Nikolai, and later came back to apologise. The guy had seen too much blood, they'd said. Don't take it personally.

When the troops came shouting and bashing on the doors on 28 March, they didn't tell people they'd end up in Russia. Nobody would have gone, Nikolai said. He wanted to make sure I understood – many people here came from Russia originally, having moved to work in the milk factory and farms in Soviet times. They had been given land. It was quite normal to have relatives across the border. But none of this meant they wanted to *go back* there.

That day, Ukrainian soldiers were already at the far end of the village, the fighting drawing nearer. Russian troops went door to door, telling everyone there would be a massive strike in fifteen minutes. No time to gather any things, just run, to the northern end of the village.

Nikolai said about sixty people gathered at the track at the end of Studentska Street, no idea what was happening. He remembered the noise of the women, their wails of fear.

'My granddaughter, eight years old, took my hand,' he recalled, voice tight with emotion. 'She was so scared.'

Nikolai was struggling to get the words out, to tell us what the little girl had asked him as they stood and waited. 'Grandad!' she'd cried. 'Are they coming to kill us?'

His face crumpled as he told us this.

After a minute he went on. He'd calmed the little girl, he said, and then after half an hour of waiting, Nikolai and his family – wife, daughter, son-in-law and granddaughter – walked with the others, several miles to Verkhnya Rohan'ka.

The Russians watched the villagers, silent, from behind their armoured vehicles. Their faces, Nikolai recalled, were hidden; all he could see were their round helmets – 'like rows of mushrooms'.

'The Russians said once we reached Verkhnya Rohan'ka we'd be put on buses to Shestakove [a village about eight miles east],' he went on. 'They said, just until it's quieter, then we'd be brought right back.'

But this was not true. Nor, it turned out, was the airstrike story. Nikolai had already grown suspicious when they reached Verkhnya Rohan'ka, he said, and as the crowd waited for the promised buses, he and his family slipped away, unseen. They hid in a friend's garden, ten, twenty minutes, and then heard the sound of engines. Nikolai watched through the fence. Not buses, but Kamaz trucks drew up. Military trucks with canvas backs. The Vilkhivka villagers were loaded on, and driven away.

The stories started circulating a week or so later: one person was in Voronezh, others in Belgorod. Some who had passports with them had made the long, roundabout journey through the Baltics and back via Poland. But that took a lot of resources.

Others in Vilkhivka confirmed what Nikolai had told us. One woman described how the Russian soldiers bashed on the door, told them an airstrike was imminent. She and her family were eating lunch. They fled, taking barely anything with them –

they'd been told it would only be a few hours before they could come back. She, too, had snuck off before the canvas-backed trucks came.

On the phone later I got hold of Svitlana, whose father was one of those taken away. She and her four-year-old had left Vilkhivka shortly before it was occupied, but he'd insisted on staying put. The trucks had stopped in Vovchansk, she said, a Ukrainian town occupied by Russians. The people were transferred to buses – which then went straight over the border.

It was a stranger who rang up to tell her that he'd seen her father in Verkhnya Rohan'ka, among the group put on the trucks. 'I cried and cried,' she said. Finally, she was able to reach her dad on the phone. He'd been in tears too – especially when he heard the voice of his little granddaughter, 'because he was afraid he'd never see her again'.

There were rumours of a camp for Ukrainian refugees in Voronezh, but Svitlana's father was staying with relatives. The problem was that in the panic to leave he'd mislaid the bag with his documents. Now he was stuck: he couldn't leave Russia without his passport and had refused to take a Russian one.

'He doesn't care about Russia,' she said angrily. 'I mean, he's pleased that our relatives are helping him, but he's very worried that the documents will take too long, that his Ukrainian passport could be taken away.

'My father doesn't understand why they did this,' she concluded, furious. 'And I don't understand. For what purpose?'

The story was a complicated one. It wasn't the same as those coming through from places like Mariupol – horror stories of forced deportation, filtration camps, torture. Estimates of how many Ukrainians had been deported varied, but it seemed likely to be in the hundreds of thousands, with some transported deep into the interior, to Siberia and the far east.

This was different, though; it was possible to believe the Russian soldiers at the lowest level really did believe they were getting people to safety. The distance to Belgorod was only forty miles or so. Of course all that mattered little; removing civilians to the occupying country is a war crime. And whatever the motivation of the soldiers, someone must have been giving the orders, someone decided to take these people to Russia against their will.

We made two more trips like this, trying to find more sources, searching for an elusive local council leader who might or might not have a list, and eventually I wrote it up for the newspaper, and then for Radio 4. It felt difficult to move on from a story when there was so much more to tell, but I hoped I could come back to it.

My last night in Kharkiv, at the end of May, was surreal. The reprieve in missile strikes and shelling, the warm summer weather, the 2,000 or so people returning by train and road every day: all of it contributed to a buzz of activity, a sense of normality returning. On Sums'ka Street, in the exact spot where I'd got out of the taxi weeks ago and found everything silent and wrecked, a hipster bar was open for business, doing a roaring trade in enchiladas and chicken wings.

The windows of the bar were still cracked and boarded up, but that hardly mattered. Many of the clientele were foreign journalists and their Ukrainian producers and military escorts; some Kharkiv hipsters were there too, hanging out, drinking fruit-flavoured beers, strong IPAs, BrewDog from Scotland . . . And a few miles away, in Vilkhivka and countless other villages where Russians had been, old women were drying meagre slices of bread, artillery cracks still sounding in the fields around, the smell of bodies still occasionally drifting on the wind. The contrast was too strange to really process.

Before I caught another train the following day, I walked through the city for a couple of hours. I watched with amazement as an actual tram rolled down the street. The mayor had announced that the metro would run again soon; anyone still sleeping on the platforms would have to leave. It all felt too fast, too optimistic.

I had planned to drop by the media centre that had been set up in the basement of a university building on Freedom Square. Natasha, a journalist I knew, was working there, and we hadn't managed to see each other yet. I set out along the winding paths of Shevchenko Park. The flowerbeds were in full bloom, municipal workers mowing the grass, couples out for a stroll.

Then all that peace was shattered by a huge explosion. It drowned out the birdsong, the strimmer's whine; its earsplitting noise had the couples ducking to the ground, where they crouched, looking around, unsure what to do. Others simply straightened up and carried on as though nothing had happened. But there was more to come.

I was near the media centre now, and it was below ground, so I made for it at a quick trot and spent the next couple of hours down there, shivering in the chilly air, as the strike continued. It was hard to tell, listening to the booms above, how close they were. Natasha jumped at the loudest one, looking at me across the table, eyes wide. I realised she was really scared. The lull and the normality in preceding weeks had somehow made this worse. I felt a childish rage, an impotent, stamp-your-feet fury. *What the fuck?* I wanted to shout, at the sky, at Russia. *What the fuck are you doing? Just leave us alone!*

Eventually I had to leave or I'd miss the train. There was heavy rain after the day's heat, torrential, and the taxi's windscreen wipers couldn't move fast enough. We went past the Palace of Culture of the Railway Workers – a unique, unmistakable constructivist landmark, with a strange fluted facade. Its windows were all blown out. 'Oh, shit, not that one,' I blurted out.

'*Da, da,*' the driver sighed.

I took a quick picture from the rain-streaked window, of the grey, damaged building, sandbags heaped up in the foreground.

The death toll by nightfall was nine, with many more injured, including a child. On the Dnipro train I scrolled through the updates. The worst damage was about a mile and a half north of the square where I'd been.

Serhiy Zhadan, Kharkiv's famous rock-star poet and novelist, summed up the heavy mood of the city in a social-media post. 'I feel sorry', he wrote, 'for people stubbornly trying to hold on to a peaceful life, and from whose hands this peaceful life slips.'

For whom was it harder, Zhadan wondered – all those who'd come back in recent days 'to the quiet sunny city', only to immediately experience the horror of shelling, or those who'd today been persuaded to come out from their underground lives, only to relive the terror of the early March airstrikes?

'War is always around somewhere,' he concluded. 'She likes to remind us of her presence.'

CHAPTER NINE

VAST RIVERS, THE KIND that flow through continents and look like seas at their widest points, hold a particular fascination for me, as do trains. The reason is simple; we don't have these things in Shetland, and I hope the childlike awe I feel on a riverbank, or watching an intercity train swoosh across a high bridge, will never fade. Best, of course, when the two are combined.

About a hundred miles southwest of Kharkiv the train had slowed, and I watched from the window, totally transfixed, as we clunked across a bridge that seemed to stretch on and on over the dark river. Lights glimmered, reassuring, in the distance. There are many bridges which knit the city of Dnipro together, taking trains and traffic across both the Dnipro and Samara rivers. The city sprawls at their confluence.

The faintest light still glowed in the sky, reflected in the surface of the river, its swirls and patterns, wide below us. It was completely dark, though, when we disembarked, the long platform illuminated only by pools of light from open carriage doors. I was trying to hurry – it was nearly curfew – and urged my feet along the cobbles, but each step required a concentrated effort, and my knee twinged badly going down into the tunnel. I thought of Oleh on the platform in Odesa - *You can't possibly carry all this*. If only I'd trained harder at weightlifting, I thought. Got stronger knees, perhaps.

The city of Dnipro was still a fair distance from the southern and eastern frontlines, but a good jumping-off point to get a bit further east, into Donbas. I had some leads, contacts I was waiting to hear back from, but it was late when I got to the small hotel, kicking off heavy boots and dumping everything in a corner, too tired to unpack. On a whim I got Radio Scotland up on my laptop. It was a Thursday night, and Anna Massie was presenting the folk-music programme. In her lovely Black Isle accent she introduced my cousin's band, a Shetland-Sweden-Norway trio called the Nordic Fiddlers Bloc. I had to laugh as I lay back on the bed, joy fighting homesickness, and listened to Kevin and his friends play their lilting, moving music.

The strike in Kharkiv had been part of a coordinated attack, with other cities coming under fire as the night went on. The sirens woke me up at 4 a.m., and I went to the window and looked out at the city as the sun crept up. The alerts faded after a while, but later that morning it emerged that a National Guard base near Dnipro had been hit; ten were killed and more than thirty injured. I spent the day writing a piece about Kharkiv for Irish radio's *World Report* and tried to find a jacket to buy, my head still fuzzy, my right ear buzzing and booming, the tinned music in the second-hand shop jangling and harsh. I put it down to exhaustion, idiotically not making the connection between hearing loss and the cracks and bangs I'd been near over the past few weeks.

I had thought of joining Bennett, but he was too far east, and in any case we were both frequently writing for the same newspaper, so being in the same place would be counterproductive. Sievierodonetsk and Lysychans'k were still in Ukrainian hands but the Russian advance was closing in on these cities, a pincer movement from the north and south looking likely. Towns were being wiped off the map by Russian artillery as they paved the way for the ground troops.

The road to Sievierodonetsk was still passable though often shelled, and Bennett's team had been using it to report from the city, which looked likely to fall any day.

'Pretty sure my luck is spent,' he'd written in a message to me, a few days earlier. It wasn't anything major – a couple of flat tyres, an uneasy feeling. 'Trust your gut,' I'd replied, hoping he'd leave there soon.

Dnipro felt like Las Vegas, with alcohol on sale and bars open late, and I met some journalists for a drink. The group grew as the evening went on, and while talking to a Ukrainian man, I mentioned I was keen to report on the evacuation efforts in Pokrovs'k, a railway town twenty miles from the frontline in Donetsk Oblast.

'Well,' he said, amused, 'if you really want, you can go tomorrow.'

He knew some army guys who were driving to Kramatorsk, a small city 100 miles east, which had become *de facto* capital of the region after Donetsk was seized in 2014. Pokrovs'k was on their way.

'They're leaving at 5.30 a.m., though,' he said. 'So you probably won't want to go.'

Half an hour later I was packing my things, and by 11 a.m. the following day I was watching the flat, fertile land of Donetsk Oblast speed by. Golden fields and blue sky, the Ukrainian flag in a snapshot. The creaky old bus was racing down the highway, overtaking everything, the wind roaring in through a broken sunroof. It was too loud to hold a conversation, and the young volunteers were glued to their phones anyway. They looked like teenagers on a school trip, snickering at videos together at the back of the bus.

We had not, of course, set off at 5.30 a.m., and I'd sat on the steps of the army building in Dnipro for a good few hours, reading Neal Ascherson's book about the Black Sea and trying to forget how hungry I was.

But it felt good to be on the road, relatively unburdened – I'd left most of my stuff in Dnipro, taking only body armour and an overnight bag. I jumped out at the Hotel Druzhba ('Friendship'). At the desk, a harassed receptionist was trying to deal with the demands of several foreigners – aid workers and journalists – and I tried to translate between them. She was mostly telling them no: No, you cannot have another room; No, there is no dinner available (or breakfast, or lunch); No, you cannot pay by card. I wasn't sure how the hotel was actually functioning – there were clearly very few staff left – but I was grateful it was. I got a small room upstairs, in exchange for most of my stash of hryvnias, and headed out.

The town felt like the set of a western, a few streets in a grid layout, dusty and hot this afternoon, and great drifts of fluffy poplar seeds, so many that they gathered in balls, dancing along the tarmac like miniature tumbleweed. In the square an old man was playing the accordion, a cheerful, old-fashioned tune, but he lacked an audience.

Pokrovs'k was once called Krasnoarmiysk, in honour of the Red Army which liberated it from Nazi control in 1943, but it began as Grishino, a railway hub in the Russian Empire. And the railway was still the heart of the town: not just the passenger station from which people were now being evacuated to the west, but also the engine sheds, repair shops and sidings.

In line with its former name, memorials to the Red Army were everywhere in Pokrovs'k, and I photographed them as I walked round getting my bearings. One obelisk commemorated the soldiers 'burned alive by Fascists' in a prison in 1943. Carved communist stars and symbols of eternal flame were everywhere; there was a large model tank atop a plinth. The layers of history in these memorials had always interested me, but now it was so much sharper, messier. That word 'fascist' was heard so often these days, used by Russians to justify their entire war of aggression, and in return used by Ukrainians to refer to their former 'brothers' who were now bombing them indiscriminately, occupying their land, and committing atrocities, just as the Nazis had done. These statues celebrating the Soviet liberators, all their lettering in Russian, not Ukrainian, all with the phrase 'fascist occupiers' in their inscriptions, were no longer straightforward.

Outside the station was another, simpler act of memory: a brick wall painted, imperfectly and more lovely for it, with scarlet poppies and ears of wheat, a soldier walking through them. Alongside were a few lines from Ukraine's most renowned poet, Taras Shevchenko.

It was to this spot that evacuees were brought most days by van or bus or ambulance – whatever vehicle could be found – from towns and villages becoming too unsafe to stay in. Or at least the authorities hoped they would come each day; they were trying to encourage people to leave places near the frontline. Not everyone was persuaded. In fact, traffic had really dropped off recently, a railway official told me.

Inside the station the windows were boarded up, sandbags heaped up against them. I walked through the echoing, dimly lit corridors as a loudspeaker voice announcing the time of tomorrow's evacuation train bounced off the marble walls and the polished stone floor.

There was a strange feeling of unreality in Pokrovs'k, of time being suspended. A missile strike would be entirely possible, and Russia had previous form in attacking evacuation points. A few weeks earlier in Kramatorsk a Tochka missile with cluster bombs had been fired into a crowd of evacuees outside the train station. The scenes of carnage were too horrible to broadcast. People were torn into pieces. Sixty-three were killed, and the international condemnation was strong. In response, the Russian authorities had flailed, first claiming a strike on military targets, then denying it was them at all and accusing the Ukrainian authorities – then saying the whole thing was a hoax. Russian state TV even put up a fake video, made to look like a BBC news report, blaming Ukraine for the strike. Finally they said they didn't have any Tochkas, forgetting they'd included them in a military parade a year earlier.

The obvious story to cover here was the evacuation effort which took place every day at the railway station. I rang around until I got a press officer for the state railway, who was obliging. I could join the train tomorrow and interview as many passengers as I liked.

Curfew was both early and strict this close to the frontline; after sunset the streets were empty. It would be a long evening confined to my room. It seemed quiet in Hotel Druzhba – until, at around 9pm, a convoy of trucks and beaten-up old cars arrived bringing new guests – the army. Not a few soldiers either; the place was now packed. I watched them file in as I perched on the front steps having a cigarette, my stomach sinking a bit. Hotels used by the military had been targeted before.

Upstairs, I lit the room with the red glow of my headtorch and lay on the bed chatting to Oleh in Odesa. I didn't mention that what seemed like half a battalion had just taken up residence, as he was worried enough already.

'You need a break, Jen,' Oleh said, for the hundredth time.

'I know.'

I said I'd leave soon, come to Odesa, then head out via Romania, retracing my steps. As we talked about the weather – I couldn't believe how hot it was, and he thought this was hilarious – I got a message from Bennett. *Yeah, my luck is officially out.*

My heart stopped. Putting Oleh on speaker, I texted back: *What??*

Bennett had stayed in the hotel that morning as his colleagues took the car for one last trip to Sievierodonetsk. On that murderous stretch of road, they'd been targeted by Russian shelling, incredibly precise, followed by further hits right next to them as they lay in the shallow ditch by the side of the road. Mykola, their Ukrainian producer, had been badly injured, with shrapnel in his right arm, and was now in hospital. They were all lucky to be alive. And Bennett was lucky that he had trusted that uneasy feeling and stayed put.

I'm so fucking glad you stayed home, I wrote to him. It felt like time to go. I could get the evacuation train, he'd find a lift out. We agreed to meet in Dnipro the next night.

Oleh was still on the line. I explained what had happened. 'Yeah, it's fucked up there,' he said. 'It's really bad, Jen, it's going to get worse.'

I assured him I'd be in Odesa in a few days, and we said goodnight. I felt heavy with tiredness, but the dogs barking outside, the soldiers drinking in neighbouring rooms and gnawing worry kept me awake.

As expected, the evacuation train was not exactly packed. Oleksandr, an enthusiastic young press officer with the state railway, met me on the platform and showed me to an empty compartment where I could leave my stuff. I'd never seen first class before, and it was *nice*: soft yellow voile curtains with little cord ties, and even a houseplant adorning the corridor.

Some of the carriages had been adapted for patients: usually these were injured soldiers or ill and elderly civilians. These ranged from compartments fitted with special beds and wheelchairs to mini medical wards, internal walls removed, medicines and equipment stacked high.

Volunteers in hi-vis were milling around on the platform, ready to help people aboard, but many of the travellers were actually soldiers on rotation. The signs taped to the window indicated that this was the Lviv–Dnipro night train, repurposed – though it would in fact be going all the way to Lviv, the city in the far west of Ukraine which was now a major hub for refugees.

With a shudder we began to move. I made my way down the long train. Children were shrieking and running up and down a third-class open carriage.

Sveta, a young woman in a denim jacket, with perfectly manicured crimson nails and long dark hair, was sitting alone, surrounded by bags. She'd come home to pick up a few things and was on her way back to Germany, where she'd been living with her sister. They'd been evacuated back in March.

Despite the warm welcome in Frankfurt an der Oder, it hadn't been easy. She couldn't get used to the food; she wanted to give up and come home to Pokrovs'k.

'We hoped of course that it would all work out, we'd come back,' she said, sadly.

But while Pokrovs'k had not fallen to the Russians, it was a ghost town she'd come back to earlier that week. And one under attack – there'd been a strike right after she arrived.

'Mentally it's been . . . really hard. I wanted to stay this time, despite the fact that the town is almost empty, despite the strikes the other day – people got hurt – but all I wanted was to stay.'

She drew back her shoulders, almost imperceptibly; pressed her palms to the Formica table. 'But look. You remember that your sister is there [in Germany], with a child. And secondly . . . Well, you already took this step, so come on, bear with it a little longer.

'I have hope,' she added, though her voice suggested otherwise. 'But I have no idea what comes next.'

The outskirts of Pokrovs'k had disappeared from view. Sveta sounded resigned to the idea that this might be goodbye for a long time. She had no family left there, and her job of nine years had, of course, gone. Time to move on. She was learning German so she could find work in her new home.

Another challenge of refugee life, she said, was explaining it all to small children. Her niece had started nursery school in Germany, which distracted her a bit, but they couldn't tell her about the war. 'We don't want to traumatise her,' Sveta said. But the little girl had not forgotten about her dad, who was still in Ukraine.

'Every single day she asks, "Is Papa coming to get me? I want Papa!" And every single day it reminds me that I want to go home.'

Two others who'd also returned just briefly were in the next booth, a mother and daughter from Myrnohrad, a mining town to the east. They were living in Dnipro but regularly made the trip back home to bring medicine to Yelyzaveta's elderly mother.

They'd tried to persuade the old woman to leave back in March.

'She wouldn't – she refused *categorically*,' Yelyzaveta said, stressing each syllable. 'She's lived in that house her entire life, seventy years. "Home is home," she says.'

Yelyzaveta and Diana would keep going like this, back and forth on the train to check on Granny, watching the maps of the advancing Russian line, playing it by ear. There really wasn't any other choice. The life of an IDP – an internally displaced person – in Dnipro wasn't exactly rosy either, they said, with high rents and little work. Diana, in her twenties, had been studying at the National University of Kharkiv.

'But it was bombed,' she shrugged. So she studied online. They had, at least, managed to take the pet bulldog with them to Dnipro.

I kept moving down the carriages. Some people brushed me away, angry at the intrusion. But one old lady beamed. 'With pleasure,' she said, when I asked if she'd speak to me. 'With *pleasure!*'

She wore a pale shawl tied in a knot at the back, a quilted jacket over her knees. She shoogled up the padded bench and patted it, 'Sit down, sit down,' and introduced her son, Lyosha. She was known to everyone, she explained, as Auntie Tanya.

Their journey was one-way. To Lviv tonight, then who knew where – they had no relatives to put them up, no idea really what awaited. But they couldn't stay in Kramatorsk any longer.

'Heavy artillery, bang bang bang, day and night, and rockets flying over our house, and sirens constantly – *constantly*. It's not like three hours of sirens, you understand, it's all day, all night, we got so sick of it.'

There was a bomb shelter under their ageing block of flats – 'But it's awful, *oy*, you can't imagine.' She lowered her voice to an outraged whisper. 'There wasn't even a toilet!'

Once, their top-floor flat in the centre of Kramatorsk had been a wonderful place to live. 'I called it my swallow's nest,' she said with a smile, 'my dovecot.'

But with missiles flying, its location became a nightmare. Abandoning the flat she'd spent most of her life in had broken her heart.

'It's been the worst day,' she sniffed. 'I've cried and cried. All of the valuables, the mirrors, silverware, which I kept from my parents' era . . . I'm mourning these things. Ah, what times we're living in.'

Mother and son struggled to understand how people could be so stupid as to believe the Russian propaganda, which alleged that Ukrainian 'Nazis' were bombing themselves. These days there were fewer of them, the ones who 'sit in the basement, waiting for Russia', but they knew a handful, Tanya told me with disdain. 'Such fools!' she raged. 'I just want to punch them in the nose when they talk such nonsense!'

It was because they watched those Russian TV channels all day, she added, trying to be charitable. 'That's where all that rubbish comes from.'

But Russia, said Lyosha, was clearly trying to wipe out Ukraine, as a nation, as a people. 'I don't get why,' he shrugged.

His mother broke in. 'By the way – we're Russian!' She was watching to see if I was surprised. (I was not.) Her father had been Russian, she explained, her mother Ukrainian, and her ethnicity, for form-filling purposes, was Russian. Whatever that meant here.

'But we've considered ourselves Ukrainian for years. We know the Ukrainian language, very well actually, we're very happy to use it.'

We were, of course, speaking Russian and not Ukrainian, something I could get away with in the east of the country – though increasingly, with the language a toxic reminder of the long colonialism which culminated in this war, even Russian speakers were spurning it.

The last person I spoke to was also a pensioner, but she was not evacuating, just going to Dnipro for an eye operation. She wanted to make clear, in fact, that she had no intention of leaving Myrnohrad, a small mining town.

'I won't abandon my home, I won't abandon my dogs. I've

only got one death,' she said, fixing me with a glare. It was already written, she added, the time of her death. Nothing could change it. 'And I prefer to die at home.'

She was bitter, resentful. Why can't the politicians sort it out, she wanted to know. Eight years of war, and no end in sight; only God would look after them, she said. 'That's the only reason we're alive – God.'

She refused to give me her name or let me take her photo. 'You can judge me,' she said, defiant and angry, 'I *am* Ukrainian, I want to live in Ukraine, but it's been like this for eight years. Eight *years* and they couldn't solve the problem.'

It was all the fault of previous president Poroshenko, of 'that lot who shouted on Maidan', she said, referring to the uprisings that began in 2013 on Maidan Nezalezhnosti, or Independence Square, in Kyiv and which toppled corrupt pro-Russian leader Yanukovych in 2014. Now, she said, they were stuck in perma-war. Her relatives had been killed; she'd seen rockets flying overhead; she no longer even jumped when planes shot through the sky. 'It is madness, just madness. Poor, poor people.'

Regardless, she would not be leaving.

'Yes, the authorities are always telling us to leave,' she said. 'Get out! Go! But with what? My pension is 2,100 hryvnias [about £50]. And we've no gas in Myrnohrad now. No water soon too.'

A flat in Dnipro, she said, would cost 16,000 hryvnias a month, plus 2,000 in utilities. Many had already come back to Myrnohrad, even those with children, because they'd run out of money. Her eye operation was costing 18,000 hryvnias; she could only get it because her husband worked and her kids could accommodate her in Dnipro.

I asked how she felt towards Russia. 'Absolutely fine. I pray for Russian *and* Ukrainian soldiers, as God loves everyone.'

And what about Kyiv?

'Exactly the same. I pray for all of them. That's all. I've said my piece. You can judge me if you want.'

For the last few hours of the journey I was typing in a train compartment, transcribing the interviews, talking to the editor about the piece. Writing on trains is a joy – there is none of the nausea of cars and buses, and the rhythm of the tracks makes a perfect 'white noise' for concentration. Or perhaps it only felt like that because I was in such unusual luxury, on a soft, padded bench, with room to stretch out. And the *providnytsia* in my carriage kept bringing biscuits and tea.

'Are you hungry?' she fussed, all concern. 'Do you need anything else?' I shook my head, tried to assure her I was fine, and she started telling me how important it was to have journalists here, covering the war. She even thanked me. My face flushed with embarrassment.

'No, I really like being here,' I said, tripping over myself to explain. 'I'm lucky to be here.' She laughed.

The train swinging onto the bridge was the sign that my stop was near. I went out to the corridor to watch it all, struck all over again by the beauty of this country. Nearly sunset again, and the light from the east illuminated the golden domes of a church on the far river bank, snug among dense green foliage. The trees reached the water's edge, where a little beach formed a white fringe against the great, slow, indifferent river. I loved the tall pylons which now loomed into view, red-and white-striped like a lighthouse, just as much as I loved the golden domes; I loved it all.

The kind *providnytsia*, giver of ginger biscuits, appeared from her little room and stood by my side, watching the view with me.

'It's so lovely,' I said, rather blandly.

There was a long silence, just the clatter of the train over bridge struts, and then she began to cry. 'When will it end? When?'

And I could think of nothing, nothing that I could say that would actually comfort her. I put a hand on her arm, and thanked her, in return.

I was so happy to see Bennett. He'd found a lift to Dnipro that morning, and we met in a pub in the centre. Mykola, his Ukrainian colleague, was in hospital; the shrapnel had caused nerve damage, and he'd need surgery. They were raising money to cover it. The two other freelancers had been criticised by some journalists, which seemed unfair. In the video of the strike, which is terrifying to watch, they clearly act with caution, taking advice from the Ukrainian military, deciding to turn back. The strike was so precise; perhaps it was the soldiers nearby being targeted, but if the Russians *had* aimed at the journalists, it wouldn't have been the first time.

The scariest part of the clip is not even the whistle and implosion of the first strike; rather, it is the subsequent shells that land metres away, as the journalists hide in the shallow ditch, injured and barely protected. The impulse would be to get up once it's quiet, to run for the car and get out of there. But that's when the second shell comes, and then the third. A 'triple tap'.

Bennett had decided to leave for a while – he'd been reporting in Ukraine since the beginning of the full-scale invasion and wanted to see his girlfriend, who had left Moscow too. The two of them hoped to live together, somewhere in Europe, but they didn't know yet which country would permit them to stay.

The pub closed, and we were making for the hotel when, around a corner, a whole crowd of people suddenly appeared. A hole-in-the-wall bar, selling little cups of fizzy fruit wine, was doing a roaring trade, and the benches and pavement outside it were full of people drinking, laughing and singing, late at night in the city. I felt I'd fallen into an alternate universe. We joined in for a bit, leaning on the railings and chatting to people. Of course the war was the main topic. But it seemed to feel far more distant for people here. The contrast with Kharkiv was striking.

'I hate all this patriotism,' an earnest man with owlish spectacles told me. 'I hate how militarised our society is becoming. The way people talk about Russians, like they're not human.' He was worried it would never go back to how it was before; he couldn't fit in to this new reality.

A drunk man was stumbling around, and when he heard my accent, he interrupted. 'Can you get me into the army?' he pleaded. I don't know who he thought I was, but I tried to explain that I could not do that. He began to cry. 'I'm from Berdiansk,' he slurred, 'Berdiansk! You know it?'

A port city on the Azov Sea, population 100,000, it lay in that part of the map that was now, temporarily, coloured red, Russian-controlled. Little news in or out.

He was sobbing, desperate. 'I just want to defend my home town. Please! Help me join the army!' He went on and on in this vein, unwilling to believe none of us could help, until he eventually careered off down the street. As it was nearly curfew time, I thought, he could well be arrested by soldiers before too long. But this was not Odesa; as Bennett and I walked to the hotel we found no checkpoints on the corners, no twitchy young men enforcing the rules.

As soon as we got in Bennett kicked off his muddy boots, crashed face-down onto his bed, still in his leather jacket, and fell asleep like that. His socks, I noticed with affection, were all holey.

There was an awful lot to do before the night train to Odesa at 10 p.m. – rewrites of a *From Our Own Correspondent* essay for Radio 4, recording the radio piece, writing an article on the evacuation train, and even more urgently, organising all the logistics of getting home. I didn't want to think about the journey from Dnipro to Shetland, the vast expanse of map that I would need to cover. It was 1,600 miles as the crow flies, but I am not a crow, and the section through southern Ukraine, across the border on the ferry, back into Isaccea and then up to Bucharest, was all overland.

Ironically, the trickiest thing turned out to be booking the ferry to Shetland, packed as it is in summertime with tourist caravans. I sat on hold with the ferry company for twenty minutes, their tinned fiddle music mixing with the air-raid siren seeping in from the street, and the absurdity of this made me giggle.

The same railway employee I'd met in Pokrovs'k was on the platform that night, striding up and down in an orange tabard, helping people get on the right train. Oleksandr spotted me, ran up and took a bag, and as he led us to the end of the long train we quickly caught up on news. He was fizzing with energy and enthusiasm for the task at hand, a man perfectly suited to his job.

It's always pretty hot in *platzkart,* the third-class open carriages of 50 bunks – but this night was off the charts. With everyone already bedded down and asleep, Bennett and I tried to make up our top bunks and stow away our bulky gear without waking anyone. This is particularly difficult if you're short: to make up a top bunk, unrolling the mat and assembling the linens, you must stand *on* the lower one, trying not to tread on a hand or foot. Sweat was running down my face as I did this, everything starting to blur. I swung myself up into my bunk after a few attempts and lay with my eyes closed, breathing in the close, humid air. I heard a stifled grunt and turned to watch Bennett, who towers above me in height, trying to fold himself like a pretzel into the space between top bunk and the carriage ceiling, his giant boots flailing around below and nearly taking someone out. He finally made it, curling up fully dressed on the bare vinyl of the bunk, and I watched, envious, as he fell deeply asleep within seconds.

At some point in the small hours the train turned south and began its final run down the length of the border with Transnistria, a sliver of Moldova ruled de facto by Russia, a strange place of KGB intrigue and Soviet nostalgia. And troops.

The little girl in the bunk below me had woken early, in order, apparently, to continue eating crisps at the same rate she'd managed the night before. The tube of crab-flavoured Pringles was opened with a pop. I groaned.

A cloyingly sweet stench of bins and fish drifted up, heavy in the airless carriage. I'd tried a crab-flavoured Pringle once, and still recalled that it was the worst thing I'd ever put in my mouth. The malevolent child munched her way through the entire tube, methodically, unhurried, as we rolled our way to the Black Sea. I sat propped against my pillow, working on my laptop and stabbing at the keys, a little ball of exhausted fury, casting disbelieving looks at the people all around who managed to sleep long, peaceful hours until lunchtime.

Oleh was waiting on the platform with a bunch of flowers and a loving smile for me, and a suspicious eye for poor Bennett, who went off to find his accommodation. I settled back into my old bedsit for a couple of days, delighted to see the courtyard again with its mangy, happy cats lounging in the heat.

The second of June marked a hundred days since the full-scale invasion. 'We have stopped the "second army of the world", liberated part of our territories,' the president, Volodymyr Zelenskyy, said. 'We will win!'

I think that, like almost everybody in Ukraine, I wanted to believe it. And morale wasn't flagging yet. But Zelenskyy certainly hadn't suggested that that victory was around the corner. There was, clearly, going to be a long, hard slog ahead.

But for a few months at least, I would be out of it all, escaping to what seemed like a whole other reality on the far edge of Europe, up on the Atlantic fringe. I felt guilty, leaving, like everybody says you will: leaving Oleh near Pryvoz market, the driver of the bus hurrying me on so there was barely time to kiss goodbye – and it was goodbye for good, we'd agreed – and then leaving Ukraine a few hours later, on the deck of the *Noviodunum*, the Danube muddy brown in the heat, knowing I had this option to get out, while so many did not.

PART THREE

LVIV, KYIV, FRONTLINES

OCTOBER–NOVEMBER 2022

CHAPTER TEN

IT HAD BEEN A strange summer back in Shetland, everything the same and yet somehow, imperceptibly, totally changed. The cabbages I'd tended so fastidiously, in the ruins of a croft house I'd used as a kailyard, had gone to seed, their lemony flowers bursting from the strange spiny shoots now swaying seven feet high in the wind. I planted peas in fishboxes, pulled rhubarb stalks from the sprawling giant slowly demolishing the old wall. My uncle was diagnosed with cancer, so I went to Fair Isle twice – in June to see him, and in September to take his ashes home. I wrote about the devastating bird flu epidemic there, the dead skuas littering the hills of the island. I made some radio features, did a little freelancing.

But much of my time was spent on plans to return to Ukraine: in particular, organising conflict-zone training, necessary if I wanted to report closer to the frontlines.

Although the Russian advance ground on through July, by late August the Ukrainian counteroffensive had started. We watched, stunned, as town after town was liberated in the territory east of Kharkiv, the Russians apparently taken by surprise, unable to stop the sweep of blue across the map. It was exhilarating just watching it, and wildly hopeful. I wanted to be right back in the middle of things.

The applications and begging letters eventually came good – I received a bursary to cover half the cost of the £1,500 course. By late September I was on an estate near Hereford, perfecting the art of bailing out of a car while masked gunmen shot at it with paintballs. The course was several days long, comprehensive and enormous fun. I talked too much during the hostage scenario, I was later told, and taken to solitary confinement, kneeling hooded in the farmyard, furiously trying to use the tricks we'd been taught to memorise details of a place you can't see.

The grand finale involved interrogations, bangs, burning tyres and gruesome fake injuries on a whole troupe of local drama students, who pulled out all the stops. 'Stop the bleeding, keep 'em breathing,' instructors intoned, over and over, and the phrase rang in my head, more useful than the confusing, ever-changing acronyms of airway and circulation that I'd tried to remember from other first-aid courses over the years.

I left the UK on a late-night flight to Poland, with an even larger rucksack than before and a very loose plan. I knew there would be live radio work I could pick up, as well as newspaper and magazine pieces. I was hoping to find the medics I'd met on the train – we'd kept in touch, sporadically, and I wanted to join them and report on their work.

I wouldn't be repeating the circuitous Danube route this time. A quick hop across the Polish border, Krakow to Lviv. Remarkably, the Lviv BookForum was being held in person; writers and journalists from all over Europe and further afield were flocking to the city to take part in three days of discussions.

It was dark when I arrived, so it wasn't until the morning that the sheer splendour of Lviv really hit me. I wandered south, meaning to catch a bus, but I just had to stop and stare, turning this way and that, trying to take it all in. The opera house, a great extravaganza of Corinthian columns, reliefs and sculptures built in the late nineteenth century, stood high on a broad avenue. Behind the tall arches and balustrades though, the windows were blanks, boarded up to protect against strikes. Chipboard and sandbags marred many of the other magnificent buildings. One of the reasons Lviv's historic city centre is so incredibly unique – and designated a UNESCO World Heritage Site in 1998 – is that it survived both the First and Second World Wars intact, unlike so many other central European cities.

Now, though, the city feared for its architecture, and for its people. Though safer than central and eastern Ukraine, and hosting many thousands of refugees, Lviv wasn't unaffected; there had been strikes on the outskirts and surrounding territory. Moscow had demonstrated, from the first day of the invasion, that it could and would fire missiles deep into Ukraine, even close to NATO territory. Nowhere was immune.

The city's twisting, tangled history is another factor in the wild architectural styles appearing round every cobbled corner. The rise and fall of empires and regimes is marked out in the buildings here – and in the street names.

Consider the street on which I stood, staring at the opera house: Freedom Avenue. Once it bore the name of Karl Ludwig, an Austrian Archduke, when this city was Lemberg. In the twentieth century alone, the avenue went through a dizzying number of names, sometimes cycling back to old ones as the town changed hands again and again. In Polish Lwów, the avenue was Legionów. In September 1939 the Red Army swept in as part of the brutal carve-up of Poland by Stalin and Hitler, then allies. Street names were all part of the relentless ideological propaganda the Soviets brought to what they termed Lvov, and the avenue was now named 1st May, for International Workers' Day. The Soviets shot or deported some of the workers and many of the intelligentsia: about 300,000 people were sent east, to Siberia, to the camps, in less than two years.

In summer 1941, the Nazis, turning on Stalin, took the city off him. Axis forces stormed through Eastern Europe, murdering more than a million Jews. Lviv, pre-war, had a Jewish population of around 150,000. Few survived.

The Germans initially renamed one side of the avenue Museum Street and the other Opera Street, though after a year it became known as the more grandiose Adolf Hitler Platz. In 1944 the Red Army returned; old names were revived and then dropped, until they settled – so ploddingly predictable – for 'Lenin Avenue' in 1959. And then, at long last, the independent state of Ukraine emerged, in 1991, from the ruins of the Soviet Empire, and that freedom was written onto the map.

This does not even cover Lviv/Lwów/Lemberg's older story as capital of the Kingdom of Galicia–Volhynia 700 years ago, nor its rule by the Kingdom of Poland and then by the Polish–Lithuanian Commonwealth of the sixteenth and seventeenth centuries, nor its brief year as capital of the West Ukrainian People's Republic, immediately after the First World War.

At the Lviv BookForum, in the basement of the Ukrainian Catholic University, under the watchful gaze of an Orthodox icon on the wall, every aspect of the war was teased out and hashed over. But the theme that kept emerging was hope. Concretely, the stunning success of the recent counteroffensive through Kharkiv Oblast had given hope, silencing the naysayers who thought Ukraine should give up, bolstering support in the West, and providing light at the end of the tunnel for all those suffering so much loss. It felt like a hopeful time, October 2022.

The hopes they spoke of went far beyond Ukraine. The guests talked of a battle between past and future, the showdown in Europe where the creeping authoritarianism of the past decades could be stopped in its tracks. There were Harvard professors and world-famous writers making this point, but it came most memorably from the frontlines. Pavlo Kazarin was a journalist from Crimea, now a soldier, and his message was broadcast on a big screen to one side of the stage, to a rapt audience. He was smiling and calm, but the message was almost prophetic.

The war, he said, was about the values on which the 'modern civilised world was built'. Are we now in a time where weapons and violence rule? He demanded. Where a state can just invade another, redraw the borders?

'If Russia gets its way, it will mean that everything is allowed,' he said. 'We are now defining what Europe is. Is it geography? Is it the standard of living? Or is this a democracy capable of remembering the lessons of history and drawing conclusions from them?'

He had tried to fight Russia with words, Pavlo said. Tried to use knowledge and facts. But the full-scale invasion made everything 'crystal clear'. He joined the territorial defence on the second day. And he knew exactly what he was fighting for.

'The finale of our war will determine the contours of our future. Contours of what we consider good and what we consider evil,' Pavlo said. 'I don't want the world to unlearn how to distinguish one from the other. That is why I am now wearing a uniform, as are hundreds of thousands of my fellow citizens.

'Some questions cannot be answered with words. One can only do this with deeds. This is our answer.'

The Armed Forces of Ukraine now had one of the highest rates of female participation in the world. Yaryna Chornohuz had been serving since 2019. She was a striking presence, even on a shaky video, with her long dreads and sharp features. An accomplished poet, she'd recently been given leave to go to the US as part of a delegation trying to communicate the Ukrainian situation to those with the power to help. She'd been struck by the 'incredible respect' female fighters like herself had been treated with.

'Although this is a war of artillery and long distances, it is also a war of great physical and moral endurance,' Yaryna told the audience. In combat positions a woman had to prove her capability in these areas, again and again.

'If you do it constantly and in a motivated way, then you gain respect and have an equal place with everyone,' she said. Not a 'female soldier' but simply a soldier. And despite the remnants of discrimination and sexism in the Ukrainian armed forces, she thought this equality would only grow. It would force society to change.

A woman with long ash-blonde hair and a pale face sat on the stage, listening to Yaryna. Taking up the mic, she talked about the women she'd met, travelling the country as a war-crimes researcher: the village mayors who tried everything to protect their residents while being targeted themselves; the volunteers working flat out to get ammo and cars and drones; the women running hotlines for survivors of rape and violence, providing psychological support.

The speaker's name was Victoria Amelina, and she had previously written novels; now she was writing a book based on what she'd seen in recent months. It would be about the women investigating war crimes, and the women surviving them.

Victoria appeared several more times over that weekend, ably chairing sessions and always making me listen more attentively. She had a dry humour common to Ukrainians, and a self-deprecatory one too. In Brits this trait can be annoying, elevated as it is to a national pastime, but in her, it was tempered by a deep well of real emotion, a startling directness. She also clearly knew a hell of a lot, weaving aspects of international law and history into her points.

Ukrainian refugees at the Isaccea port, crossing
into Romania, March 2022

Valentina, the kind translator, at Isaccea port
during the refugee crisis, March 2022

Maksym and his mum Katya, Isaccea border crossing, March 2022

Destroyed residential block, Kharkiv, May 2022

Kharkiv metro station and trains transformed
into living quarters, May 2022

Ruins of Vilkhivka school, May 2022

The author with Nataliya Zubar, Vilkhivka, May 2022
(*Credit*: Zhenya Titarenko)

Yulia and Misha in their basement, northern Kharkiv, May 2022

Vlada Chernykh, call sign 'Aïda', drone operator and medic, November 2022, she was killed three weeks later near Bakhmut

'Kim', a young volunteer in the Khartia brigade, on a drone mission in November 2022

Ihor, medic, Donbas, November 2022

Kam'yanka after occupation and liberation, November 2022

A bicycle dangling in the debris of a flat, missile
strike site, Kramatorsk, March 2023

Bohorodychne convent, Donetsk region, March 2023

Tetyana Oharkova and other PEN Ukraine volunteers drop off
a crowdfunded jeep with the army, eastern Ukraine, March 2023

Sunrise on Independence Square, Kyiv, March 2023

In the whirlwind of socialising over that weekend, I got to know Victoria a little, along with some of her colleagues at PEN Ukraine – an organisation which had become a virtual focal point for writers and intellectuals during wartime and was involved in a great deal of practical, on-the-ground activities. Talking to Tetyana and Volodymyr, husband-and-wife scholars, I heard about the intrepid literary activism PEN Ukraine was undertaking – delivering books and humanitarian aid to recently liberated areas, trying to support writers under occupation, tracing the missing and the dead and promoting Ukrainian literature and language under the hardest circumstances imaginable.

I had a feeling I'd see these people again, that the connections I'd made almost by chance would endure. More immediately, though, as the festival came to an end, I had to get to Kyiv. On the last night I found a lift; Remy, a French correspondent, was leaving early in the morning.

We were almost the only vehicles on the road. The first indication of what was happening came shortly after we'd stopped, to get a coffee about halfway along the 300-mile route. Out here in the countryside there were no sirens, nothing but a news flash on your phone screen to indicate that, not too far away, absolute hell was raining down.

Kyiv was under attack. Several other regions were reporting incoming missiles too, but a strike on the capital was the biggest news. Rockets had hit a busy area during rush hour; there were many casualties.

I was itching to get to there, and get to work. From the speeding jeep I messaged editors at home. It was still early there, three time zones away, but I'd be in Kyiv soon, I said, and could report live or gather material. 'Be careful,' came the usual instruction.

As we approached the city the roads were almost empty; it felt tense and unpredictable. Rumours swirled of further attacks, of kamikaze drones overhead. Soldiers blocked one road, and we backtracked, took another, until we reached the cheap hotel I'd booked. 'You'll be alright?' Remy asked, with a raised eyebrow. I assured him I would.

Kyiv's air defences had apparently intercepted some of the missiles and drones, but a few had got through: there was damage to the central station and to a popular pedestrian bridge connecting two parks. It was after midday when I got to the site of the worst strike on the Taras Shevchenko Boulevard, where, on a multi-lane arterial road, the neoclassical university building sits in splendour, its walls painted a princely red. The blasts had sheared off chunks of the red plaster, and in the road where one missile had landed, an organised chaos reigned. City workers in orange hi-vis and hard hats swarmed everywhere like worker ants, dangling from cherry pickers to snip the tangled overhead wires, pushing rubble from the deep crater into flat-bed trucks. The blackened cars and lifeless bodies the morning's pictures had shown were long gone.

I saw another crater in the children's play park nearby, where a woman in a headscarf was raking up autumn leaves and bits of shrapnel. The blast of this missile had flattened the carefully planted flowers, destroyed a swing and blown out every window in the eight-storey neoclassical building opposite.

Scenes like this were familiar to me now, from Kharkiv earlier in the year, from Mykolaiv. But, naively, I hadn't expected it in downtown Kyiv.

That assumption had been widespread, though. I spoke to Roman, a Kyiv resident in his forties, and he pointed up at one of the shattered windows, where a strip of curtain flapped in the wind, darkness inside. That, he said, was the apartment of a friend who had only just returned to Ukraine, his wife and child with him. All three had escaped unharmed that morning – physically, at least.

He himself lived nearby. 'This was the alarm clock for me,' he said drily. 'I woke up because the walls shook.'

He felt Kyiv was still relatively safe, protected as it was by air defences. The problem that morning was the scale of the attack. More than eighty rockets in total were fired at Ukrainian cities.

'They do it in three waves,' Roman explained, 'so the first wave is intercepted, but before you can reload, the others are flying through.'

Better defences from the West were the answer, he added.

Russia, for its part, was calling these strikes 'high-precision'. One missile had certainly landed with precision on the intersection – right at the peak of rush-hour traffic. Among the dead were a paediatrician coming off night shift, only identifiable by the make of her car, and a policeman going to work. When I mentioned this during a live report to Radio Scotland later that day, the presenter was taken aback. *'Rush hour?'* he asked, incredulous. Yes, I said, there are a million people in this city; they go to work. I wasn't trying to be flippant – it was something I'd been thinking about a lot, perceptions versus reality. It was difficult sometimes to convey what was going on here, in all its complexities and nuances. Of course there's rarely time for that on air, and 'Normal Life Continues' is not a headline, while 'Rockets Kill Nine in European City' most definitely is.

Complicating this was the cynical use of any glimmer of normality in Ukrainian cities by propagandists. Russian trolls were hard at work creating posts showing 'normal life' in Kyiv: queues at McDonald's, people in shopping malls and so on – 'proving' that the horrors of the war were all fabricated by the hysterical Western press. The posts would look like they'd come from some 'alternative' media site in the UK, some 'independent' journalist, who was nothing of the sort, and I'd seen people I knew sharing them. It left me speechless.

I found a young man surveying the debris-strewn park, and was taken aback when I heard his American accent. Daniel was from California, but he had fallen in love with Kyiv and had lived here for years until the invasion forced him to flee. He, too, had only recently returned.

'I love it so much here,' he smiled, despite the fact that we were looking at a climbing frame surrounded by shrapnel and scorched trees. 'I came back to see my friends, to get reacquainted. To be an observer. But actually this is my adopted home.'

That morning, in bed on a nearby street, he'd slept through the whole thing, but had dreamed about it.

'It was so strange,' he said. 'I was dreaming about war, explosions and screaming . . . But I turned on my phone and realised these were real noises . . .' He trailed off, staring into the distance, as though he were still processing this.

Eventually he turned to me again. 'I'm not leaving,' he said, though I hadn't said anything. He'd lost the laid-back Californian drawl and spoke urgently, angry now.

'I'm shocked, yeah, but not surprised. This is what the Russians do, this is their playbook. They get humiliated – the Kerch bridge – and they just lash out.⁵

'Look at this –' he pointed ahead of us – 'it's a *playground*! They hate everything. They hate Ukrainian people because they won't capitulate, because they want to be a free country, their own country! And I'm with them.'

---

5 Two days earlier the bridge linking Russia to the occupied Crimean peninsula – a crucial supply line for its military – had been badly damaged in an explosion which killed five people. The Ukrainian Security Service later claimed responsibility.

It turned out the contingent of British writers from the BookForum had also arrived in Kyiv that morning, but at the worst possible moment. Two doctors and a journalist had taken a night train, which crept into the city moments before the strikes. They'd been rushed from the train down into bunkers below the main train station and waited it out.

Now, early afternoon, it seemed we'd all have to return underground. Government text alerts and forwarded messages from military experts were unequivocal: *Another strike expected in one hour.* I'd walked down to Khreshchatyk, the main boulevard, in search of lunch when I got this ominous little text, and began quickly weighing up my options. Vehicles had vanished, and I wouldn't make it to the hotel in time if I walked.

The streets were emptying of people, a palpable tension building in the air. The looming buildings on either side and the sudden, horrible silence began to unnerve me. I made for the metro, joining the hundreds hunched down on the stone floors of the platforms for an hour, but the strike never came, and soon I was back in the warm evening sun, people milling around like it was any other day. It felt like cat and mouse, like a game with no point to it.

The power flickered off at night, planned outages plunging first one part of the city into darkness, then another, as the authorities tried to balance the struggling grid, and I lay in the darkness scrolling through updates: strikes in Zaporizhzhia, Dnipro, Ternopil', Lviv. Thermal heating plants and power stations had overwhelmingly been the target of this wave. Russia's winter campaign to freeze Ukrainians into submission had begun in earnest.

There was no power in the morning, and I hung my headtorch in the bathroom to wash by its dim red light. Another alert was audible, alongside the birdsong and the sound of workmen hammering on a roof nearby. I went down to the basement for the first of many live reports over the phone that day.

It was evening before I got outside. The stars I'd seen above Kharkiv during the blackout were brilliant once more, above the cobbled streets of Podil, Kyiv's downtown district. But any wonder I felt then had evaporated now. There was absolutely nothing beautiful, I realised, about a cold, dark city; it quickly starts to feel like a deeply unsettling place.

For a few days I was busy with requests for live interviews, as Ukraine dominated the news, but soon enough interest waned. Then, with perfect timing, I received an invitation. The PEN group was making a trip to the de-occupied territories east of Kharkiv. Did I want to come along?

CHAPTER ELEVEN

I BREAKFASTED LIKE HENRY VIII on the day I left Kyiv. I'd never seen food like it. Not just honey, but a honey*comb*, skewered, slowly dripping. Exquisite *salo*, the fatty slices transparent, melting on the tongue. Fancy cheeses I cannot pronounce. I wasn't really meant to be there, at the most expensive hotel in the city, but late the night before, after another slew of text messages warning of a missile strike, my friends in a TV crew had snuck me in – the hotel has an excellent bomb shelter. It was not the last time I'd have cause to reflect on the spontaneous kindness and camaraderie of other correspondents while in Ukraine.

The PEN Ukraine group left Kyiv that morning, rather later than planned, the ten-seater laden with musical instruments and carrying an assortment of novelists, local and foreign journalists and several academics. The number of philosophers on board – including a professor from the national university – was a constant source of jokes.

We also had with us a crowdfunded jeep. Trucks like this, fast and manoeuvrable, were the number-one item requested from the frontline, and PEN Ukraine, like many volunteer groups, was constantly trying to buy them. This jeep would be handed over to the military in the east of the country.

If we ever got there. As dusk fell I was biting my nails, increasingly anxious – I was supposed to be on air that evening, giving a TV report for the BBC, but we were still driving towards Kharkiv. I needed to get there, set up and find a good spot with a good connection. I had a feeling this might prove harder than it sounded.

The city, when we reached it, was ghostly and dark. Thirty per cent of the power grid had been taken out in the strikes earlier that week; Kharkiv residents had spent days without water and gas. I recognised Sums'ka Street, the theatre, the church and other places familiar to me, though they were hard to make out in the gloom. Mobile Internet was off, GPS was jammed, and the sirens started to howl across the city as we reached our destination. Never mind, someone said cheerily, we were going underground anyway.

I bolted down the steps into the Art Area nightclub and into a warren of corridors filled with people, all milling around and being as noisy as possible, buying drinks at the bar and filing into the main space where a band was already playing. 'This won't work,' I was muttering. But the alternative was broadcasting from the dark street with air-raid sirens blaring. It had to be down here in the scrum.

I ran up and down through the crowd several times, as if this would solve the problem, all the while holding my phone aloft, moving it around above my head like some octogenarian trying to make the magic box work. Eventually, next to a pile of coats, I got two bars of signal.

I seized Tetyana from our group as she squeezed by and asked her to hold the phone steady with me in the frame, and simultaneously to stop people ambling through the shot, which she cheerily did. I had earphones plugged into the phone and waited for the studio to count me in, trying to rearrange my face into a calm and normal expression. It was all over four minutes later; I ended the report on the happy note that, despite everything going on above, despite the Russian border being twenty miles away from where I stood, here in an underground club in Kharkiv people were packed in to discuss culture and values, the mood exactly as resolute as when I'd left a few months ago.

Later the producer sent me a photo of the studio gallery that night, a bank of screens with one showing a little image of me in the nightclub. It was distinctly weird. I knew that gallery well, had spent many shifts looking at that bank of screens with all the live feeds, watching the correspondents standing by in Washington or Seoul or Moscow, and I'd wished fervently to be on the other side of the screen. I didn't want to be a TV correspondent, I just wanted to be *there*, reporting, somewhere, anywhere. And now – if briefly, and somewhat chaotically – I was.

The event in Art Area was of course a fundraiser for the armed forces, and it felt a bit like the bunker gig back in May. Natasha, the journalist I'd last seen as we hid from missile strikes in the press centre the day I left, was standing at the back, and she greeted me like a long-lost friend.

Serhiy Zhadan and Sviatoslav Vakarchuk were on stage – two rock stars talking about philosophy and war. Natasha whispered Russian translation into my ear. Both could sell out stadiums, but here they were in this crowded basement talking earnestly about the future of Ukraine to a few hundred people. Vakarchuk, a former deputy in the parliament and a well-known celebrity, had shown up in Kharkiv a few days into the full-scale invasion, Zhadan was saying, when things were impossibly dangerous; he'd brought an armoured car with him. This guy *gets* Kharkiv, was the message. Vakarchuk nodded, pleased.

The series of concerts and discussions was called Fifth Kharkiv – a phrase of the scholar Yuriy Shevelyov, born 1908, who had lived nearby. He'd written about his city's past and present, its transformations, its identity as a Ukrainian city so often repressed then re-discovered in the 1920s.

'It seems to me this is exactly what is happening right now,' Zhadan said. He himself was a renowned poet and novelist, deeply involved in Ukraine's literary scene. Despite the shelling, the danger, they were still gathering together to debate the values on which this future was being built, and building on the foundations of Kharkiv's Ukrainian past.

'This is the Kharkiv phenomenon,' the poet said. 'Despite the war, continuing with cultural life, with the intellectual life of the country – it seems to me that this is terribly important.'

They talked back and forth for an hour or so: on how to live in the present, or how to remember to live at all when all day and every day you felt you *should* be volunteering, working, fighting for victory, for a future. How history would judge it all.

'We can maybe have an objective assessment in one or two hundred years,' Vakarchuk said. 'We're kind of "live on air" right now, you know? We're making history. We have our Cromwells, our Churchills, our Oscar Wildes – all on the move together.'

It was getting late, and I was starting to sag, adrenalin all fizzled out. But when Vakarchuk began to sing, I felt a jolt of recognition.

Kokhannya, kokhannya . . . It was that same song, from the bunker.

Love, love, Vakarchuk sang, to the hushed room. *From evening to morning . . . Just as the sun sets, just as the sun sets, love disappears.*

His voice, rising in ad-libbed grace notes then sinking back to the wistful melody, was so haunting, rough with emotion then soft as a lullaby; it rose and fell and the people standing in that packed space, some murmuring along, seemed to rise and fall with it, until the performer drew out the last line into a fluid improvisation of dark, minor notes, like a jazz singer in some smoky club.

No one could quite figure out where to put me that night; there wasn't room in the apartment where Tetyana, Volodymyr and Vakhtang were staying, nor in the hotel with the others. 'I'll sleep on the floor!' I'd insisted, but they looked at me with horror. After much heated discussion it was decided I could go to Slovo.

'Slovo?! Seriously?' I said, jumping up with excitement. I'd read about this legendary building, bound up so closely with the grim history of Kharkiv's cultural scene. I couldn't believe I could *stay* there.

Some girls in a red sports car gave me a lift, driving madly, screeching round the dead, dark streets under the stars, blasting out music. Traffic lights were blank, trams had ground to a halt with the recent strikes, and the road was theirs.

Budynok Slovo, the 'house of the word', is situated near Derzhprom. In early Soviet times, when Kharkiv was the capital of the Ukrainian Soviet Socialist Republic, Moscow's policy of *korenizatsiia* – 'nativisation' – prompted a brief flourishing of a Ukrainian avant-garde, playwrights and poets and journalists attracted to this bustling city of industrial and trading fame, allowed to write in their own language at last. The policy was the Bolshevik's attempt to endear this restive republic, and all the others, to their rule. In this political environment, writers were elevated. Slovo was designed to be a true 'house of the word', the building even shaped in a Cyrillic 'S'. The flats were spacious and well equipped; some even had telephones.

This special treatment came, however, with the heavy caveat of state control which was followed by repression – a story familiar across the Soviet Union. But in Kharkiv, in Slovo, the axe fell quicker.

Stalin grew tired of *korenizatsiia* and opted to wipe out the native intelligentsia instead. In the early 1930s, the party line shifted abruptly; Ukrainian 'bourgeois nationalism' was the new enemy. The purges began. The Soviet Union under Stalin's paranoid control regressed to Tsarist ways. Russification and centralisation, brutal orders issued by Moscow and carried out by its secret police.

So frequent were the arrests in this one building, and so quickly were the disappeared replaced with new, terrified writers, that some flats have two or three names associated with them, names of the 'Executed Generation', as it later became known. Almost all those taken away were shot or died in Russian concentration camps.

Their lives and fates are meticulously documented in the Kharkiv Literary Museum, an organisation more radical and activist than the name perhaps suggests. Its work began in the early 1990s and goes well beyond displays and interpretative panels: the whole event that night had been put on by the museum, and it ran the flat in Slovo as a literary residency. Reconnecting Kharkiv to its past – its *Ukrainian* past – was a political task, and an urgent one. Literature, here, was a living, burning thing.

My enthusiasm for a night in Slovo faded when I realised I'd be the only one in the flat. As the others were cracking open a box of wine and tuning the guitars by candlelight a mile away, I climbed into bed, shivering in the blackout, hungry, and tense. I am, to my shame, a little bit afraid of the dark. It's the curse of an overactive imagination; things creep up, distorted faces appear where they shouldn't be. As the sirens came and went through the small hours, I lay awake, thinking about the people who had inhabited this block, perhaps this room. And then, in the dead of night, a sharp noise made me sit bolt upright in bed – a creaking, a footstep surely. Rustling. I fumbled with the headtorch but the red light left the shadows all around impenetrable. Something moved right next to me, and I shrank back, breathing fast. Then I looked over the side of the bed, holding the torch aloft.

A tiny mouse was looking up at me, all comical ears and whiskers. He bent his furry head to nibble at the crumb of a cracker I'd had for tea, held tightly in his little paws. 'Hello,' I said quietly, hoping he wouldn't run away. He was the sweetest thing I'd ever seen, a little emissary of the real world to stop me getting lost in the other realms.

I fell asleep finally as the dawn started to creep into the sky. An hour later, Ivan from the museum arrived to cook for someone in another flat, intent apparently on banging every pot in the kitchen in succession, so I got up, packed, and stomped off into another lovely sunny morning.

Mala Danylivka, Derhachi, Bezruky. Suburbs north of Kharkiv became fields and sparse villages, all bearing the marks of the last eight months of war. The Russians had tried to reach Kharkiv down this route in March 2022 but got stuck. The town of Derhachi held, so was subject to endless shelling.

We scuffed around a destroyed municipal building, peering into empty window frames. Between partially collapsed concrete ceilings, there were little glimpses of a cartoon butterfly painted on the wall, a mural of a winding river through idyllic countryside.

I climbed over the debris to get inside, curious, though not curious enough to follow two men up the broken staircase to an upper floor. In the stairwell was the town's crest, hand-painted on the wall: '1660', it proudly proclaimed, with a Cossack and three corncrakes. These rare and rasping little birds apparently gave Derhachi its name; they nest here on the bend of the Lopan' River, which snakes its way down into Kharkiv.

Among the buckled metal and shattered glass, something bright and colourful caught my eye: a celebratory placard made of fibreglass, cracked in two. 'Day of Derhachi's Liberation!' it read.

Liberation from Berlin's forces, it meant, not from Moscow's. It marked seventy years since the day in 1943 when the Red Army freed the town from Nazi occupiers. Outside, I found a white slab with names of the dead from 1943, an inscription about fighting the Fascists and the usual red Soviet star, paint peeling. This plinth too was damaged by shelling. A Ukrainian flag flying ten feet high alongside was nearly torn in two. The whole scene struck me as a grim still-life of the competing stories of the past and present.

As we travelled further north, a strange noise entered the minibus, a high-pitched drone like a light aircraft, a vibration that gnawed deep in your skull. Tank tracks, scored deep into the asphalt, created this strange music, which continued all the way to the little town of Bezruky.

Previously this had been an attractive place to live, on the suburban rail line from the city, with stands of old pines circling the neat grid of streets. Their tall crowns swayed gently, evergreen, but the birch trees below were a blaze of autumn's colours, their leaves carpeting the sandy ground; already a sharp edge in the air had us blowing into cupped hands. I walked around another imposing war memorial, 'ETERNAL MEMORY' inscribed in gold on black marble, and half of it blown away.

Bezruky had been back in Ukrainian hands the whole summer. But in all those months, neither the gas nor the electricity connections had been restored. The challenges were obvious: a tall concrete pole carrying cables was held together in two parts only by the thin metal rods inside, making it look as though the upper sections were floating. The railway line too was a mess. But still I couldn't help think of the incredible speed with which that intersection in downtown Kyiv had been repaired, of the army of municipal workers who had descended to fix the damage in little more than a day. As in Vilkhivka, that lakeside village I'd reported from in May, the worry in Bezruky was a winter with no heating. And that winter was not far away.

From Bezruky the Russian border is only half an hour by car in normal times, and tanks rolled through these streets on the first day of the invasion. Messing up the asphalt was the least of what they did in Bezruky. In June, after they'd been pushed back to positions nearer their border, Russian shelling killed a little girl as she read a book. Her name was Marharyta Haponenko, or Rita, as her granny called her.

Rita's granny, Alla, was still in Bezruky. One of the Ukrainian journalists in the group interviewed her outside the small house, and we all stood around, listening to the horrific story. It was '*kassetnaya*', she said. A cluster bomb. You couldn't hear them coming – no time to get into the cellar. Alla's daughter – Rita's aunt – had died of shrapnel wounds a week later. But the eight-year-old girl died right there, at the door of the house where she'd been reading a book.

She loved reading, loved her school, the Bezruky Lyceum – loved everybody. A star, an angel, Alla said. She ended each sentence with a slow shake of the head, looking at the ground, repeating, 'It's very hard. It's very hard.'

I didn't record her, but I still remember exactly how those words sounded as she repeated them quietly, almost like a chant.

Duzhe vazhko,
Duzhe vazhko,
Duzhe vazhko.

I stayed in the museum's other apartment in Kharkiv that night, with Tetyana, Volodymyr and Vakhtang. The flat had been the home of the linguist Shevelyov, he of 'Fifth Kharkiv' fame, and had been damaged in the shelling and airstrikes earlier in the year. In the stairwell – a grand old tenement stair with ornate ironwork and patterned tiles – the glass from the windows still lay in a heap underneath the boarded-up frames. I moved slowly up the stairs by the light of my mobile phone. Not that the windows would have let in any light; the street outside was pitch black too. Walking down Rymarska Street to get here, I'd only occasionally seen a faint glimmer in some solitary window, smothered with curtains and cardboard.

Inside, the windows were similarly sealed with cardboard and parcel tape, but happily, the heating was on. I slept a little more soundly, glad of the voices murmuring through the wall, the company of humans rather than mice and ghosts.

We left early, heading east this time. The highway runs all the way to Donetsk, though we wouldn't be going as far as the frontlines – just seventy miles or so to Izium. But that took hours, because the road was, in places, completely destroyed. The high-pitched scream of rubber over tank marks was the least of it: some of the fiercest battles to retake this territory only a month earlier had been on the motorway itself, leaving behind giant craters, burned tanks and cars, and minefields that ran right up to the asphalt on either side.

Guided, vaguely, by soldiers at the innumerable checkpoints, our philosophers' bus took long detours down dirt tracks, finally reaching Izium at lunchtime. The big sign loomed, the town's name in blue and yellow, peppered with bullet holes. All around, the shops and petrol stations lay in ruins, and hulking concrete blocks formed barricades and checkpoints.

The occupation here had been brutal. Russian forces used Izium as their stronghold, a logistics hub, but in the struggle to take it, back in the spring, they'd bombed it so relentlessly that not a single street seemed to be untouched. So many had died here, elderly people especially, left without medicine, without rescue, in the ruins of their flats. And most had been buried in one place – in the forest on Shakespeare Street.

I'd been chatting to Maksym Bespalov as we drove along. A writer from Dnipro, now living in Lviv, he knew my friend Ivanna from college days and had written books on his two great loves: the Camino de Santiago pilgrimage trail, and Ireland. We had a lot in common, and I liked Max immediately, liked his open, friendly face, his easy enthusiasm.

But he fell silent as the pine trees began to enclose us, looming on either side. We turned onto Shakespeare Street. This was the edge of Izium, a fringe of pine forest. When we got out, the peace of the place was striking, birds singing in the trees and a sharp, fresh pine scent. The winding paths on the sandy ground were needle-strewn and dappled with sunlight.

But as we walked towards the forest's edge, we could see, and sense, that something was very wrong here. Under the trees, the ground was heaped into mounds; deep tracks where some heavy vehicle had made a mess of the little paths. My eye was drawn to a strange shape, a little further along, and it took a minute to realise it was a Ukrainian tank, lurking under camouflage.

This had been a Russian position. Between the mounds, deep hollows had hidden vehicles, which were now all filled with rubbish. Crushed tins of beer, plastic bottles, wet wipes, rusting tins of food. Deeper into the woods, more disturbing rubbish lay in piles. Blue and white surgical aprons, gloves, discarded masks. And then came the sea of wooden crosses.

Nearly 450 bodies had been exhumed here, weeks earlier. The Ukrainian authorities had taken them for testing; they wanted to identify every person before they were properly reburied by their loved ones.

Some had been found in pits, Ukrainian soldiers executed by

the Russians, hands tied behind their backs. Many were civilians, some buried in coffins, which now lay open and askew, their satin linings filling with pine needles. Police tape was still strung between trees and spooled all over the ground. Our group spread out, nobody talking. I picked my way along, reading the inscriptions on the makeshift crosses, many just planks of wood nailed together.

Max and the others were looking for the grave where, perhaps, their friend and colleague had been buried. Volodymyr Vakulenko, a poet and children's writer, had been abducted by occupying forces in his village near Izium in March. Now, after liberation, there was still no sign of him, but on the records kept by the gravediggers, his name was listed. Number 319. The record, though, was incomplete, raising more questions than it answered.

The forest offered no clues, either. On most of the grave markers, only the scantest details were scrawled in marker pen. A number, perhaps an address, a date of birth. I stared at them. These people had lived through the Second World War.

> *Peshkova. 03.03.38–16.03.22*
> *Skoyarov, A.I. 30.09.36–12.03.22*
> *Old man, 35 Lenin Avenue*

One marker, numbered 299, bore a photograph of the old woman who had been buried there. In it, she was holding up her own family photographs. Her striking face was angular and stern, with hooded eyes. And her empty coffin lay, cast aside, in the shallow hole, strewn with plastic bags and a bedsheet.

Some of the crosses were sturdier and bore the official black-and-gold notices of the local funeral director. Three of these were clustered together, leaning at drunken angles in the empty hollows. I stopped to read them properly. Elena and Dmitriy, a couple in their early thirties, killed on the same day. But right behind, Olesya, nearly six years old. Same surname, and patronymic Dmitrievna. An entire little family, killed together on 9 March 2022.

Later, on a website that documents Ukrainian victims, I found an entry for Olesya. She died under the rubble, it read. Her home was in a long block of flats, no. 2 Pershotravnya. Russian airstrikes had simply obliterated the middle of the structure. Families had sheltered in the basement, onto which the five concrete floors collapsed. It took a month to dig the bodies out. The dead included Olesya's mother, father, sister, grandmother, grandfather, great-grandmother and aunt.

I found Max back near the edge of the woods, squatting down to examine the rubbish left behind by the Russians. Printed on almost all the ration packets, the foil wrappers of peanut butter and stewed pork and boiled vegetables, was the same logo, a red circle with orange figures, waving arm in arm. Around it was the slogan '*Druzhba Narodov*', 'friendship of the peoples'.

This phrase was an old Marxist maxim, revived by Stalin in the 1930s to promote a myth of brotherly love and equality between the Soviet Union's disparate nationalities. It still carries weight in Russia; people still believe the big lie. In Ukraine it had long sounded old-fashioned; now, it seemed sick.

I picked up a foil jam packet and read the back. It listed the place of production – another Lenin Avenue in a grim town in western Russia – and said it was produced under order from '*MEAT FACTORY "FRIENDSHIP OF PEOPLES"*' in occupied Crimea.

Max turned over a rusting can with his toe. He had a look of utter contempt on his face. We walked to the road. It was a relief to be under blue sky again, away from those empty graves and upended coffins. I couldn't imagine the horror experienced in September by those who had had to dig it all up, parcelling up the rotting remains of more than 400 people. The smell, apparently, had been indescribable.

I asked Max if he'd found grave 319. He had, but it had told him nothing; it was just another hole in the ground lined with bits of rubbish. He didn't sound hopeful that Volodymyr was still alive, but they had to wait for the DNA results from the Kharkiv lab. However – there *was* a chance, a rumour, a very faint hope, that the poet was in a Russian prison. This is what Olena, his mother, was clinging to.

The whole group had piled into Olena's flat, and taken up seats and spots on the carpet around her husband Vasyl, sitting like children being told a story. He was benevolent and gentle, with pure white hair and magnificent eyebrows, and as he spoke he stroked the back of the teenage boy next to him, who was watching cartoons on TV, but also was glancing at all of us, nervy and unsure. This was Vitalik, fourteen years old. He and Volodymyr, his father, had been inseparable.

Vitalik broke into a loud wail, rocking back and forth with agitation, and Vasyl murmured to him. 'Grandad's telling what happened,' he said softly, 'shush now.' The boy sank back.

The flat was a few floors up in a multi-storey block – the only one in the village, Olena had explained, when we were struggling to find the address. Kapytolivka had been hard to reach. Izium, which straddles the Sivers'kyi Donets River, was in such a state that getting from one side to the other was difficult: the bridge had been blown up. A diversion took us over a shaky pontoon, wooden slats a foot above the river, and then checkpoints held us up for a while.

What had happened in Kapytolivka fitted the pattern of bombardment, occupation and brutality common to towns and villages all across this eastern part of Ukraine, and in the south. They'd had a grace period, a week or two of uneasy limbo, before the war reached the village. During that time Olena and Vasyl begged her son Volodymyr to leave with Vitalik – as did his friends and family elsewhere in Ukraine.

Volodya, Vasyl recalled them saying, *Please, take the child and go.*

Volodymyr, nearly fifty, by all accounts a stubborn and resolute man, would not go. He had a disability, from injuries sustained years earlier, and as sole carer of his son Vitalik, who has severe autism, he thought the Russians would leave him alone. This was a fatal miscalculation, and a strange one for a man who, by all accounts, understood that Russian military culture wasn't known for decency and mercy.

But really, it seems, Volodymyr wouldn't leave because he felt he shouldn't *have* to leave. This was his home, after all; he was so deeply rooted in Kapytolivka that he'd started adding a 'K' to the end of his name. He wouldn't abandon it. 'I won't let them rob me,' Vasyl recalled him saying.

In addition, the writer felt it was important that people with strong pro-Ukrainian beliefs stayed in the east. He was needed here. He'd just keep his head down.

Olena described the first days of the invasion in Kapytolivka. It had begun with airstrikes. Planes screaming overhead, days in the cold basement of the apartment block, no gas or water. After the air raids, the Russian columns entered on 7 March. Volodymyr was living at his father's house, a few streets away, with Vitalik.

When the occupying troops arrived, what did this outspoken patriot, writer of Ukrainian literature, enthusiastic participant of the Maidan revolution do? Did he keep his head down?

'He shouted so that everyone could hear him,' Olena said. '*Everyone* heard. He shouted: "*Rashysty pryyshly!*"'

The Rashysts have come! To shout this on the street was a wildly risky thing to do – especially for a man who had previously said to friends that, if it came to occupation, he'd likely be snitched on by someone in the village.

Volodymyr, true to his profession, had kept a notebook filled with observations from these weeks. He wrote about walking miles with Vitalik to take food and supplies to 'our guys', when those guys were still in control of the territory; about the sounds of war coming closer, 'like an angry viper'; about looking up to the sky, in a moment of exhausted despair, and seeing cranes flying overhead, free and beautiful, a portent, he thought, that 'everything will be OK, everything will be Ukraine'.

We know what he wrote, because the notebook, covered in his dense scrawl, was later recovered. He'd buried it underground, under the cherry tree in the garden, after his first arrest. That had been towards the end of March, his mother told us. They took Vitalik too. I looked over at this anxious boy, non-verbal, strung tight as a wire, reliant on his grandparents for absolutely everything, and tried to imagine him being arrested by troops.

'Under what pretext was Volodymyr arrested,' someone asked.

'For "nationalism"!' Olena shrugged. 'For the position he held.' Volodymyr's strong pro-Ukrainian views, she admitted, made him stand out here – not because the place was pro-Russian, but people tried to stay out of it all. Most here spoke Surzhyk, a mixture of the two languages common in the countryside. Volodymyr railed against it, going into shops and telling them to speak only in Ukrainian, telling them to switch off the Russian propaganda playing on the TV. It didn't endear him to people.

'He could go a little bit overboard,' his mother said, uncomfortably.

When father and son were arrested they were separated. Volodymyr was interrogated and beaten, then both were released. Olena believed the Russians made a mistake in taking Vitalik too, which meant they returned the pair home.

Because of this mistake, we have the diary. Volodymyr knew they'd come back for him, knew his fate was sealed. The house would be searched for any 'incriminating' literature. And so he wrapped the little diary in plastic, along with some of his own Ukrainian-language books, and he dug a hole under the tree.

The next day the soldiers came, a gang of them, dragging him away from the open fire where he was cooking, throwing him into a minibus. Its door was hanging off, and it was daubed with the letter 'Z', according to Volodymyr's father, who saw this all unfold. And that was it. Volodymyr disappeared without a trace.

By foot, by bicycle, all summer, miles and miles a day, Olena and Vasyl searched. They went to the checkpoints, to the headquarters of the occupying troops, to the new self-styled 'authorities'. And begged for information.

They promised they were looking for him. 'Go home, don't worry,' they said. 'We're looking.' But why was it so hard, she kept asking, to simply search the basements where the occupying troops kept prisoners?

Olena was living for rumours, for the scantest bit of information. Some people were released from the makeshift prisons and torture cells (twelve such sites were later discovered in Izium alone). And they hadn't seen him there. So where the hell was he?

Since the Russians had arrived, there had been little information in or out of the occupied territories, leaving relatives in free Ukraine to guess at what was happening to their loved ones. One of these was Iryna, Vitalik's mother. She'd raised the alarm and alerted writers' organisations; PEN put out a statement calling for his release.

Behind the curtain of occupation, wild rumours swirled, as they will do in a vacuum. It was during the summer that Olena first caught the rumour, a bright, sparkling thread of hope: the rumour that Volodymyr was not in Izium. He was awaiting trial in prison, either in occupied Donetsk Oblast, or in Russia itself, the story went.

All this time, as this woman in her seventies was walking miles to be told nothing, she was also trying to keep the family alive in a war zone, with no gas, no heating, no water connection and dwindling stocks of food. Vitalik was constantly scared, frequently hysterical, she said: there were helicopters, explosions, the inexplicable nights in a basement, the inexplicable absence of his father. He was nearly killed in shelling.

'You're a strong woman,' one of our group said to her, as we got ready to leave. 'Many people give up in such situations.'

Olena sighed. 'I don't even take it as a compliment, because I just have to be . . . I'm needed.'

And she looked strong. Resolute. She talked of Volodymyr's character, his stubbornness, as though it were something unique to him, but it was clear to me where that came from.

Then she said suddenly that she had to believe he was still alive – 'Because he's my only child.' And she looked, briefly, broken by grief.

She and Vasyl saw us all out onto the street, the crowd of us clumping noisily down the stairs. They hadn't seemed to mind the intrusion. Olena hugged everyone.

'Thank you, I thank you all,' she said, so sincerely. 'Even sympathy is very dear to me.'

The writers had brought things for the family, sweets for Vitalik; they would help financially, and promised to come back.

But the main thing for Olena, it seemed, was simply that basic human need: being listened to.

The couple waved us off, white-haired Vasyl looking stately, hands clasped behind his back, gravely nodding. Olena had tears in her eyes. Some of us did too, as we drove away.

The atmosphere in Shevelyov that night was emotional and tense. People wanted to talk, to make sense of the past two days. For some, this trip was the first time they'd seen the carnage and devastation of de-occupied territories. And I think the grief and anger of Olena stayed with us; I still felt her hand on my arm, where she'd placed it earlier. It was that she was so kind, I thought. So sincere and warm, after everything she'd been through.

Soon a ton of people turned up, and a *kvartyrnyk*, a flat party, was underway. Wine eased the tensions, helped the talk flow freely, and Volodya and Vakhtang took up instruments and played. A young woman dressed all in black showed me a stack of postcards, prints of her artwork.

'Take one!' she offered. They were striking, thin red lines forming shapes on a black background. A Molotov cocktail bottle with a heart inside, and underneath in fractured Ukrainian capitals, 'BLAZING FEBRUARY'. A glowering Shevchenko, the national poet, hair ablaze.

I picked up a card with Kharkiv's crest, its archer's bow. 'CITY OF STRENGTH', it read. The artist was called Dina Chmuzh, and she showed me, on her phone, pictures of her poems and art painted onto the chipboard of bombed buildings.

Talking to her, I realised Dina had painted the very mural I'd admired that morning, in the arch below the flat. I'd been struck by its strange, almost mythical symbolism: a woman sitting straight and proud at a long, red table, attended by a host of crows, the cracked and crooked windows and walls of the city forming a backdrop to it all. Manuscripts lay scattered before her, glasses of dark wine casting long shadows. I'd wanted to look at it all day, and had had to make do with a quick snapshot.

I thought of the 'Kharkiv Banksy', Hamlet, who had been painting his work onto walls here for years, with his black-and-white line drawings, strange little vignettes and poignant questions. Or of the cluster bomb scar on the street outside which someone had turned into the petals of a flower. It was this, all this, that made Kharkiv feel so alive, so mid-transformation. Graffiti that took the form of poems, of questions about how to live, musings about the war and the future, all painted straight onto the chipboard and plaster of the broken city; it reminded me of the activists I'd seen in May climbing a ladder and unscrewing the hated 'Moscow Prospect' sign, replacing it with the image of Ukrainian philosopher Skovoroda. They pasted their new street sign straight onto the boards covering the window frames, in that bombed and ruined part of the city centre, literally remaking the city, cementing its meaning and loyalties.

'What was he like?' I asked Max, later that night, as we drank wine from mugs in the kitchen. I'd heard so much about Volodymyr Vakulenko's disappearance, his possible death. I wanted to know about his life.

'He was a very special man,' Max said. Then he corrected himself. 'He *is*. He *is* very special. A very idealistic man.'

Max had admitted to me that of all the possible versions the most likely was that his friend was dead. But he had to hope, and at least talk as though he could return from wherever he was.

Their friendship went back some fourteen years, when Max was a young wannabe writer and Volodymyr was a 'punk in a leather jacket'. Ukrainian literature was flourishing – not like it was now, with state funding and international interest, but underground: there was a radical scene of self-published zines and online communities, with Volodymyr involved in everything. He organised literary festivals all around the country, which had a big impact on people like Max.

'He was just central for emerging Ukrainian authors,' Max said. The two had talked often, 'about everything', the older writer encouraging the younger. 'Everybody thinks he's a little bit crazy, too maximalist. But we also like him because he's him.'

'What are his ideals?' I asked.

And Max replied at once. 'For all of the good versus all of the bad.'

It sounded like a perfect epitaph. But I didn't want to say this.

We talked about the visit to Olena and Vasyl. How she'd been so moved by Volodymyr's colleagues all turning up en masse, despite the difficulties of reaching Kapytolivka. How she'd said that the hugs and kind words meant more than material help.

Max put down his mug and shook his head, wiping tears away. 'My heart broke.'

CHAPTER TWELVE

A STRANGE SENSE OF déjà vu hit me as the philosophers' bus made the 250-mile journey back to Kyiv. The city we were speeding towards was under missile attack. We read the news, on our phones, from the safety of the motorway.

It wasn't only Kyiv. The strikes were coordinated; waves of Iranian drones, too many to shoot down; cruise and anti-aircraft missiles hitting power stations and grid infrastructure all over the country.

But attention was once again on the capital, in part because that morning a drone had exploded on to a 120-year-old apartment block, killing a young couple sleeping inside, along with their unborn baby.

In these circumstances, it was hard not to be moved by the first glimpses of the city as we crossed the river. High on the tree-covered hills up ahead, the towering titanium statue, *Mother Ukraine*, held sword and shield aloft, the whole structure seemingly ablaze in the setting sun, the sprawling monastery's spires and domes glinting alongside it. Between the two, and higher than both, was a 300-foot flagpole, from which the largest Ukrainian flag in the world rippled slowly, backlit and golden-hued, the sky above all pale rose and blue. Bombastic memorials to war and country usually leave me cold, but this was so epic and defiant.

The power was on when I got in to the rented flat, but I knew not to count on it lasting. Sirens sounded through the night, drones apparently shot down over the suburbs, and around 9 a.m. the next morning, as I was drinking my usual muddy coffee, explosions rang out, distant but certainly in Kyiv. I scoured networks for news and spent the rest of the day doing live reports for radio stations in the UK.

It already felt horribly normalised, this new reality, and we were only two weeks into Russia's winter campaign to plunge Ukraine into darkness and cold. It had been terrifyingly effective, in one sense: 30 per cent of power stations had been destroyed, half the nuclear reactors were off anyway, and a week earlier Zelenskyy's government had stopped exporting electricity to Europe in a bid to keep the lights on at home, which was costing the country dearly. In Lviv the authorities were buying up wood-burning stoves to distribute among basement shelters, for fear of people actually freezing once the temperatures started to plummet. There was not nearly enough gas for the winter.

Among all this detail the bigger picture bore repeating: with airstrikes and rockets, a military superpower was deliberately targeting the infrastructure of a neighbouring country in an attempt to make life there unliveable.

But Russia's desperate strategy was, in another sense, not effective at all. The Ukrainians I knew had lived through hell already. Cold and candlelight wasn't going to suddenly break them.

On a bit of a whim, I took the train back to Lviv, to study Ukrainian for two weeks. Though I could get by in Russian in the east, it was becoming less welcome everywhere, particularly among the younger generation. The switch to Ukrainian had been a slow one, gathering momentum over the years, but Putin had managed to turbo-charge it with his invasion.

I got to know Lviv a bit, walking miles along its cobbled streets and, every day, through Stryiskyi Park. I don't think there can be a better place to watch the season turn. The big landscape park was a blaze of colour, ever-changing, totally mesmerising, and it stretched right down to the Catholic University where I had lessons.

Something about the autumn days in this park, as well as the strange and charming old streets layered with history, cemented Lviv as slightly other-worldly, almost spectral, in my mind. The flitting, dancing light as leaves fell in flurries down in the dark ravine at Stryiskyi's heart; the way the pink-hued creepers and twisting vines seemed to overgrow the park's boundary and colonise the winding, cobbled streets around; the shushing of my feet through deep carpets of ruby-red and bright yellow foliage. Red squirrels, in Scotland so elusive, would come right up to me as I sat on the moss under a tree. They'd perch there, fearless and expectant, so close I could marvel at their long, finger-like claws and vestigial thumbs, the plush white of their bellies, and the flash of their fiery coats when they suddenly took fright and darted.

I watched the leaves turn and begin to fall in earnest on my walks through the park. One morning, I felt the first cold frost, a sharpness in the air I could almost taste. The grass was fringed white, and my breath billowed upwards. Usually I'd delight in this, I'd kneel down and peer at the rime's patterns on skeletal leaves and relish the coming winter months, but now it felt distinctly ominous. News that nobody wanted.

Here in Lviv at least it was relatively safe; the sirens which sent us to the university basement always faded without incident, and the power outages hadn't reached us yet, either. It felt strangely distant from the war. But near the fabled Rynok Square, next to tourist attractions and crowds, was the church where, day in and day out, the bowed heads and stifled sobs of funeral processions came out of its dark doors, one column after another, a stark reminder that this western region too was paying a terrible price.

Curfew, one night, was shifted from 11 p.m. to 12 a.m., and there was a celebratory atmosphere in the city centre. I was by then staying in a crummy hostel; I'd wasted a whole day pitching stories into a wall of silence, and trying to sort out things at home in Shetland. Sub-tenants, post, tax returns; things you really need to be present for. My neck had seized up, a wisdom tooth was trying to kill me, and I had prickling, searing neuralgia down one side of my face. I set off stomping round the narrow, winding lanes, vaguely seeking food, but too irritated to eat. Then, turning onto Virmenska, I heard the singing.

'Full-throated', you might call this type of folk singing, but that wouldn't be quite right. In Ukrainian it is *bilyi holos* – 'white voice'. At its strongest, it's almost controlled shouting, akin to that wild keening for the dead we once did in Scotland. The throat is open, and the notes are loud and strong, often sung as polyphony. It came from singing in the fields; there are traces of it all round central and Eastern Europe.

Two women were singing, their parts taking turns then coming together, deep and powerful. Strangers were stopping to listen, entranced. I sidled up, joined the cluster of people, and when the song ended introduced myself, and asked if I could sing with the group.

It was several hours later that I left, throat aching, feeling a warm glow of happiness. Among the singers had been an Appalachian folk musician who spoke – and sang – fluent Ukrainian, and he'd found some of the lyrics on his phone so I could follow along. And suddenly, because of music, the language made sense. My frustrations – I'd been finding it difficult learning Ukrainian as a Russian speaker – briefly melted away. As the evening went on, sitting round a table on the cobbles wrapped up warmly and drinking berry liquor and hot tea, we even sang Scottish songs –

the first two verses of 'Ca' the Yowes', a Fair Isle favourite, with harmonies. It was the most magical rendition I'd ever heard, and I recorded it on my phone, wanting to remember everything.

I walked back to the hostel and found the corner of Serbska and Ruska Streets blocked by a crowd of people. A busker was leading them, and I moved through the crush to hear him more clearly. Everyone was beaming, swaying, strangers dancing with each other on the cobbles. At the end of the song the busker shouted out the names of occupied places – 'Donetsk, Luhansk, Mariupol: they are Ukraine!' – and wild cheers went up. Then, as though spontaneously, the crowd began singing the national anthem, all the voices rising together above the narrow, ancient streets.

I left the strange peace of Lviv for the capital in early November, staying a few nights in Kyiv, where the atmosphere was markedly different. Rolling blackouts were really making life difficult. The authorities were trying to manage demand, but there was a sense of increasing desperation behind the resolute facade. Oleksiy Kuleba, the head of the region's military administration, warned that a total blackout could be on the cards, lasting up to two weeks. 'We are already preparing for this,' he said, grimly, but really only so much could be done. Portable generators were being imported as fast as humanly possible; the city hummed and coughed with their diesel power. But still the missiles came, from the seemingly inexhaustible stockpiles of the Russians, and still the engineers across the country raced to fix what they could.

I was staying in a hostel at the bottom of Andriivskyi Descent, an ancient steep street that runs down to the old trading quarter of Podil. The location, and no doubt the cheap bunks, had apparently made the establishment a haven for young people, mostly American, who wanted to come and experience the war.

'Are you a journalist?' I'd ask, as we ate in the common area, and they'd reply, with a smirk, 'Sort of.' Mostly they seemed to get drunk, pick up girls, and post selfies from 'war-torn' Kyiv on social media, garnering an endless stream of admiration and 'Stay safe!' messages from back home. It was a phenomenon in Lviv too, but this crowd was creepier. 'I'm CIA,' one leering young American told me repeatedly, as he followed me down into the basement kitchen. Never has the sardonic Scottish response 'Are you, aye?' been more apt.

Some of these foreigners were 'here to fight', they said, and they'd kitted themselves out in eBay's best military chic, and were hanging around waiting for their 'in'. Occasionally, real mercenaries came into the cafe on the ground floor: Czechs or Brits, usually, with much more practical, worn-in gear, and with real guns slung across their backs. The wannabes would stare longingly at them.

Meanwhile in the real world, and despite all the odds, people were getting on with life, even having children. I'd seen my friend Marta in early summer, when she was six months pregnant. Camilla had been born in late September, and Marta and her husband Alex were settling in to life as young parents.

I visited them in their flat in a twenty-five-storey tower block. Marta ushered me in, whispering so as not to wake her daughter, but took me in to see her, tiny in the cot, still at that scrunched-up new-baby stage, little fists clenched in sleep.

It was such an antidote, that one afternoon spent in normality, such a contrast to the blur of hostels and trains and work I'd been in for a month. We sat and talked in the kitchen, voices low, about how they were managing life – timing everything around power cuts, from the heating of bottles to the walks outside – until Camilla woke and began crying, a little mewl of annoyance. Alex brought her through. She had a fuzz of black hair and deep, dark eyes.

Marta was explaining their procedure for air-raid alerts: hide in the bathroom, the corridor, or the bomb shelter. The bomb shelter was a long trek down many flights of stairs. So, like most people, they did their own 'risk assessment', interpreting the details on Telegram channels. Flights near Belarus might just be training, so keep an eye on it; if missiles or drones had been launched, get into the basement. They waited it out in the corridor sometimes, following the 'rule of two walls' (the second wall, hopefully, absorbs whatever projectiles get through the first).

It seemed impossibly difficult, managing these myriad threats with a small baby in a high-rise flat. But Marta was exuding stoic calm and even happiness. They would get through it, she said. And look at this beautiful baby, just look.

The city was dark as I walked home, car lights and headtorches the only illuminations, or occasionally a brightly lit shop-front, the telltale hum of a generator close by. A few people were out, picking their way along the pavements and dashing over pedestrian crossings which had become a free-for-all in the absence of traffic lights. Sofiiska Square, flanked by the monastery walls and its ornate, baroque tower, felt forbidding in the gloom. Its expanse was interrupted by ghostly faces peering from the posters propped up on the cobbles. I moved closer to try to make out the text, the names and birthplaces, nicknames and deployments, of the dead soldiers commemorated on these rows and rows of memorials.

It was bitterly cold one night as I left the hostel on an endless quest for Internet connection. One cafe in Podil had a generator, and I made a beeline for its bright lights, joining the rows of people working on laptops round every table. It felt a bit like a swanky office. I sipped a tall glass of sea-buckthorn tea, made from the plant's sweet, tart orange berries and full, apparently, of vitamin C.

I'd arranged to speak to Victoria Amelina, the novelist from the Lviv forum, who actually lived in Kyiv but at that point was on the road for work, or volunteering, which were really the same thing for her. I wanted to write about the long search for Volodymyr Vakulenko, and it had been Victoria who dug up his diary, shortly after Kapytolivka was liberated.

She was exhausted but talked to me on the phone at length, keen to share the story, and to explain the context. It clearly meant a lot to her; she'd kept an acorn in her pocket from the garden that day, when she'd helped Volodymyr's father find the right spot. But I got the impression that every single victim of this war that she met meant a lot to her. And as a war-crimes researcher, she met a lot.

'They always try to give you apples from the garden, show their hospitality although they have nothing, give you a cup of tea,' she said. And then she so perfectly described the thing I'd been trying to put into words for months. 'I have a writer's imagination, so I would just imagine the horrors happening anyway,' Victoria said. 'It's like when something happens to someone you love and you imagine them in hospital, but when you get there you see that this person is hurt but they're alive, and it's easier. Well, it's the same with the cities and villages.'

This was how I'd felt, precisely, about Kharkiv, and why it had been so much worse to watch it from afar in March and April, why coming back in May, despite the danger then, had lifted so much of that fear. It hadn't really made sense at the time, but Victoria understood.

We talked about Vakulenko for a long time that evening. She kept in touch with his mother; Olena was still waiting for results of the DNA test. But this whole story of writers being murdered, of marauding soldiers dragging villagers from their homes and torturing them for being pro-Ukrainian, this whole story, she said, was one of impunity, not only now but in the past too. Russian impunity, Soviet impunity, and silence.

'We didn't do a good enough job to make sure something like the Second World War could never happen again. We only looked at one side of the story. There were two monsters, Hitler and Stalin, and the regimes behind them, but in Nuremberg only the Nazis were tried. There was no justice for the Soviet regime.'

This had led, she said, to the 'cult of great victory' in Russia. 'You might know, they have this motto,' she said. 'In Europe it's "Never Again", but theirs is "We Can Repeat" . . . I know it well – my first language is Russian so I watched a lot of TV as a kid; I know how violent this narrative is. Unfortunately Russians never learned what being a Nazi *means*.'

Specifically, she said, the crimes committed in Ukraine during the twentieth century had gone unpunished: the Holodomor famine and the murder of writers in the 1920s. The world turned a blind eye, both to these Soviet-era atrocities, then later to Russia's aggression in Chechnya, Georgia, Moldova, Crimea. It could have been halted, the Russian war machine, she was sure of it. But the world had shrugged.

I told her about my brief stay in Slovo, with its ghosts of that lost generation.

'Yes!' she cried, 'I stayed there too! It's so important to us. Those people managed to leave such a powerful heritage behind them. After Ukraine gained independence, we drew a lot of inspiration from their works. And you know the Kharkiv Literary Museum was a very important part of that cultural process, in 1991.'

I said I'd be going there soon, to look at Volodymyr's diary, and she was pleased. She was working on her own diary-book, about the war, justice, and women – if she could ever find time to work on it, she added, laughing.

Victoria wasn't travelling only around the liberated territories but also internationally. Her mission was to make people finally understand what was going on in Ukraine: this wasn't some dirty little civil war but rather centuries of imperialism, rampant and unchecked, coming to a head.

'I know it's very difficult for a foreigner to understand the context,' she said. 'Of course I can read novels about Great Britain and Ireland, but all the nuanced literature about Ukraine was untranslated. It was a mystery for everyone, what this place is.'

She'd been in Dublin recently and reckoned 'they get it'. They'd invited her over, published her in the *Irish Times* and in literary journals.

'They seem deeply interested, like you are, in history and culture,' Victoria said. Ukraine and Ireland, she felt, had a lot in common; she was looking forward to going back there. In better times. I said I'd tag along – I couldn't imagine a better road trip.

I made my way back to Kharkiv after a few days. The night train left at 11 p.m., and I watched, incredulous, as my fellow travellers in the compartment slept peacefully throughout the clanking and blinding lights at each provincial station – 2.30 a.m., 3 a.m., 3.30 a.m., 5.10 a.m., until finally the lemon yellow of Kharkiv's station facade appeared in the half-light of a wintry morning. Back at the Ryleev, the matriarchs and resident cat greeted me warmly. I settled in to work for a few days, chasing leads that could get me further east and doing live reports for radio.

Every scrap of attention at this time was on Kherson. The Russians had taken the southeastern port city early in the war and established a ruthless regime there, with reports of widespread torture and repression occasionally reaching the outside world. We'd seen photos, taken surreptitiously, that showed propaganda posters adorning advertising boards throughout the city: 'WITH RUSSIA – FOREVER'. The school curriculum had been changed to reflect Russian 'truth' and children were now taught in the Russian language. As the only regional capital the Russians had actually managed to capture[6] in this botched invasion, Kherson was the jewel in their occupation regime.

But a Ukrainian counteroffensive was edging ever closer to this city on the Dnipro River, prompting a hasty Russian retreat from the right bank on 9 November, hours after the puppet leader of Kherson, conspiracy theorist and blogger Kirill Stremousov died in a mysterious car crash. Two days later, the blue and yellow flag was flying outside the city hall, and footage emerged of people crying and celebrating, hugging the soldiers. 'We knew you'd come,' a woman says in one video, sobbing as she clutches the soldier tightly.

Like every journalist in the country, I wanted badly to be there, but access was extremely difficult, even if I had found a group to join. Some correspondents were even stripped of their accreditation for getting in to the city without permission. I gave up on the idea and stayed in Kharkiv, where people were celebrating too. The Kefir basement bar was packed that night, the mood ecstatic. Anything, it seemed, was possible now. No one knew then how Kherson would be punished.

---

6   Russia partially occupied four oblasts by this point: Luhansk, Donetsk, Zaporizhzhia and Kherson. The capitals all bear the same names; of these, Zaporizhzhia remained under Ukrainian control, and Luhansk and Donetsk had both been occupied since 2014. Mariupol is not a capital and in any case, they'd reduced it to rubble.

CHAPTER THIRTEEN

BACK IN MARCH, WHEN I'd interviewed Bohdan, the actor I'd first met in 2018, over Skype, he'd told me about the bakery in Kharkiv that he and his friends were sleeping in; they'd been distributing bread across the city each day, dashing out between artillery strikes and aerial bombardments.

It turned out to be more than a bakery, almost a social centre for the many volunteers and activists who had stayed in Kharkiv. As the first snows came, slushy and grey, the floor-to-ceiling windows of Pakufuda were like a beacon at the end of Independence Avenue, right around the corner from Derzhprom. Inside it was cosy and welcoming, with a mezzanine, comfy chairs, board games and extremely good pastries. I took my radio mic along one day to interview Lily and Tanya, two of the young owners. Lily was businesslike, the sleeves of her baggy jumper rolled up, ginger hair pulled into a bun. We sat at an upstairs table.

'We want to stay open, because, firstly, we really love this project,' Lily explained. 'It's kind of like our soul.'

I looked around the mezzanine: hipsters working on laptops, kids playing board games, a dog peacefully asleep under a table. It felt like someone's living room.

Tanya said she'd noticed more returnees in the last couple of weeks. 'I don't know why – maybe other cities have more problems? Or perhaps they just miss it,' she smiled. 'Every day I see old faces I haven't seen since February.'

We went down the narrow stairs to the bakery, and I stopped to breathe in the wonderful smell, a hit of cinnamon and raisins, of rising dough. There is nothing more comforting.

The diesel generators could keep the coffee machine and fridges running, but the biggest of the ovens guzzled power and was reliant on mains electricity. Lily was explaining the system when, as if on cue, the power cut out. We stood in the darkness for a second, laughing, but it came back on. She shrugged. It happens.

A man in chef's uniform resumed pouring flour into an industrial mixer. 'Oatmeal and raisin cookies,' said Lily. 'For soldiers and volunteers. They need sugar and tasty food.'

The team regularly prepared thirty-kilogram boxes of biscuits, serious calories with which to battle the cold, and these would go to soldiers, but also to children in areas near the frontlines.

A hammock and fairy lights were in the far corner, originally installed on a whim, which proved prescient. When the bombing started on 24 February, the basement became home to more than forty people, Lily said. She'd evacuated by then, returning a little later, but had left the keys with a friend in case the building was needed.

The group had cooked communal meals, slept in rows of sleeping bags and baked as much as possible. Their bread fed the soldiers defending Kharkiv and fed the people hunkered down in the metro.

Back in March the problem had been finding flour and staying alive. Now it was power. The strikes last month left them in the dark for eight hours at a time, and Lily said at that point she'd considered leaving again.

'But I don't want to. A lot of people have stayed here. They want to have a normal life – with pastries, with croissants. So we carry on.'

The baker opened the door of the huge German oven; it made a roar, and out slid four golden loaves in tins. On the long table, sourdough rounds were proving in their baskets, dusted with flour.

The bakers had discovered that Ukrainian flour and other ingredients were as good, if not better, than the imported stuff they'd previously relied on. That was a good lesson.

When Lily and the other owners first opened the cafe, it was challenging, she said – problems with staff, training, getting the pastries right. 'I thought then, "If only I'd known it would be so hard, I wouldn't have done it!"' she laughed. 'Then the war started. And I thought, "Ah. *This* is what a problem is."'

The sound of children laughing came through a door at the end of the basement room: it was a games room, a safe place underground for playtime.

The thick walls of the old building made it a good shelter. But they also kept the heat in, much better than the thin walls of Tanya's apartment.

'If there's electricity and we can use the ovens, it will be warm inside. I think a lot of people could stay here,' she said.

These girls, I thought, really had built a hearth.

I was finding warmth and determination all over the place, when what editors expected was fear and despair. This had often been an issue, and I tried to explain that the resilience I described wasn't an individual phenomenon but society-wide. The more Russia attacked Ukrainian society, the less inclined people were to despair. They only got angrier.

Dmitriy, a language tutor, invited me to visit his parents, in the south of the city. Their district had been hit a couple of times but was relatively quiet now, and when I got there I was struck by how lovely it was, with blocks of flats and rows of mature trees, right on the edge of a small forest. And *proper* forest, I thought as we walked alongside it, not the grim, uniform plantations that blanket Scotland.

Nikolai and Lyubov (Kolya and Lyuba for short) were retired engineers in their seventies, and kindness itself. We spoke at length, the four of us, as the light faded outside – mostly they wanted to hear about Scotland, about the island I came from, and my impressions of Ukraine.

But their own lives, to me, were equally fascinating. In their careers both had travelled widely around the Soviet Union; they had Russian relatives, spoke Russian. Their lives had been so bound up with that country. But now, although they hadn't switched language (Lyuba noted, apologetically, that their Ukrainian wasn't perfect), they certainly had no love left for 'big brother' Russia – none at all.

We drank black tea with jam, tea so malty, so tasty that it is still vivid in my memory. She'd made treacle slices, which were also delicious, and urged me to eat another every five minutes.

When I spoke to them in later months, the pair had perhaps hardened a little, but at this point both expressed a kind of bewildered fury, which I'd seen in so many people already. 'I will never, ever forgive them,' Kolya said quietly, referring to the Russians. 'Some "brothers" they turned out to be.'

Lyuba was on the verge of tears when we spoke about the war, with anger as much as sadness. But she felt sure of two things: Ukraine would win, and she and Kolya weren't going to leave their home.

On the way here Dmitriy had shown me the damage from the shell that landed in late summer: a detached house was gutted, and the windows were all blown out on the corner of the block of flats. But, he shrugged, no one died, and repairs were being carried out.

What about the winter fast approaching, I asked them. The power cuts and heating issues? Were they worried?

Not really. They'd prepare as best they could, following the advice from the authorities about battery chargers, insulation, food supplies. The bath was kept full of water – Lyuba showed me – so they had a reserve.

Actually, they really wanted to talk about the summer, about the future, rather than this temporary predicament. They had a *dacha*, a country cottage, where they grew vegetables, fruit, even grapes. It was in an area which Russia had occupied, but thanks to the Ukrainian counteroffensive, they'd been able to salvage what they could of the harvest. Kolya was making wine.

'Please come back, you must, in the summer, when it's warm again!' Lyuba said, holding my hands in hers as we said goodbye. We'd have a barbecue at the dacha, she said; it would all be wonderful. I wanted so much to believe that it would.

Dmitriy walked me back to the metro. It was sleeting a little, and nearly dark, and I noticed my throat hurt again, a lurking cold I'd been keeping at bay. My route home took me down the massive Poltavskyi Shliakh arterial road, deafening with traffic, and at the crossing I watched an ancient truck struggle up the hill, making the most almighty noise and surrounded by a noxious black cloud of its own exhaust fumes. It had a tank lashed to the top of it. The tank had seen better days, too.

The green light pinged, and I dashed across the wide expanse of lanes and tram tracks, unable to avoid a lungful of smoke. The effect was quite immediate: I felt my chest tighten, all those angry bronchial tubes suddenly constricting in protest. By midnight I was wheezing, breathing in painful gasps, and only finally slept when I remembered about the codeine in my emergency kit. I managed a BBC interview in the morning by sipping strong black coffee throughout, but for three whole days I was stuck in bed, coughing my lungs up, and very pissed off.

The Kharkiv Literary Museum was closed but the director allowed me and a French journalist to visit, in order to see Vakulenko's diary. The notebook of thin graph paper was carefully wrapped but still bore the signs of its time hidden underground, the pages slightly warped. Each one was covered in minuscule writing, his slanting script spilling into the thin margins, additions written vertically down the edges, the text dense with crossings-out.

The writer had also buried his own books, and here in the tissue-paper wrapping was one of the children's titles: *Three Snowy Stories*, featuring on the cover a plump snowman in a top hat and scarf, smiling. There was also a book of poetry with a Cossack on the cover against a blue and yellow background. Victoria Amelina had told me the soldiers who searched the house after they took Vakulenko had removed books – those with national symbols of Ukraine on them, like the trident and the flag's colours. 'Blue and yellow ribbon equals Nazi,' she'd said. 'This is how genocidal logic works.'

The windows in the museum, which was an old townhouse in the centre, were boarded up, the displays removed. The collections, that invaluable archive that documents, among other things, the work of the 1920s renaissance, were boxed up on the first day of the invasion and moved down to the basement, along with some of the staff, also seeking shelter from the bombs.

Tetyana, museum director, wore white gloves to wrap up the items again, holding the notebook almost reverently. We talked about the museum's work, which now took the form of cultural events like the 'Fifth Kharkiv' debate I had attended in the basement.

'It's not a new identity for the city,' she explained, 'but it's broadening our identity, removing the Russian imperial identity. It's like . . . a Kharkiv of dreams, of the future. That's what Fifth Kharkiv is.'

Like Victoria, she talked about the past – uncovering it, understanding it, finally.

'Actually literature, and the history of all this' – she gestured around at the museum – 'holds the answer to the big question, "Why?" It was written a long time ago. And in Soviet times we didn't know it well, but now we see.'

Those asking 'why' need only look at this history, according to Tetyana. The answers were all there in the attempts by Moscow – from Tsarist to Soviet to 'modern' Russia – to wipe out the cultures of its colonies, like Ukraine.

'Ukrainians are changing the past as well as the future,' she said. 'It's a cultural front.'

It was cold in the museum but colder outside. I made my way down Pushkinska Street, coughing and swearing at my phone. The signal was constantly cutting out, the GPS almost always wrong – apparently it was being jammed to interfere with Russian drones. A bar was open at the end of the street, windows warmly lit and inviting, and I ducked in to use the WiFi. Ordering a mulled wine to warm up, I suddenly realised that I'd been here before, six years earlier. The streets realigned in my head to how I'd found them in 2018, and then I knew exactly where I was, and how to reach Nataliya Zubar's place.

When I got there, Nataliya ushered me in, talking at her usual rate of knots, wanting to show me the new kit she and Zhenya had bought to document the war. Over the summer they'd been making films in the villages we'd been to, and I recognised the burnt-out school, the lakeside houses. One film followed a group of boys of primary-school age as they played at being soldiers: toy guns and checkpoints, oversized helmets at angles on their little heads. It's natural, I suppose; kids play out the reality around them, looking at what 'being an adult' means and copying. But it was a hard thing to see.

The lack of GPS made getting home difficult; taxi apps thought I was in a village a mile away. I made it, mostly by foot, just before curfew, and desperately wanted to sleep, but was waiting to hear if I would be going to the northern front in the morning. A fellow freelancer had put me in touch with a brigade; it was a volunteer group and open to journalists if we weren't too much bother and brought our own body armour. Of all the countless possibilities I'd been pursuing, only this one now looked likely to come to anything.

At midnight the press officer finally confirmed – the team would leave tomorrow morning for a surveillance mission, and I could come too. I couldn't know the location – just 'north'. The young man on the phone laughed. 'Nearly in Russia, actually!'

The drone team was getting supplies at a petrol station when I met them. The five were in high spirits, joking around as they leant against the green-painted jeeps, eating sandwiches and free coffee. There was a flight attendant, an IT whizz, a project manager, a PhD student – all Kharkiv kids in their twenties or early thirties. They asked me only to use their call signs, not real names, so I was introduced to Masson, Lego, Mother, Aïda and Kim.

For a while I rode in the back of an open truck, bouncing along the main roads out of Kharkiv, wind whipping my hair, and a broad grin on my face, chest cold totally forgotten. Then we changed vehicles and for the next hour I sat with Masson in the cab of a jeep. The boys perched on the back, faces hidden behind army hoods and buffs, holding tightly to the large wooden crates lashed to the bed of the truck which contained the drones.

Masson had a wispy, dark beard and a dazzling white smile. I could imagine him, charming and efficient, working as a steward on a Ukrainian airline, as he had until the 2022 invasion. Then all aircraft were grounded and he faced a stark choice: leave or take up arms. There was a brief window of opportunity for cabin crew and pilots to work abroad. Masson was a pacifist, and he grappled with the decision. But not for long.

'In my soul I couldn't go far from home, where my family is. And hundreds of thousands were fighting for freedom – I had no right to leave,' he said. 'The most important question for me was what I would tell my children in the future if they asked what I had done.'

He'd never imagined taking up arms before that moment, he said. The 'anti-terrorist operation' – the fight against proxy Russian forces in the east, beginning in 2014 – had felt far away, a distant war.

'But actually it was very close,' he added, rueful.

Anyway. He brushed this all aside. 'It's a past life,' he said. 'War unfortunately changes people, morally. It's awful, and people get used to it. To all this cruelty. You want to return to that life, but it would be hard.'

The biggest discovery, Masson said, was that the Russian military could make so many mistakes. It amused him.

'We thought the Russian army was a monster, unbeatable,' he recalled. 'It was David and Goliath. But now we've studied them, fought them. Now we understand it was all propaganda.'

Outside, another badly-damaged village. 'Tsyrkuny,' he said, with a jab of the head. 'From here they launched rockets and mortars at Saltivka.'

He began to describe the damage in that massive 'dormitory'

district of Kharkiv. 'I know,' I said. 'I was there in May. It was awful.'

He grunted, agreeing. What the Russians had done was unforgivable, he said. And yet people called for 'negotiations'.

'Would you tell us to sit down with Bin Laden? Russia is a terrorist. Night-time rocket attacks on residential flats, with people sleeping?' He let out a *pfft* of disgust. 'They know the coordinates.'

I asked about his pacifism, intrigued. He was by no means the first young man I'd talked to who had held, and abandoned, this belief.

'Well I thought the most important thing was to resolve things peacefully,' shrugged Masson.

Now, after everything Russia had done, this belief belonged to that past life that now felt so distant.

'I have only hate left,' Masson said flatly. 'No human feeling.'

We slowed to negotiate craters on smaller roads. Barbed wire stretched across open fields, sodden brown and pitted with shell holes. The border was close, and beyond that lay Russian positions – the targets. We set up in abandoned Russian trenches, their wooden ammo boxes forming walls.

It could have been eighty years ago, I thought suddenly. A scarred landscape of soil mounds, trenches and scorched trees; young people in ill-matching khaki; wooden crates and old guns. But then they got the Starlink out, and we were firmly in the twenty-first century.

I hadn't seen for myself yet how these portable satellites actually worked. Ukraine was awash with them – I even knew friends who were buying them to use in cities, since the mobile signal and broadband were no longer reliable in the power cuts. On the frontlines, thousands of donated Starlinks had been a game-changer, allowing communication between positions and the rear.

The Starlink was a little flat dish which Masson unfolded and set up quickly. The blonde woman, call sign Mother, was kneeling in the mud, bent over a laptop and shouting instructions to Kim as he adjusted another dish on a tripod, up on a mound of earth nearby.

Kim was the youngest, in his early twenties, a joker. He came down from the ridge and helped the others unpack a small white plane from a crate, slotting its long wings into place like a giant Meccano model. This, they explained, was a drone made to order in western Ukraine. Named after folk hero and outlaw Oleksa Dovbush, its quirk was that it could only fly if launched from the back of a speeding pickup. So they clambered up and fixed it to the roof of the cab, sprinkling a little Coke from a plastic bottle – 'for luck'.

There was an infectiously light mood among the group as they got the drone ready, everyone cracking jokes as they worked. Everyone except Aïda. This young woman, a star student at the city's pharmaceutical university, was serious, sombre, and totally focused on the task. She wore a medic's patch on her helmet, but today she would be a drone pilot, and now she stood ready with the handheld console in her hand. Strands of her long brown hair framed her face where they'd escaped the fleece hat and helmet she wore, silver earrings just visible behind her scarf. I'd later learn she was also a crack shot and the first woman to enter the brigade's field section.

'Jump up,' Kim said from the flatbed of the truck, offering a hand. I did gladly, feeling the wind rush a minute later as Masson put his foot down. We needed to reach forty miles an hour, and the road was not really ideal, all bashed up by armoured vehicles and shelling. I got a vivid flash of being a kid on the back of the trailer in Fair Isle on baling days, bouncing through the fields at hair-raising speed. We'd jump off while it was moving to gather up the silage bales, pushing them end over end to be collected. I was momentarily lost in this memory, smiling like an idiot, when something clipped the top of my head. I ducked and the truck screeched to a stop.

The drone had come loose, and, instead of taking off, had flipped backwards on to us. The men jumped down to gather up the splintered fragments of the Dovbush from the road and then gathered round to watch a post-mortem: Ilya, the press officer, had been filming it all from the back of the truck. The conclusion was that the 'feet' attachments had been too weak. The lucky Coke had not helped. Deflated, they returned to the women to report back.

This drone, cobbled together by volunteers in a workshop in Ukraine with 3D printers, was a good example of the messy, makeshift nature of Ukraine's resistance, and a sign of how tech-savvy and inventive this country was. But although the Dovbush was cheap and quick to make, it was not without its flaws.

Mother was undaunted when we came back bearing bits of plane. She exuded a no-nonsense practicality, an air of a headteacher taking on a rowdy class. I felt sure she'd have rolled up her sleeves, if it wasn't so bitterly cold. 'We can't use it now because we lost the motor,' she said brusquely, but added that the advantage of the parts being 3D-printed was that they could be adapted. They'd give the workshop feedback and await a new, improved Dovbush.

Surveillance mission over, the team moved to the next task: bombing. We'd have to wait until it was dark, though. I shivered, and the battery in my camera bleeped pathetically.

The light was already fading as Aïda worked in the dugout, preparing the mortars, which, it was hoped, would find their targets of warehouses and buildings being used by the Russian army a few miles away. Though the surveillance mission had failed, they still had enough information to go on, and this bombing drone would be launched from a tripod, not a speeding vehicle.

She was oblivious as I took pictures of her working, completely absorbed in the task of attaching a handle to the shells using sticky tape and pliers. Oblivious, too, to the whistles and booms of artillery that would occasionally break the silence, just distant enough to ignore. Tucking her hair behind her ears, she held each shell up for close inspection before passing it carefully to Kim.

Suddenly the whole team tensed up, calling to one another across the trenches and staring at the sky. Thick cloud cover revealed nothing. But the noise was unmistakable. It was the buzz of a drone.

'Ours?' someone shouted.

'Definitely not ours,' Mother shouted back, her voice clipped and urgent.

A long silence, only the clicks of safety catches releasing, and that strange, high-pitched buzz. It seemed to be right above us, but still invisible, and I felt incredibly exposed. There wasn't really anywhere to run; the trenches were shallow, the trees bare and burnt. *Not nice when the tables are turned, is it,* a voice said in my head.

'Orlan?' Kim asked.

'Orlan,' came the terse reply.

A few more minutes of listening intently, guns trained at the sky. Orlans are Russian drones shaped like planes; they can carry shells. Not good news.

And then it simply faded away. Mother reported it on the radio. We moved about half a mile down the line of trenches, and they set up the tripod for the bombing drone. The light drained from the colourless sky until only our headtorches and a glowing laptop screen, showing grid coordinates, were visible.

It was quiet for a while. The temperature had dropped below zero with an added wind chill. I was wearing most of my clothes, and it wasn't helping.

In the lull, Kim talked me through their part in this 'drone war'. The brigade operated in Luhansk too, a much more active front to the east. The little Dovbush wouldn't work there – no long roads for launching, too dangerous. Smaller drones could be launched by hand, though.

'Earlier I worried about technical problems,' Kim laughed, referring to the drone feet snapping earlier, 'but now, loss of equipment – well, thank God it's only technical, you know? People are fine. Thank God.'

He preferred working with quadrocopters and had undergone more training in their use. Lighter, smaller, they could fly much lower and be controlled much more precisely, their course corrected to the slightest angle.

Some other soldiers, older men, had turned up in a vehicle, and one of them approached us, holding up a headtorch. 'Good day,' Kim said, politely and in Ukrainian. We'd been speaking Russian all day – perhaps so I could understand, but as they were from Kharkiv, I suspected they might always use Russian together.

It was noticeable with this group, the politeness. In the hours I'd spent with them, they'd rarely even sworn, and there was none of the macho posturing you might expect among young guys with guns and an exciting mission. I wondered where they'd all end up, and how it would change them.

Just as it was finally pitch black, bad news: missile strikes across the whole country, several in Kharkiv.

'So?' I asked, feeling I was missing the obvious.

'Both sides will have turned on radar,' someone said. 'The drone can't fly.'

And with that, now distinctly dejected, the Kharkiv kids packed up their drone and its tripod, their sticky-taped shells and laptops, and drove home to their city.

CHAPTER FOURTEEN

I WAS BEGINNING TO suspect divine intervention, as for
the third time in six weeks I found myself out in the countryside
when missiles were hitting the city. Even more ironic was that
it wasn't any old countryside but the militarised Russian border,
surrounded by craters and shell holes and trenches.

When I got back, Kharkiv was tense and in almost total
darkness. Only the odd generator-powered shop-front or hotel
provided light, or the headlamps of the sparse traffic. Phones
had no signal, no location, nothing. A hundred missiles across
the country, they were saying, and it wasn't only Kharkiv
without power.

It was a relief to find the Ryleev Hotel windows ablaze with
light – or the basement dining room, at least; the generator
could power one bit of the building at a time. I perched on the
radiator to thaw out, still in my boots and jacket, while one of
the women made me fried potatoes. The little kitchen was just
off the dining room, so I could see her dancing with a colleague
to some loud, cheery music as the pan sizzled. What a lovely
place to come home to, I thought, turning to defrost the front
of my legs.

Now there was a heap of writing-up to do, yet more pitching,
a radio script and editing, and plans for the coming week. I was
hoping to get home for Christmas, via Düsseldorf for a reunion
of a journalism exchange I'd been on years before. But that
would mean first going to Kyiv to return the body armour I'd

borrowed, then to Lviv, then Krakow and north via Berlin. It was a lot to plan, and I was dreading the journey; I still had a bad cough and felt wiped out by whatever I'd caught.

In the midst of all this, though, a chance to go to Donbas cropped up, so I dropped everything to take it, not least because it would mean a road trip with Ivanna. There was a team of medics she'd been helping, sending supplies and equipment as needed. She'd even got them an old ambulance. Till now they'd never met, and she wanted to take some supplies down to Donetsk Oblast herself. It was a risky journey, and she didn't want to go alone.

The date of departure kept changing, but on 18 November I packed up my room at Ryleev, gave the matriarchs a present and a promise to come back soon, and took my bags across town to Ivanna's flat. The car was packed and ready before we went to sleep that night, so we could get up early and have a good head start.

We didn't count on the weather, though.

The temperature had plummeted overnight, and the little car, a small and slightly battered Mitsubishi hatchback, was covered in a thick layer of ice. You couldn't even see in through the windows, and little icicles had formed along the wind deflectors. 'Shit,' I said weakly.

Ivanna looked at me, an eyebrow raised. She was obviously wondering if this was a sign.

'Are we crazy?' she asked me. 'Is this a bad idea?'

We knew the road would be difficult, at least on the stretch I'd already seen, as far as Izium: shell holes, missing bridges, long detours. But we'd be going much further this time, east into Donetsk Oblast, down through Kramatorsk and then south to a town a stone's throw from the city of Donetsk, which was held by Russian forces.

And it was snowing.

'Really,' she said, as we looked at the ice-bound car. 'If you think it's too bad, we don't have to go.'

The heroic car survived the ice, the slush, and the shell craters; even the pontoon over the bridge in Izium. Ivanna was gripping the wheel and inching the car across, a gap between the planks beneath us showing racing water a foot below. 'I hate pontoons,' she muttered.

Izium, 80 per cent of its buildings destroyed, was a bleak sight from the car windows, under a heavy sky. A few figures walked through the icy streets with shopping bags, heads down. The only route through was as bad as it had been in September, and the car plunged at wild angles into the deep waterlogged holes. I watched an old Lada emerge from one, amphibious and slick with mud.

The road rises and falls through a series of valleys after Izium. As we came over the crest of a hill, rumbling across scarred and pitted asphalt, we had a view of the whole ravine, the town spread out along its slopes, and I really thought I was seeing things. Through the blur of diagonal sleet and the overworked windscreen wipers it looked like the whole place had been razed to the ground. Low patches of mist were like wisps of smoke hanging over the houses. Everything was drained of colour except the sickly faint brown of dead grass and the black silhouettes of scorched trees and burned-out cars.

Ivanna slowed, and we crawled through the valley, not speaking, the settlement becoming clearer. And I saw that yes, it *had* been razed to the ground. Each little house we passed was a skeleton of wooden beams. And when you looked further into the valley, the devastation stretched on and on, nightmarish, whole streets of blackened ruins winding into the mist.

This had been Kam'yanka. Perhaps it could be again, but it was hard to imagine how. A phrase that people liked to throw around

– that a place had been 'wiped off the map' – came to mind as we drove away. It was an annoying phrase because it was rarely true. 'Oh, Kharkiv has been wiped off the map!' people would say, melodramatically. And of course Kharkiv was alive and kicking. But Kam'yanka was dead.

There wasn't time to stop. We had to get to the medics' base before dark, and there could be long delays on checkpoints given the restricted access to frontline areas. We took it in turns to drive, through dense coniferous forest full of foxholes and tattered tarpaulins and dead trees, crossing into Donetsk Oblast. Along with the Luhansk Oblast, this makes up the area often referred to as Donbas.

Each of the road signs we passed had some heavy, awful significance. Sviatohirsk was where the monastery, ancient and remarkable, had been shelled repeatedly, killing monks and a nun. Lyman, like Izium, made us think of mass graves. And in industrial Kramatorsk, grimy through the rain-streaked car windows, all I could picture as we passed the red-brick railway station was the cluster bomb attack in April, the horrific images of human beings torn apart, bleeding, dying, on the forecourt here.

Finally we reached mining country, the flat open steppe, and the sun briefly appeared. It cast a burst of golden colour over the stormy sky then sank, a burning red smudge, behind the collieries, the headstocks and spoil tips.

'*Terykony*,' Ivanna said, nodding at the little conical hills of mining waste. I nodded and with great enthusiasm tried to describe the West Lothian shale bings, half a world away, but so similar. We drove through a tiny town dominated by the mine workings in its centre, the red scree slopes of its *terykon* looming over the low buildings.

Until this point, checkpoints had been breezy, the men standing guard in a happy mood despite the cold and wet. Ivanna would chat to them briskly in Ukrainian, they'd all have a chuckle, and we'd drive on. When I asked what the joke was, she laughed again. 'Oh, they think we're mad! Crazy girls, driving stuff to Donbas . . .'

Nearer the frontlines though we were taken into a small hut by the road for a longer questioning, by a stern woman who made copies of my accreditation and passport. After a while we were allowed to go through, and finally, not too long after dark, we made it to Kurakhove, where Yevhenii – Zhenya – led us to the secret base. GPS off, no photos.

After unpacking the boxes we sat down for bowls of hot plov, that comforting, oily Uzbek dish of meat and rice. Zhenya was a major in his thirties, a gruff but warm-hearted man; alongside him was Yevhenia, a sergeant and doctor aged twenty-eight. At the end of the table sat a broad-shouldered Viking with a sandy-coloured beard and gentle smile. This was Ihor, and I laughed when he said he'd been a dentist, because it was so incongruous.

'It meant I already had the background required to be a medic,' he explained. When the war started it had been an easy decision, and training didn't take long – American tactical medics had carried it out. The courses had been good, he said, but there was a glaring problem – they were trained with equipment the Ukrainians didn't have. Like what, I asked?

'Certain types of bandages, splints . . . We need an oxygen concentrator.'

Ivanna had been trying. She was their magician, their fairy godmother. Needless to say, on this first meeting, they were happy to see her.

We talked about families; Ihor had relatives in Moscow. They didn't talk anymore.

'They told us we should lay down our guns and be patient and everything will be good, because they're liberating us,' he said, shaking his big head sadly.

Yevhenia's story was terrifying. Her parents lived in a village which was occupied by Russian forces for six months, and a pair of her army boots (she was already a soldier then) had been in the house before the troops arrived. Her parents had hidden this incriminating evidence – in fact her dad had buried them, so scared the house would be searched.

The whole time she didn't know if they were OK. 'It was awful,' she murmured. 'I worried every day.' Then in September the Russians were driven out and she got just one day of leave, racing to see her parents. 'I cried,' she admitted. 'A lot.'

She never managed to find the boots afterwards: too well-hidden underground.

A pot belly stove and camping beds with scratchy woollen blankets made for the most welcoming sight after a long day. I snuggled up, full of plov and ever so tired. Then I coughed all night.

It was cloudy the next day. Clouds meant no reconnaissance drones, so probably no shelling. A quiet day, explained the young soldier, leaning against the wall of the farmyard they were living in.

'That's good!' I said, naively.

He shook his head bitterly. 'No. I want it to go faster. Otherwise it will never end.'

I hadn't thought about it like that. He was fed up, and missing his family. Everyone scuffing around this place was. We'd come out with Zhenya in his van, winding through little villages, hamlets really, visiting soldiers at their positions. The Russian positions were about ten miles away.

'What do you need most?' Ivanna asked at each stop. The answer was always the same: family.

Round the back of one house, well camouflaged under mud-coloured nets and tarps, a massive truck was parked up, its tyres nearly as tall as me. Under the coverings lurked the surface-to-air missiles which can take down everything from attack drones to helicopters. These had a 50 per cent success rate, a soldier told me, but if they fired them, they had to move, fast, before the retaliatory strike came.

The owners of these little houses had fled, and the soldiers had moved in, as happens near frontlines – but they weren't trashing the cottages. Everything was clean and orderly in those we visited – if full of guns and grenades. In one, a cosy home where the walls were lined with dark wood, a carved staircase led upstairs to bedrooms being used by the brigade. I studied a wall of family photographs for a while then noticed a bowl of bullets below them. In the substantial garden, a vineyard and fruit trees were a hint of the happy lives people had led here once. Often there were notes left for the Ukrainian armed forces, the soldiers told us. 'Please use the house, there are potatoes in the cellar,' and so on.

Not all the civilians had gone, though. In Yelyzavetivka, a cluster of houses either side of the long straight road, I heard Vasyliy and Anna approach before I saw them, their bodged-together two-wheeled tractor coming down the road with a loud *put-put* and the couple perched on a cart behind it.

I talked to them for a bit. This had always been their home, they said, and now it was their children's home too, and they had no intention of leaving. 'Where would we go?' he shrugged, the same refrain I'd heard so many times.

Cracks of artillery nearby formed the backdrop to our conversation, and neither so much as blinked. Anna's mother had been wounded not long ago, and her sister too. The ambulance couldn't take them to safety because its tyres were blown out and the crew injured. And her uncle – he had died. Anna had to view his body in the morgue. 'We saw all this with our own eyes,' she said. Her face was drawn and tired under a big woolly hat.

But it was still better than the unknown, for them. Soldiers brought food and diesel and sweets for the kids. 'We've plenty of firewood,' Vasyliy shrugged. They both had a sort of wry detachment from it all. After all, it had been eight long years like this.

As we drove on, I was trying to imagine the team's work – evacuating wounded soldiers to safety – in this environment, racing down these long, seemingly endless roads, rutted and potholed. I felt like we'd been driving forever that day, and of course we hadn't been as far as the contact line from where Zhenya and his team might have to collect people. How long did it take to get a casualty out of the 'red zone'?

The big man shrugged, and didn't really answer. The road was the only way to evacuate people – helicopters were easy targets – so you just dealt with it. Not everyone would make it.

The Russians' favourite target at that moment, of course, was energy infrastructure, and Kurakhove was a sitting duck. The tall striped chimneys of the thermal power plant towered above the small town, spewing twin plumes of smog. I watched them from a small pier on the other side of the reservoir, another temporary base. One of the soldiers living here, nicknamed Apostle, pointed out at the water. 'A man was killed there by shelling in June, while he was swimming.'

There was a video, apparently. Lots of people in the lake, making the most of the hot weather, and suddenly they're screaming, flailing around, great chutes of water exploding upwards. Cluster bombs again, it was thought.

On this evening, though, it was peaceful. At about a mile's distance across the lake, the plant, with its forest of electricity pylons, looked hazy, a distant mirage. A skein of wild geese was making its slow way overhead, their cackles reaching us through the cold air.

Apostle had a calm, grave demeanour, watchful eyes looking out from under his hood – a man whose call-sign fitted perfectly. He had laid out a feast of roast chicken, smoked fish from the lake, spicy carrot salad, marinated tomatoes – plus a bottle of *horilka,* to warm the soul, and to toast the things that mattered. It was wonderfully, almost absurdly, domestic – I thought of Zhenya earlier in the day pointing out the beehives he tended. They kept pigs too, and had been drying a haul of mushrooms from the woods. All these scraps of normal life, here amidst the noise of heavy guns, the permanent threat of strikes, the sudden dashes to rescue wounded soldiers.

'The most important thing,' said Apostle, philosophical now, 'is *byt.*'

Byt is a small word with great meaning: everyday life, a sense of home, normality, habitual comforts.

'This is the foundation,' he said, and he gestured at us all, sitting round the table together. 'After all – we're people, not animals.'

It was there in the hut by the shore, drinking with Ivanna and the medics and Apostle, that I got a message on my phone from Iryna, the ex-wife of the missing writer Volodymyr Vakulenko. Iryna was Vitalik's mother, and she lived in central Ukraine. I'd been hoping to interview her.

'A lot has happened recently,' the message said. 'Hope has been replaced by darkness.'

My heart sank. I realised I'd been hoping, too, for this man I'd never met.

The next message said that Volodymyr's mother Olena had seen a photograph; an American journalist had found it. It had been taken before Volodymyr's body was buried in grave 319. So he had been there all along. No Russian prison, no trial – they'd shot him and left him by the side of the road. Olena had known the picture was him from his ring and tattoos.

'I saw it too,' Iryna wrote. 'I recognised his sweater.'

'I'm so sorry. I'm truly, truly sorry,' I wrote back.

I ducked outside and called Olena. I told her, too, how sorry I was, and it felt, again, inadequate. But she thanked me and said that yes, we could drop by tomorrow, she would like to tell me more about Volodymyr.

I felt deeply sad. I'd liked Olena so much when I'd met her back in October. The strength of her hope then had been palpable; I kept thinking of what she said as we left. 'I have to believe, because he's my only child.' For that last glimmer to be snuffed out, for it all to come crashing down, with a photo of his dead body – and after all that time. My heart broke for her.

Inside, someone asked me what had happened. My face, I guess, gave it away. I explained, briefly. Someone proposed a toast to his memory, and we all raised our glasses.

Back through Sloviansk and Kramatorsk, through the scarred forested land of northern Donetsk Oblast, back through those horrible woods of foxholes and shattered tree trunks, the fields pitted with thousands of black, waterlogged shell holes. We reached Kapytolivka, Olena's village, by late morning.

She welcomed us in, and we sat in the living room, where Vitalik was watching TV, laughing out loud at cartoons.

It was a week ago, she began slowly, that she had seen the

photo. 'They had a lot of doubt about whether to show me, whether it would be worth it or not. But yes, you can't hide from the facts.'

The photo was proof he had been shot and left by the road. The man who buried the dead had taken photos, hoping it would help relatives identify the victims later.

Olena had been ill with Covid too, and was only able to withstand all this, she said, thanks to the injections she was getting for her heart and nervous system. She'd have to withstand more, as the funeral was 'looming on the horizon', and would take place as soon as Volodymyr's body was returned to them, 'for the burial, a normal, *decent* burial'.

Everything had taken so long. The investigation, establishing the basic facts. Journalists had done a lot of the digging. The DNA results still weren't back. 'Unbearable,' she said, 'waiting, waiting.'

She had so many people to be angry with. The people who told her he was in Russia, to start with. 'If they shot him, it means he never *was* taken to Russia! Where do people *get* this information?' she asked, furious.

Then there were the Russians, who had fobbed her off, again and again. She remembered a commander sitting across from her.

'We're looking,' she intoned, impersonating his bored, disinterested voice. 'We're looking, there's no information.'

And as he said this, she remembered, he had looked not in her eyes but over her head. He wouldn't even look at her.

'And I saw this, and I knew that he knew *everything*. What happened to my son, where my son was, *everything*.'

This was late April or early May. Volodymyr was almost certainly dead then. The body, the records showed, was buried on 12 May.

'And yet I continued to search, all through May, all of June, July *and August*,' she almost spat.

Meanwhile Russian soldiers were repeatedly searching the house where Volodymyr had lived with his father – 'Oh, a hundred times. Looking for what? Weapons, Nazi symbols.' Her voice was disdainful.

She recounted what they'd said to Volodymyr's father as they turned his house upside down: 'Why on earth would you raise a *nationalist*?'

'What are you talking about?' the old man had replied, bewildered.

'Oh,' the soldiers had said, 'they've told us *all* about you here. We know everything about you.'

And from this she guessed that it was locals who'd pointed the finger. She even had a good idea who. The man was long gone, in Europe somewhere.

There would be no justice, it seemed. They'd shot her son – but who would answer for it? They'd lied to her face, and she had to live with it. Someone had sold out her son, for what? For pettiness, for preferential treatment, for cigarettes – we'd likely never know.

'Everything, as they say, is God's will,' Olena said. She fell silent, as though thinking the same thought I was having – *How, how on earth could this be God's will?*

'But he was my only child!' she burst out. 'And can it really be right that parents should bury their child? It seems to me this is the most terrible thing that can happen in life.'

She'd thought, in March, that the air raids were the worst that could happen. Terrifying. They'd crouched in the basement with planes screaming overhead. Then the cluster bombs. But, she said, she'd live through it all again. If he could just be alive.

And now how to tell Vitalik. Or whether to tell him. Would

he understand? He knew something, of course. The two had been inseparable. Even when the boy was little Volodymyr had taken him along to literary forums, conferences, readings. In fact, Volodymyr had planned it all out, Olena told us. When he reached old age he and his son would move to a care home, and that way, be together forever.

'And he didn't even make it to fifty,' she said. 'He was always saying that he'd have a long life. He'd show me the life line on his hand – "Look how long it is!"'

Her voice trailed off, speaking to herself, or perhaps to her son, berating him quietly. 'And now what have you done? What have you done, what have you done . . . *Bozhe moy*. My God.'

Before we left I asked about something Iryna had told me – that Volodymyr had really loved nature. '*Oy, bozhe*,' Olena said, and she described the hours of work he'd put in to tidy up the village, clearing litter from a sacred spring near the church, from the bus stops. 'People are so *passive*,' she said, shaking her head. 'They chuck stuff, throw litter everywhere.'

Her son had created a tiny park in Kapytolivka. 'Everything had just started to take,' she said. 'It was coming into bloom. The lilacs and the bird cherry, in his little garden. Then the jackals came with tanks . . . They drove over it. But part remains,' Olena said. 'And spring will come, and we'll still be living, we'll put it in order, this little garden' – she was crying now – 'and we'll put up a plaque.'

In Kam'yanka, that ruined valley of blackened houses, we stopped for a bit, walked down a potholed road, because two cars had gone that way so we reasoned it wasn't mined, but still, we didn't go far. Fog hung over everything.

As I paid closer attention, photographing my surroundings, all the traces of Russian occupation began to appear. A rank dugout, a dark hole in the ground, sodden brown fabric draped over the sandbags, rotting in the damp air. Next to it, an empty bottle, size forty-three boots and a splayed paperback – detective stories in translation. A Russian soldier had been reading Agatha Christie.

Further on, I found a gate sprayed with the letter 'Z', the 'calling card' of Russian soldiers. A shining German microwave, lying in the grass. Given the widespread looting for which the Russians were now infamous, it was easy to imagine how it had got here. The retreat became a bit too hasty for its bearer, perhaps, and he had to run away. Or maybe he was shot. I struggled to care.

We stopped again on Mount Kremenets, on the approach to Izium. All I'd seen of this area was the destruction as I'd driven through, but now Ivanna helped me understand its complicated beauty; a history that is all bound up with Tatars and Cossacks and military battles. From here the most spectacular scene stretched out on all sides. Rolling hills, covered with dense dark trees, the mist and fog patches moving slowly through the valleys and slopes. Nearby the nature reserve began, the river winding through forests, monasteries scattered through it all. This spot had been home to a holiday resort. There had been a faux-Gothic hotel called the Seven Winds, with pointed arches and dormer windows, where you could eat dinner watching the sunset. Guests could enjoy a spot of windsurfing, or mountain-biking in the countryside. Ivanna had come here with friends, many times.

Now she stood, in her big army jacket and boots, a small figure in the rain, looking at the ruins. Everything was wrecked. She got out her phone, video-calling a friend to show her what had become of their favourite place. I left her alone and walked up to the crest of the hill. Here, I'd read, people had snuck up during the occupation of Izium to try to catch a signal on their phones, at enormous risk.

The war memorial that dominated Kremenets was one of the

strangest, and biggest, I'd seen. It was made of three enormous concrete obelisks, all jutting angles and looming overhangs. Suspended between two was a sculpture, like a steel ribbon of human beings brandishing guns and knives, in tin helmets and peaked caps, reaching and striving heroically as they always are in these monumental pieces. But around them, attached by thin threads of dull metal, were the curved wings of small birds, incongruous in this martial scene.

That the hill had been heavily shelled was obvious not only from the craters which had smashed up the chalky ground but also from the considerable damage to this memorial. A chunk of the metal sculpture had fallen to the red marble plinth below, a little heap of broken birds which perfectly framed the graffiti on the obelisk behind: 'Glory to Ukraine', someone had written in spray paint, reclaiming this monument from the Soviet past.

The last stretch of road was the worst. We took turns to coax the car at a crawl over the dirt track of a detour, and it tipped dramatically into each giant crater, sickening thuds emanating from the chassis. Each one could have been the end of the Mitsubishi. Even back on the highway I struggled to keep us in a straight line, and not only from the tiredness clouding my vision. As night fell a dense, freezing fog had settled. I gripped the wheel, extremely conscious that beneath the fog, flanking the road, were the skull-and-crossbones signs warning of mines.

We talked about the people we'd met, Zhenya with his bees, Ihor, Yevhenia. Ivanna told me something I'd missed the day before – Zhenya had told her that tending the bees kept him steady, kept his mind from lingering on the men he'd not been able to save.

And now she'd worry about them all. This was why she hadn't met them earlier, in a vain attempt to limit the spiralling number of people she worried about every day. Another spot on the map, now, that she'd keep an eye on. That twist in the stomach when a certain place comes under attack. I knew well what she meant.

'But we're human after all,' she concluded, echoing Apostle yesterday. You had to embrace it, the new friendships and connections, the worry and the love.

I was thinking about this when I got on the train, the first of many in that long journey home. As usual, I couldn't sleep, and had time to think. I kept coming back to how much richer my life was because of the people I'd met. I'd worry about Ivanna, and I'd told her this many times; she brushed it off with a laugh.

I understood more about 'degrees' of worry now, about the way perspectives shift depending on what you've seen, where you've been, what you might have risked. To worry about her in Kharkiv seemed almost silly when she was worrying about people on the frontline. But I would, because I cared about her, and I was always scared of losing people.

But Ivanna knew well the futility of spending all your time worrying. It doesn't help anyone. And I tried to bear this in mind as I made my way back to Scotland.

PART FOUR

DONBAS

FEBRUARY–APRIL 2023

CHAPTER FIFTEEN

'OH SHIT,' MY PASSENGER in the pick-up truck said. She was leaning over to peer at the temperature gauge. The red pointer was trembling near the big red 'H'. 'Shit, shit, shit,' she repeated, her South African accent thickening.

I pulled on to the hard shoulder of the *Autobahn*, and we cranked open the bonnet, waiting for the freezing air to cool the hissing, steaming engine. It was dark. It was sleeting. We were somewhere near the Polish border.

My companion was Mary-Ann: artist, activist, sock-puppet extraordinaire. We'd nicknamed the pick-up Vinnie; according to Stout family lore, I told her, you always have to name cars or they'll let you down. Now I came to think of it, all our family cars had died, spectacularly, much like Vinnie was doing now.

Every ten seconds a lorry passed inches from us, blasting us with wind and deafening noise. I was hungry and tired and now bitterly cold. I shone my torch on Mary-Ann, who was trying to unscrew the radiator cap, and was almost annoyed to see she was grinning from ear to ear. 'You've got to laugh, Jen,' she said. I grudgingly accepted that she was right. I would try to be a bit more Mary-Ann-ish.

For the next hour, with multiple pit-stops, I coaxed and cajoled Vinnie to Poland. We finally limped across the border to the motel at about 10 p.m., doing a steady fifteen miles per hour and steaming gently. Just in time to get a plate of *gołąbki* – cabbage rolls stuffed with mince in a thick savoury sauce – with sauerkraut and pickled beetroot and marinated tomatoes. I ate with huge contentment. I was back in the right part of the world.

The rest of our jeep convoy was in the truck-stop cafe too, having a beer before bed. Our group, nearly twenty-strong, included two priests, a tour guide, a fisherman and several businessmen, all volunteering to drive 1,600 miles across Europe. The idea was simple: medics and soldiers in Ukraine desperately need jeeps on the frontline, for speedy evacuation and manoeuvres. Right-hand-drive vehicles don't hold much export value in Europe so sell for less. The charity Jeeps for Peace was therefore buying up old models in the UK, driving them to Ukraine, and handing them over to the army. They'd made several trips already. When I heard they were setting off at the end of February 2023, I asked if I could tag along. Beats flying, I thought.

The fact that many of the pick-ups came from farms – Vinnie's mud-encrusted interior was testament to this – was the little spanner in the works. After quiet lives being driven a few miles a day, suddenly they were being driven across Europe.

We'd started early that morning in the port of Amsterdam, driving off the DFDS ferry. After twelve hours on the road, Vinnie had not been the only casualty, but the other jeeps could at least be patched up.

It felt like a scant few hours of broken sleep before we were up again, slipping across the pitch-black and icy asphalt to our trucks. Vinnie had to remain in Poland, in disgrace, until a mechanic could assess the damage, so I jumped in with the priests, who had a slightly swankier model: leather seats and a Bluetooth radio. We set off, listening to a folk/electronica band from Skye, their trippy mix of Gaelic laments and dance music a perfect soundtrack to the ethereal morning. Mist still swirled in the fields, but a huge burning sun was rising slowly behind the black branches of trees, everything in silhouette around us on the motorway, the empty dark sky slowly flooding with orange light. I saw my face in the rearview mirror lit by this light, and basked in it, thinking of the dreich dark days of the Shetland winter which I'd just left. Up there, at sixty degrees north, winter feels relentless. Now I'd jumped all the way down to the fifty-first parallel and it felt practically spring-like as we sped along the highway. I could have sung aloud with happiness.

At the next fuel stop, we discovered this vehicle was leaking diesel, quite catastrophically, when it was topped up. It seemed to be fine once back on the road, though. So we hammered on. The priests were good company; they'd had to live together during lockdown and now bickered like an old married couple. 'Oh that's it, just drive *over* the pedestrians,' the younger one muttered as we navigated the streets of Przemyśl, and I laughed in the back, listening to the rector of one of Edinburgh's biggest churches swear at the traffic lights.

The convoy regrouped at Medyka on Poland's eastern border as the sun set. As on previous trips I could feel that nervous tension building as we inched closer to the barbed wire of the border, at least among those who hadn't been to Ukraine before. The tanks in the queue next to us perhaps heightened this, though on closer inspection they weren't really tanks but armoured personnel carriers, old British models now daubed with Ukrainian colours, secured with rusting chains to a flat-bed truck. A little glimpse of the immense flow of military aid that had been moving across the long border for the past twelve months.

Paperwork held us up on the Ukrainian side for hours; it got late, and very cold. The small cafe in the border complex was our saving grace as we enjoyed hot plates of borscht and nips of vodka from the women there, who smiled, wryly amused at the antics of all these slightly giddy Scotsmen. But it was funny – the combination of petty bureaucracy and human kindness, those two universals, had served as a reminder that normal life extends to countries at war too. You expect a war zone but find the same queues of bored truck drivers, the same aggravating delays over a misspelled surname, the same ebb and flow of everyday life.

A few days later, the volunteer drivers all returned home, having had an experience they'd never forget, meeting soldiers from the brigade, dancing to Ukrainian folk music and even doing stints on camera for a local news channel.

Mary-Ann, the South African artist, stayed in Ukraine for a while. I think she fell in love with the place. I wasn't surprised, because Ukraine suited her – the emotional honesty of people, the frankness. I'd put her in touch with a children's writer who had been on the PEN trip to Kapytolivka last year, and on their first meeting they ended up in a church where the funeral of yet another soldier was taking place, crying together, sharing all the grief.

Mary-Ann's project had started in Scottish prisons, where she was working in art therapy. The men there had told her they wanted to do something to help Ukraine, but in their position felt powerless. So she started making origami sunflowers with them; in the end, they turned out huge numbers of these little paper badges, which had a little barcode in the centre to raise money for art kits. She believed, very strongly, that children who'd survived war and occupation should have access to art materials, believed it could be transformational. I left her in Lviv, in safe hands, and undoubtedly in the right place.

I was going east again. Back on the night trains with another set of body armour from Reporters Without Borders stowed under the seats next to the scuffed old rucksack I'd come to hate quite passionately. I was wiped out from the long drive but full of plans. The first was ambitious: I was writing about the jeeps and wanted to track down one of ours to finish the story. It was said they had a sixty-day lifespan, as most of the vehicles went to Bakhmut, where the artillery was most relentless, and were blown up or burnt out after a few weeks.

The idea that somewhere round the hell of Bakhmut you might see a right-hand-drive pickup from a farm in Aberdeenshire had gripped me. It was a great story, the physical embodiment of all the solidarity of the past twelve months. But unsurprisingly, no one I spoke to would allow me to go to Bakhmut. Kramatorsk was the compromise; the Ukrainian organiser of the convoy said I could meet some of the brigade there for an interview.

I'd driven there once, with Ivanna, on that icy, foggy November journey to Donbas and back. So why not do it again? She was abroad for a month, and I was going to stay in her flat in Kharkiv. 'Use the car,' she'd said casually. The heroic little Mitsubishi sat waiting for me.

Natasha, my journalist friend, met me off the train in the morning. We drove through the city, up Sumska Street and over Freedom Square. Things had obviously improved in Kharkiv, the hard winter nearly over, the power supply almost reliable, trams and metro running. Government billboards declared, 'Kharkiv is living and working!' alongside some slightly unctuous adverts with crocuses and a greeting 'for the best women in the world' from the mayor himself – it was nearly International Women's Day.

This time it was not ice thwarting my journey but a flat battery. The hero-car coughed weakly and died. I found jump leads and rang Natasha, who arrived minutes later with more friends and a car, reliable as ever but looking concerned.

'Are you sure you should drive to Kramatorsk on your own?' she asked, as we hooked up the two vehicles.

'No,' I replied, laughing.

But actually the only part worrying me was driving through the city. I'd still not figured out the intersections where distant, tiny traffic lights strung high above flashed arrows I couldn't interpret, and what felt like a thousand angry drivers beeped at me to get a move on. It was a relief to reach the outskirts, which were still marked by the battles for the city a year ago.

'*Zi sviatom,*' the soldiers on checkpoints said to me, with irony. 'Happy holidays!'

It was a reference to Women's Day, one which the petrol station attendant had made as well, as I explained why I couldn't stop the car (in case it died again), and why the fuel cap would only open if you yanked that bit of wire that stuck out of the boot.

'Where is it you're going?' he asked, seeing the flak jacket and pet food (for strays), the bottles of water and spare blankets in the car. When I explained, he laughed, shaking his head in disbelief. 'Picked the right day for it!'

The highway down to Izium and on to Sloviansk had been patched up, in parts, though there was still a detour at Chuhuiv. It went through residential streets, one-storey little houses, and some kids had chosen a hairpin corner for their playtime checkpoint. They brandished plastic guns and scowls. I waved at them, and one waved back, but the other boys just stared, eerily perfecting the contemptuous glare of bored soldiers in their battered tin helmets.

An impressive temporary bridge had been erected over one particularly smashed-up bit of the highway, and the shaky wooden-slat pontoon over the Sivers'kyi Donets River was gone, replaced by a more solid version. No water racing underneath the car. But the burnt-out tanks and upended cars along the roadside remained. Essential fixes only; the rest would wait till after the war. It made sense but gave everything a sense of limbo.

Traffic thinned out, the military cars replacing civilian ones in a Frankenstein army of repurposed and refashioned vehicles, sprayed matte green, in every shape imaginable: old Soviet Ladas, lurching high-roof Sprinter vans, battered pick-up trucks, grey Kombis from the 1960s and a wide array of tractors. A Land Rover raced west with blue lights flashing – a makeshift ambulance – and occasionally I'd watch an armoured personnel carrier roar past, draped with camouflage and deafeningly loud.

It was evident which vehicles had come from the front. Riddled with bullet holes, sheared apart by shrapnel, bumpers and doors ripped off. At a junction an old Toyota was being dragged on bare rims, the metal screaming and sparking as it bounced over the already damaged asphalt.

Sloviansk and Kramatorsk lie close together, two sprawling towns of heavy industry, with foundries, steel mills, machinery plants. Both had been captured briefly in 2014 by Russian-backed militias and were retaken a few months later. People here had known war for a long time.

I squinted into the low sun, which had emerged from the dark storm clouds billowing overhead; the road shone, a silver path after the heavy rain. The light still glimmered faintly when I arrived in Kramatorsk, smokestacks looming across the river. After it took on the role of regional capital in 2014, the attendant rise in population had brought more funding and investment. But now it was a garrison town. Bakhmut, where so many people were dying every day in a terrible, grinding hell, was only twenty miles away, and Kramatorsk was full of soldiers on rotation.

Its proximity to the fighting also meant it was full of journalists – including Bennett, my American friend from the Moscow programme. And he wasn't alone – Mykola, the Ukrainian fixer who had been injured when the team was targeted in May, had recovered and was right back in the thick of things. I could stay in their flat for a few days – great news as I'd found nothing else.

There were out on a story when I arrived, but Quentin from the BBC was in the city and had agreed to be key liaison. I'd rung him, slightly frantic, from the middle of Kharkiv traffic, and he'd offered to help without batting an eyelid. We'd never even met before. I found myself wondering once again how on earth I'd do this without all these friends and colleagues so willing to lend a hand.

Booms from the direction of Bakhmut rang out as we talked in the car park of his hotel. Something briefly lit up the sky. Access to the front had become increasingly difficult, and he and his team had been stuck here for a week, waiting for permission.

After dropping off my things at the flat, I dashed out to get a bowl of soup at Ria Lounge, the pizza restaurant at which, I'd been informed, 'everybody' ate. And right enough, it was packed with foreigners and press and soldiers and volunteers; next door the supermarket was equally busy, the checkout queues full of men and women in uniform carrying stacks of energy drinks – the whole of Donetsk Oblast was dry, no alcohol allowed.

I made my way home in the dark, shining my headtorch on the pavement ahead and on the shop-fronts and flats I was passing, the weak spotlight showing broken windows and police tape. The air-raid siren had started up, and it seemed to come from every direction, rising and falling over this military city. I quickened my pace.

But Kramatorsk wasn't the target that night. Once again, it was the city I'd only just left; at 4am Kharkiv and many other cities across the country came under a massive coordinated attack with cruise and anti-aircraft missiles and swarms of cheap Iranian drones. Many had been intercepted, but not the Kinzhals, the hypersonic weapons that fly under the radar of air defences.

From Kherson, too, the news was grim. Relentless shelling of the city was killing the residents who'd endured so much already. A bus stop was the latest target, four dead.

I drove to Sloviansk early, to meet some soldiers who'd taken delivery of a British jeep. It was an old Land Rover pick-up, not painted yet. Vasyliy was in his fifties, and he had the most fantastically expressive face, weather-beaten and full of wry amusement, and a plush white beard that gave him a gnomish look.

Dmitriy was much younger, wearing a US Army field jacket. He praised the jeeps, especially the versatile L200s; you can mount a machine gun on those, he said, approvingly. But mostly they were used for evacuations and getting people from one position to another, with speed.

'It's always like this – *faster, faster, faster,*' said Dmitriy. '*Again, again, faster, faster* – well, that's manoeuvres, that's war. And for evacuations, for the wounded, we need something like this' – he gestured at the roomy Land Rover – 'or an ambulance.'

The vehicles had a short life expectancy. 'They break down, wheels get blown, they're always coming under fire – today you have one, tomorrow it's gone,' he said, adding, philosophically, 'Well, what can we do?'

Keep requesting more and hoping they'd arrive, it seemed.

'How many, in an ideal world, would you need? For your battalion?'

Dmitriy puffed out his cheeks. 'Ideally? Well. A thousand. But then maybe the war will go on for two years, and a thousand won't be enough. We simply have no idea. Thank God people are helping, that's all I can say. Europe, America, the whole world. I thank you all.'

The pair were diplomatic when it came to the situation around Bakhmut. There had been mutterings of discontent about the government's decision to keep reinforcing the town even as the Russian line approached in a pincer movement around it.

'It's difficult,' they both said. 'Complicated.' They'd continue to hold it, as the army command had ordered, Dmitriy told me. 'As long as possible,' he added, several times. 'As long as we're given enough ammunition, we'll hold it. It all depends on how much we get.'

'Artillery?' I asked.

'Yes, of course, we need more shells. We just have to hope for the best, though.'

'As long as we can'; 'hope for the best' – Dmitriy, despite his caution, had really summed up the mood here. Late last year there had been an almost giddy optimism, the country still high on the stunning success of the counteroffensives, the broad swathes of map turned from red to blue. Yes, a hard winter ahead, but real hopes of an end to all this. Now though, the feeling was of settling in for the long run, not daring to predict an end date, but grimly getting through it. Every soldier knew that the chances of dying if you were sent to Bakhmut were high. Neither side released accurate casualty figures, but it seemed that tens of thousands on both sides had likely been killed there; the toll was estimated to be higher on the Russian side, which was partly made up of Wagner mercenaries. The private military company, funded by the Russian state but held at arm's length to do its dirtiest work, was apparently sending wave upon wave of ex-convicts into battle, freshly sourced from Russia's penal colonies.

Kramatorsk felt quite lively that afternoon as I walked around with Bennett, but it was mostly soldiers, not 'normal' city life. The economy here was running on the pay packets of all these troops, with cafes and shops doing brisk business. I passed a shop selling military gear, generators, boots. A sign stuck to the door boasted of the most sought-after item: 'GREEN SCOTCH TAPE'. This was the current signifier, the tape Ukrainian soldiers wound around their arms and stuck on their helmets; sometimes it was blue, or yellow. Russians wore red and white.

A woman we stopped to speak to told us about the strike one month ago; a rocket had flown straight into a block of flats on Marata Street.

'Absolutely awful,' she said. 'People were killed. Have you seen it?'

We shook our heads, and she led us down the street and round a corner. 'Go in, take a look,' she said, and left us to it. We found an appalling scene. The central section of the substantial old block – it looked like early twentieth century, brick-built, with decorative moulding on the outside – had been completely torn away. I stood looking up at the wallpaper in what had been eight flats, their contrasting bathroom tiles all on display.

'Jesus Christ,' Bennett said quietly. For a while we took photos, picking among the debris. So many household things, little bits of home life, intact but scattered around the heaps of rubble and rebar. Children's shoes, a bathtub, a telephone. A yellow Teletubbies toy. A block grater, completely squashed flat. In a window frame, among the bricks and dust, someone had placed an artificial red rose, carefully balanced on the open pages of a dictionary. There were candles in storm lanterns on the ground, a small shrine to the three killed here.

Bennett went to start dinner in the flat, and I walked on a bit. Further along Marata Street I met two young women, Dasha and Ira. They were fashion-conscious university students and wore the outsized fleecy jackets popular everywhere and knee-high black boots; one was studying medicine, the other teaching. They claimed to be totally unperturbed by the war carrying on around them. It registered as an inconvenience in their young lives.

'Spring is coming, the air is fresh,' Dasha laughed. 'We got used to all this ages ago.'

I wished them luck, and they strolled off. I watched them pass the destroyed block, barely glancing at it; to them, this was simply how the city looked at the moment. Up through a pleasant postwar housing scheme, the five-storey blocks separated by flowerbeds, I spotted a small armoured vehicle, its gun turret covered in tarp, parked rather conspicuously alongside the flats. The woman walking ahead of me stopped to look at it, and as I drew near she turned to roll her eyes.

'Not exactly hidden, is it?' she said. We talked as we went on up the hill, about her life in this frontline city. It sounded rough. Not much work, and not enough money by far. Humanitarian aid came through, but in the form of food, not cash. And if it was hard here, how would you manage in Dnipro or any of those big cities?

'Those who evacuated came back. It was too expensive,' she sighed.

Others I spoke to in Kramatorsk echoed this sentiment and complained bitterly about the authorities putting pressure on them to evacuate when it didn't seem to be a viable option. The population had more than halved, and those remaining would just 'sit it out', they said. No one liked to talk about the fact that both Kramatorsk and Sloviansk lay in the path of the Russian army if it managed to break through at Bakhmut. But in theory it could happen, and it would mean absolute carnage here. I asked about this and got shrugs in response.

The occasional but deadly strikes were a more pressing concern, but there was a marked fatalism about these, too. Because Russian-held territory was so near, a rocket might hit before the sirens ever sounded, and the common wisdom was that it was better to die in the open, or in your own bed, than to be crushed, or to suffocate, in some dank cellar. 'The basement won't save you,' I heard, again and again.

I had some sympathy with this. Proper bomb shelters were one thing, but the shallow basements underneath crumbling post-war prefabs were not a place I ever felt safe.

It was all, as usual, a question of perception, of your own personal analysis of the risks. To someone in Western Europe, all of Ukraine would seem horribly dangerous, whereas someone in Lviv, enjoying a degree of normality, might look at those choosing to stay in Kramatorsk and question their sanity. And then in Kramatorsk, twenty miles from the fighting, you could feel safe compared to those living in a 'real' frontline town, where life was a daily hell. And this was where I'd go tomorrow.

CHAPTER SIXTEEN

WHAT WAS SUPPOSED TO happen was this: I'd jump in a minibus with some volunteers who, every day except Sundays, drove to heavily shelled places and took civilians out to safety. There were many such volunteer groups all over Ukraine, some made up of foreigners. Pete Reed, a former US Marine, had been killed a month earlier getting people out of Bakhmut. He wasn't the first.

This evacuation run was going to Chasiv Yar, a small town eight miles from Bakhmut but not nearly as dangerous. Another journalist had given me the number of Vlad, who was in charge, and I'd asked if he'd let me tag along. He'd called back late last night: 'Be at the petrol station outside Sloviansk at 8 a.m.'

I arrived twenty minutes early; I hate rushing and wanted to get a coffee. But the parking lot was already full of jeeps, people in flak jackets with 'PRESS' across them milling around, clearly about to go somewhere. I parked the little car, threw on my own vest and helmet and ran up to them.

'Are you going on the evacuation run?' I asked.

'Yes, yes,' the harassed Ukrainian driver said in English. 'It's leaving now.'

'Well, can I jump in with you?'

He looked non-plussed. 'I guess so, yeah.'

I squeezed in the back of the jeep, alongside other foreign reporters. The convoy moved off.

I had a feeling something was a bit . . . *off*. Twenty minutes went by. The roads got worse, potholed and muddy, as we began to climb a long hill. I looked at the map on my phone, perplexed. I didn't want to annoy them, given the driver was less than thrilled about having me there.

I cleared my throat. 'This is a funny way to get to Chasiv Yar.'

It was, in fact, the opposite direction.

There was a silence in the car. Then a French reporter said slowly, 'We're not going to Chasiv Yar.'

The driver turned to look at me. 'Who are you supposed to be with?'

I gave the name of Vlad and his group.

'You're in the wrong convoy,' he said.

'Oh!' I said. 'Shit. Where are you going?'

'Siversk,' came the blunt reply.

There was another long silence. It was obviously too late to turn back, and they couldn't really chuck me out. Though the driver looked like he might want to.

I apologised profusely and tried to ignore the hollow feeling in the pit of my stomach that was my body shouting *this is very bad*. Siversk was much further away, up near the border of Luhansk Oblast; it was in the middle of what looked on the map like a pocket, surrounded by the red of Russian-held territory. I'd persuaded an editor to take a story from Chasiv Yar on the basis that it was coloured green on the insurance company's 'risk map', indicating my policy was still valid there. Siversk was firmly in the red zone, though to be fair, the map was pretty arbitrary; shells were hitting both towns regularly.

Worse was that I was a distinctly unwanted passenger, and the volunteer organisation running the trip apparently didn't like random, lone reporters turning up unexpectedly.

'The press officer will need to speak to you when we get to Siversk,' the driver said tersely. 'He's going to be pissed off.'

I agreed that this seemed likely, and quite understandable, and then kept quiet for a while, as the jeep thudded and lurched through mud-filled craters and we crawled higher into the chalk hills.

Once, Siversk had a brick factory and 10,000 residents. What we drove into that morning was just a ghostly remnant of that town. Most of the buildings I could see were destroyed or damaged. The convoy stopped on an unpaved residential street which had been churned to a river of black mud.

I found the press officer and tried to be charming; he was fine with it, once I explained. Or he just had more urgent matters to attend to.

The convoy had disgorged quite a number of other reporters, plus some volunteers who seemed to also be taking pictures and videos of proceedings. 'Why don't you have a fixer?' several people asked me. I hadn't realised it was so unusual to report alone here.

The evacuation from this address had been pre-arranged – the charity had already been in touch with the family, and they were packed and ready to go.

You could hear the battles, which didn't sound so distant here – an unnerving backdrop of rumbling explosions and closer cracks. Everyone – volunteers and press – was wearing bulletproof vests and ballistic helmets and carrying tourniquets.

The children and adults appeared, laden with bags, and now I realised a benefit of working in the way I had done over the past year – I'd managed to avoid being in a media scrum. Journalists crowded around the evacuees as they made their way to the bus, shutters firing incessantly until eventually a volunteer put an arm across the chest of the pushiest photographer. 'Come on man, that's enough now.'

I'd drawn back and found myself standing next to some neighbours who'd come out to wave the family off. Serhiy and Sveta didn't want to join the evacuation. Not yet, anyway. They had built everything they had here, practically a small farm – pigs, hens, dogs, cats.

'It's too hard, to abandon all that,' Serhiy said. He had a sympathetic face, creased with worry, and I noticed his right hand was tightly gripping the right, trying to control the tremor running up one arm.

'Parkinson's,' he said. 'I do have medicine, it's just not helping any more. It's the stress, it's this insane situation; every day you don't know when something's going to land, or where. Only God knows, as they say.'

Sveta added that her parents were old now; they were here too, in this town in which they'd all grown up. She couldn't leave them behind.

'We'll hold out,' her husband said. 'Every day we pray to God for the preservation of our people, and our soldiers.'

We watched the bags being dragged out of the house next door, loaded into the minibus, the little girl standing so forlorn by her mum's side. Serhiy suddenly asked where I was from, how old I was, and it seemed only reasonable to share a bit about my life in return. After a few minutes we said goodbye, and Serhiy added quietly, 'God bless you.'

The other reporters had fanned out a bit now, filming the street and the convoy. I knew I had to talk to the family, or the story would have a giant hole in it. I approached the mother, who was watching from the verge as the boys fixed a tow rope to the bus. It was, predictably, bogged down in the sucking mud.

Her name was Olya, and she was thirty-eight. She was happy enough to chat, explaining that they'd decided to go because the shelling had got too intense. Her seven-year-old daughter was too scared. The girl was wrapped up in a puffer jacket, her long blonde hair falling over her shoulders. Olya had four kids.

'I thought we could wait it out,' she told me. 'But we need to be somewhere quieter. And now the situation in Bakhmut, they're saying it's really bad.'

She didn't voice the fear out loud, that Siversk could be next in line if Bakhmut fell. It wasn't necessary.

They'd go to Kramatorsk tonight, then further west to Dnipro, and she didn't know where after that, though the volunteers had promised they'd be taken care of.

'We'll be on our travels,' Olya shrugged.

One of her sons was asking her about some item of luggage he wanted to take, and she broke off to have a brief argument with him. I looked around, at the brick house – already looking derelict, as they'd boarded up the windows – and the neat wooden fence that ran around it. I tried to imagine leaving like this.

Olya turned back to me. Her expression was so conflicted - exasperation, resignation, but also a real, upright sense of pride. I noticed her long and elegant golden earrings, and the colourful clips holding back her curly hair.

'This might be a stupid question,' I said, 'but how are you feeling right now?'

'Not very good,' Olya said with ironic understatement. She looked around, at her kids waiting by the gate, at the empty, muddy street, the power cables dangling, useless, from their posts. No gas, no power, and yet they'd lasted this long. In fact, they'd nearly outlasted the whole street. 'So we're the most steadfast,' she laughed, but it was only partly a joke. She was proud that they'd clung on.

The bus was freed from the mire, and they called Olya to come. The family traipsed off round the corner and climbed aboard, and I got back in the jeep.

The next stop was not so smooth. Near the railway station, where the overhead wires hung in a tangled mess over the tracks, there was a bunker dug into the wasteland, more of a foxhole, with steps leading down to darkness. A woman came out, and the charity's co-founder Misha, perhaps not for the first time, tried to persuade her to leave. She quickly became incoherent with rage, screaming at him, refusing to go. I asked one of the group what was going on.

'There are two kids living down there with her.'

'Are you serious?'

He nodded.

Misha went down to negotiate with her in the bunker, followed by a French reporter. I waited above. A tiny kitten, just a fuzz of pale orange fur with huge brown eyes, was darting around our feet, and I crouched down to talk to it. At first it shrank back, but after a minute it let me stroke its back and its little Batman ears. I felt its spine under the patchy fur. The animal was physically vibrating with fear, trembling constantly, and when an outgoing bang resounded around us, I felt the kitten flinch under my hand.

I looked around at the abandoned railway tracks and destruction and the rubbish on this patch of waste ground and could not quite reconcile my mind to the fact that children were living here, in a hole in the ground. But I didn't go down to the bunker. It didn't feel like a good thing to do. This woman seemed half-crazed, deeply traumatised. What right did I have to elbow my way in and get a front seat?

Misha emerged and indicated we should leave. They'd come back in a few hours for the kids, he added. It had all been worked out. Meanwhile the guys from my jeep wanted to do more reporting in Siversk. We drove over the railway bridge; below it, soldiers were standing knee-deep in mud, and a dark green armoured personnel carrier was being towed out of the mire. Rays of sun had briefly emerged from the dark clouds, glinting off the rooftops of the town spread out before us, but it only highlighted the incredible damage the place had sustained. We came across makeshift graves in another piece of waste ground. Plastic rubbish was piled in impromptu dumps and blowing away in the wind. Presumably communal services had long since stopped operating. I was reminded of something Olya had said earlier. I'd asked what Siversk had been like. 'It was beautiful,' she said. 'Once.'

The hospital was still open, though. It was a normal provincial hospital with a few wards, a long building with trees all around it. Some craters we passed in the hospital grounds looked fresh, the earth black where it had been blown up. At the main door, on a bench in the sun, a little row of old ladies sat wrapped up in shawls and coats. They didn't seem to be patients, but I was just introducing myself when it came: that menacing whistle, high-pitched and descending, and the first bang.

'*PRILYOT!*' a man's voice shouted. '*PRILYOT, PRILYOT!*'

It means, roughly, 'arrival by air' – 'incoming'. The little old ladies had risen from their perch and were shuffling inside – painfully slowly, it seemed to me, but time had started to stretch weirdly. I'm not going to push the babushkas out the way, I thought.

Once in, we were ushered underground. Nothing crumbling about this basement – it was a proper sturdy shelter, and I was glad of it. Down the stairs, into the dark, low-ceilinged corridor, and suddenly I sensed thick smoke, felt a little stab of panic. I hate being underground; all the scenarios of being trapped here without air raced through my mind. But then I noticed it was *pleasant* smoke, wood smoke, rich with fuzzy childhood nostalgia. We passed a little room, and I saw the big old boiler, the janitor adding wood to a furnace. No wonder all these elderly people were sheltering here: safe *and* warm. There had been no mains gas in Siversk here since the invasion began. Firewood meant survival.

Down a long corridor, packed with supplies – bottles of water, food, medicines – and it was clear the remaining staff slept here sometimes, from the toiletries and basins of water next to camping beds. I talked to a woman sitting on one of the beds, a nurse. She didn't want to be quoted: she apologised, but said they've had rather a lot of foreign journalists. I could well imagine. At the end of the corridor, next to a pile of coats, a tiny old woman was waiting out the strike. I took her picture, and she told me not to, so I apologised and put the camera away. The other foreign journalist began filming her, his camera hovering inches from her face. 'I think she's had enough of journalists,' I said, to no avail. I felt a bit sick with the whole thing, us descending like vultures on this picked-over place, recording their misery and then leaving.

Once it was quiet above ground we left. On the ridge of a hill outside the town, we pulled over to let a tank pass us on the narrow track, and from here an incredible panorama opened up, a Donbas landscape of lakes and forests, smokestacks and small houses, and on the hazy horizon, the strange, angular shapes of *terykony*. These though were bright white, not the conical, rust-red spoil tips I'd seen before. These were the chalk mines. I'd read about the nature reserve that covers the steep white slopes along the river. Coal is not the only richness that lies under the Donbas soil; mineral deposits here are world-renowned.

In Kramatorsk a few hours later, I ate a burger and passed out on the bed for half an hour, then got to work. Bennett and Mykola came in, clattering through the door and trailing mud. 'How'd it go?' he shouted from the kitchen.

'Went the wrong way and got lightly shelled,' I yelled back.

'Damn.' His face appeared in the doorway. 'All good?'

'Yeah, fine.'

'Cool, cool. I'm making stew.'

Never any drama with Bennett. In any case, he and Mykola had experienced much worse last year.

I rang the editor who'd been so wary of me going even to Chasiv Yar, wondering how to phrase this. 'So, a funny story,' I began.

'Oh, *God*,' I heard him say.

I explained how I accidentally went to Siversk and what happened there. He listened, groaning and shouting 'Fuck!' at various points in the story, which he found distinctly not-funny. I did understand; it's an editor's job to be cautious, and a reporter's job to be on the ground. But I was back in one piece and going to file a good long story, just in time for the print deadline.

My buoyant mood lasted as long as the writing-up, after which I was suddenly deflated, exhausted; then, all night, violently ill. I could blame it on the burger, on Bennett's stew or on adrenalin, but in any case it was inconvenient, and when I got up to pack in the morning it was with little enthusiasm. My hands were shaking, eyes blurry from lack of sleep. I was going to join up with the PEN Ukraine team again: Tetyana, her husband Volodymyr, and Vakhtang. Professors and scholars in their philosophers' bus. They'd driven a jeep and their minibus over from Kyiv with supplies and a jeep to deliver to frontline positions here. I found them at a petrol station in Sloviansk and jumped in, happy to be reunited.

We were heading to Lyman, not far to the northeast, but the strict checkpoints and blown-up bridges made the journey longer. First the jeep was handed to soldiers in Raihorodok. Then they took us under military escort to Lyman.

Five months had passed since this strategic railway town had been wrested back from the Russians, but it was frozen at that point in time, as though the battles had only just raged through it. Shelling continued regularly from the Russian-held territory, and in two hours we saw no more than a dozen people.

The drizzling rain never lifted; it never seemed to get properly light. We picked our way through the gloomy streets. Life here had once revolved around the railway, which was built in Tsarist times, growing in size and importance as coal exports from Donbas increased. It was a big industrial junction of locomotive and wagon depots, workshops and sidings, and the station itself had a long neoclassical facade, with three big halls joined together, tall pediments above the faux brick columns.

I climbed up the metal steps of a footbridge which ran about thirty feet in the air across the tracks. The middle section of the bridge was damaged, but this bit seemed OK. I admit that I just wanted the picture badly; I'd caught a glimpse from street level, between trees and fences, but up here I had an uninterrupted view of what remained of these grand station buildings.

The pediments were like a row of rotten teeth, roofs gone and crumbling bricks exposed. Beneath the crumpled scraps of what had been the roof, I could see straight down to the barrel-like wooden shell of the vaulted ceiling below. Scorch marks and shrapnel bursts marred the pale-green facade, and the bright 'LYMAN' lettering had been knocked askew.

I turned to photograph more railway buildings half-collapsed, red and beige bricks spilling on to the tracks. Looking back at the street I'd come from, I could see the row of shop-fronts all gutted by fire, by shelling, by strikes, by the hell that must have rained down on this place for so many months. The little figures of my companions were coming towards the bridge, hoods up in the rain, and one was calling up to me. I cupped my ear.

'Come down, you'll get shot by snipers!'

I retreated quickly.

Strange little snapshots of the town emerge online if you look. Searching for mentions of the station, I found a poignant post on the website of the Lyman city council.

'Dear residents of the Lyman community!' the post began, and I imagined the harassed railway worker typing this out late at night (the timestamp said 10 p.m.). It stated that anyone wishing to catch the free daily train to Lviv and other western cities should come to the station for 6 p.m.

This was 'in connection with the difficult and tense situation', it said, which seemed quite an understatement. The date it went up was 10 March, when shelling was relentless and Russian forces were advancing towards the city.

Similarly, I found an evacuation advert still taped to a mangled shop-front. It promised safe passage out of Lyman, help with housing in safer regions, support for families. 'All free! Call this number!'

I wondered how many had taken up the offer. As in Izium, the mass graves exhumed after liberation offered a glimpse of what awaited civilians who didn't leave. Hundreds had died, young and old, lacking the most basic medical care, heating and food, and under intense bombardment. Torture and execution by the occupying forces couldn't be ruled out, either.

As we drove around the near-deserted streets, splashing through the mud and rain, a strange shape caught my eye. We got out to have a look. Wedged at an angle through a broken paving stone was the tail fin of a Uragan rocket, which scatters high-explosive fragmentation submunitions. In other words, this was the remnant of a cluster bomb, sticking out of the mossy sidewalk on a residential street. And indeed all through Lyman the evidence of these devastating 'bomblets' was clear – a wall we'd just passed had the burst, scattered shape of their impact gouged into its concrete.

I missed out on a lot of no doubt crucial conversations that weekend because of my frustrating inability to speak Ukrainian – or at least to understand rapid, conversational Ukrainian. But in a cafe in Sloviansk, a soldier friend of Volodymyr and Tetyana's did speak to me briefly in English – and said something I knew I'd never forget.

She'd been fed up, she said, a few months ago – cold and miserable, frustrated with the war, with commanders, with everything. Missing her daughter, who was abroad. But now she'd reached a new stage of acceptance.

'I've made my peace with the war. Everyone has. We're resigned to this shit.'

She and her comrades still believed victory was inevitable, she said. 'But we all know that we probably won't be alive. We won't survive this.'

I stared at her. There was no emotion, no tears. Entirely calm, she added, for the avoidance of doubt, 'By the time the war finishes we will all be dead.' And then she speared a chunk of cake with her fork, and ate it.

I wanted to object, somehow. Throw my arms up, protest. *You can't say that! You're too young!* But it would be like objecting to the wind or the rain. For her, this was just the likely outcome. Better to accept it than fight it.

The base we stayed on was large, half HQ and half hospital, its location kept strictly secret because of the frequent missile attacks on medical facilities. In the morning I left early to find a good Internet connection. I was due to be on Radio Scotland's weekend show, talking about everything I'd seen over the last few days. I found a cafe and ordered what I thought would be pancakes and cottage cheese, but I hadn't paid much attention to the menu as I focused on typing out notes for the interview. The cafe was empty except for some soldiers demolishing massive plates of sausage and cheese. Then a crockpot arrived. The crepes – *nalysnyky* – were indeed stuffed with cottage cheese, and sultanas, and sugar. But then they'd been baked in a soupy sauce of butter and sugar and perhaps also cream. It was a heart attack in a pot; it was so sweet my teeth ached. It was heaven.

Full of sugar, I bounced my way through the radio interview. The presenter, Fiona, who knew me quite well, had seen me posting online about another Ukrainian culinary delight – *salo*, the cured bacon fat that melts on your tongue. The night before, at the base, I'd discovered that this delicacy also came in a garlic-flavoured paste, a whole plastic tub of it, and I'd been over the moon. 'You've really fallen in love with the country, haven't you,' Fiona said, down the line from Glasgow. And I had, without question.

Back in Ivanna's little car now, I followed Tetyana's minibus on the route that was becoming so familiar, back to Kharkiv. It was here, in particular, that I loved so much, I thought, as I drove along, singing along to La Rue Kétanou. This northern slice of Donetsk Oblast, where it turns into Kharkiv Oblast, this forested, misty-valley paradise, the Sivers'kyi Donets River snaking through it all, past chalk hills and escarpments: it all made my heart race, and I'd only ever seen it in wartime. I'd only seen it scarred and burnt and littered with rusting tanks and the open wounds of mass graves, and seeing it in wartime made me love it more. I could only imagine how beautiful it would be again one day.

The area is home to the Holy Mountains National Nature Park, and the Sviatohirsk Lavra is probably its most famous landmark. On the banks of the river, the forest rising steeply behind it, the monastery's walls are painted white and the little roofs spearmint blue; alongside it a small, perfect cathedral seems to have grown into the sheer chalk cliff, and indeed it has, because the cliff is an ancient cave complex. 'Switzerland on the Donets', as Chekhov probably did not really call it, but he easily could have. I'd always wanted to see it.

Now it was better known for horror stories: monastery walls crumbling under intense shelling, bodies being pulled out after airstrikes, nuns dying of shrapnel wounds.

We didn't go there, but to a village just upriver, Bohorodychne, which means Mother of God. The church on the hill is named for an icon which first appeared in the eighteenth century, *The Mother of God, Joy of All Who Sorrow*. The first church was built back then, in 1847. It was pulled down during Soviet rule, then the remains were bombed by the Nazis. Only in the 2000s was it rebuilt, a five-domed and fairly flashy big church, with baroque columns, green marble, mosaics. The original icon was returned, and the past restored. But it would turn out to be a temporary reprieve.

Entering Bohorodychne on the muddy road, the scene looked a lot like Kam'yanka, the destroyed valley settlement that I'd driven through with Ivanna last year: apocalyptic, dark, lifeless, every building ruined, along the road and on the slopes of the surrounding hills too, as though each square metre had been shelled and shelled. Here and there, I saw some fragments of normal life, strangely intact and awash on the sea of debris. A white children's trike, left at an angle on the side of the road as though the rider had only just jumped off. A table with a chair pulled slightly back, visible through the gaping hole where a wall had been. The red velour tablecloth was getting wet in the rain. More salvageable buildings were draped in UN-stamped tarpaulins, awaiting repair. Long, tall fences surrounded the gardens, made of thin metal and stapled to frames. These corrugated sheets were pierced by many thousands of shrapnel holes and hung askew, twisted and bent, banging in the wind.

But the church. We reached it and stood in silence for some time. The scene was the most complete definition of the word *desecration*. One tower was ruined, partially collapsed; the other was riddled with shrapnel, the facade and mosaics blasted away, by airstrikes, apparently, targeted directly at the church and adjoining convent in May, when Russian forces were trying to take the site. The basements had been full of people sheltering from the bombs. Perhaps that is what makes a destroyed church such a shocking sight: a plea for sanctuary brutally disregarded.

The gleaming golden cross that had topped an onion dome lay in the rubble of bricks at my feet, and the dome itself had crashed through the wrought-iron gates. To see it up close was so strange, its layers peeled back, diamond-shaped gold leaves and neatly nailed pieces of wood underneath forming the onion shape.

The smaller domes on the other tower were black skeletons, their gold all burnt off. Great arcs and sprays of shrapnel pitted every lovely, sky-blue wall. We climbed inside the ruin, feet crunching down into a thick layer of brick and plaster shards. A couple of walls remained, arched and soaring; it must have been an impressive space.

'You know this church belonged to the Moscow patriarchy?' Volodymyr asked. It was true – the whole Sviatohirsk Lavra, of which Bohorodchnye convent was part, had been on the Russian side of the split in the Orthodox church in Ukraine; its bishop had sometimes gone so far as to have openly supported Russia's propaganda and actions in eastern Ukraine. Much good it had done him.

A large, handsome dog appeared in the doorway, something close to an Alsatian. He picked his way among the rubble, looking hopefully at us. His dark coat was shaggy and thick, but beneath it he looked skinny as hell. Why on earth hadn't I brought dog food? I knelt down to see if he was friendly, and he immediately leaned his weight on me, practically resting his head on my shoulder.

The others began filming for their website, and I went back outside, photographing the remains of the church tower, convent and cemetery for an hour. I couldn't go far for fear of land mines; we'd been warned that the woods further uphill were full of them. The dog was by my side the whole time, trotting obediently next to me. Occasionally he looked at me, pleading, head to one side with that forlorn expression Alsatians are so good at. 'I've no food,' I kept saying. 'I'm sorry.' We climbed over the debris where Russian soldiers had set up camp. Rusting tins, sodden mattresses, green army ration packs. It was all mixed in with charred, once-precious items from the church – an intricately-patterned censer, its shine tarnished to a dull blue-grey; a small wooden icon cross, so badly burnt that only a shadow remained of the painting of Christ. All just rubbish now.

On a sheet of rusted metal someone had sprayed, in childlike English letters, 'Hell.' As I knelt to photograph it, the dog limped across the frame. I hadn't noticed his limp before. I wondered what had caused it. Wondered if he had been here – in hell – all this time, all this long year. Waiting, perhaps, for his owners to come back.

A gust of wind blew suddenly, a great howl through this blasted space, and it set the countless bits of broken fence around the village banging and groaning, the warped metal screaming and straining against the wind; the clamour was suddenly so loud, so creepy, that I was totally unnerved. I felt something like dread settle in my stomach, looking around at the desecrated church, the dark and deadly tree line in the distance, the glowering sky so oppressive above, at this desolate, terrible place where everything beautiful and comfortable had been so completely destroyed.

Then the dog came up, whined, licked my hand. I smiled at him, this warm, solid, living thing, and we went to find the others.

Tetyana and Volodymyr were talking to a local man who'd turned up; to my enormous relief, he fed the dog, and said he did it every day. Only five people, he said, had clung on in Bohorodychne; everyone else was gone.

Maybe the summer would bring some back, I thought. But it was hard to imagine the place reviving any time soon. Too grim, too hard. Reconstruction, realistically, was a long way off; there wasn't even gas or electricity here. It felt like what I'd seen on the highway: patch up what's urgent; the rest has to wait. Until that unknowable, distant date when no one is trying to kill you.

I felt wired and angry as I got in the car; the sudden loud bangs of those fences had been making me flinch. I realised too that the dog had been such a brief comfort, and that I'd forgotten how much I needed it. As a small child I'd been inseparable from the collies on our croft, curling up alongside them to sleep, and a memory of that long-lost comfort had come flooding back.

Soon it would be dark in the village, pitch dark, no people, no warmth. I imagined the dog there, abandoned in the dark, trying to find somewhere to curl up among the broken glass and mess, and I wanted to scream.

Slowly I put the car in gear and drove away. And in the rear-view mirror I saw him. Sitting a little way up the hill, very still, watching me go.

CHAPTER SEVENTEEN

BY EARLY SPRING THE power in Kharkiv was back on, the grid patched up after the 9 March strikes. The occasional blast in an industrial estate notwithstanding, things felt almost normal. Or perhaps just compared to Siversk. My risk perception was, admittedly, a bit skewed.

But Nataliya agreed. I went round one evening – 'You must come and see my winter garden,' she'd said, and it was quite amazing: a closed balcony so full of elegant and enormous foliage that it felt like stepping into a carefully tended jungle, lit by strings of fairy lights.

'Oh, Kharkiv is almost normal,' she said in her nonchalant way, reaching over the table to offer me a bit of Brie. The Russians, she thought, were 'testing the air-defence systems' daily, hence the sirens, but people were blasé about it now. She laughed, telling me how, during the 43-hour blackout earlier that month, she and colleagues from the Maidan Monitoring NGO had gone out to film the effect on the city, and had come back with nothing.

'Almost every cafe or shop was working on generators; there were no long queues. The hospitals were all working on generators too. People were walking in the parks – we even heard a conversation like, "Oh, we have no electricity, no water and no gas. So let's go for a walk in the park!"'

In the Nikolsky shopping centre next door, which had been hit by missiles last year, everything was open again. 'Even the swimming pool on the roof!'

Not all the international shops had returned, she said, specifically mentioning H&M in a wistful tone. Nataliya has a soft spot for H&M.

Though her flat was in the epicentre of the heaviest bombing in the first weeks of the invasion – she'd described that Nikolsky strike as like 'Armageddon' – Nataliya had stayed put all the way through, each near miss making her more incensed and resolute. She was wearing a *zalizobeton* t-shirt with the striking Derzhprom design I'd first seen in the bunker concert back in May. A lot of people wore it, and with the desert colours and resemblance to a battalion insignia, it lent a military air. With this and her flaming red hair she looked quite formidable this evening.

But actually I'd caught her in a philosophical mood.

'You know what's interesting?' she asked. 'That I started to love this city more than before. And I even started to accept people around me. Previously I loved the city, but not the people.'

'You have quite high standards for people,' I butted in, teasing slightly. But she was serious.

'I felt myself absolutely an outlier. I have been a dissident for all my life, and now I'm starting to feel part of this city, which is a very strange feeling, actually. I had never felt part of a majority.'

'When did that start?'

'I think it started a year ago, when I saw the resilience of this city,' she said, thoughtfully. 'When I saw what almost everyone who stayed here was doing to combat the enemy – a lot of civilian resistance, both volunteers and municipal workers, doctors. It was outstanding. And this heroic resistance . . . It became a legend of the city.'

'Like a self-fulfilling prophecy?'

'Yeah, a self-fulfilling prophecy. And now the mayor mentions it all the time; we have all these slogans and billboards praising it.'

The mayor, Ihor Terekhov, was no favourite of activists in the city like Nataliya. In the past he'd been on the anti-Maidan side, supporting corrupt president Viktor Yanukovych. And he always spoke Russian – even when the legislation ordered that official public business be conducted in Ukrainian. He was close with Hennadiy Trukhanov, the Odesan mayor I'd interviewed in what felt like the mists of time, but was about a year ago.

But now Nataliya had nothing bad to say about Kharkiv's mayor. He was speaking Ukrainian these days, she added.

I suggested, cynically, that it might just be a political move.

'Yeah sure, but it's not only political, it's also part of resistance,' she insisted. The war had changed people who had previously looked more favourably on Russia, kept an ear open for its propaganda. A rocket strike on your apartment block, or on a school, has an instant and transformative effective.

People who once said things like, 'Oh, I consider myself Russian, I have relatives there,' she explained, would suddenly be cursing Russians. 'Like, "Fuck Russia, I hate them!"'

There was, she went on, this strong sense of *personal* outrage: how dare these Russians try to destroy Kharkiv's flower gardens, its beautiful avenues? The mayor, she added, was no exception. 'It's apparent that Terekhov loves this city.'

Nataliya talked about the ways in which Ukrainians were uncovering their own history and traditions. Russification had erased so much, but the traces lingered. Nataliya's family, dissidents and intellectuals, had spoken Ukrainian behind closed doors. It was a political choice, but also linked to the fact that they came from the villages – her grandmother was a *tselyuk,* a word for a villager that also has a 'bumpkin' or 'hillbilly' connotation to it. As a result, the Ukrainian language had lived on in the family.

However, at school, university or in public, she had always spoken Russian – even, she said, playing in the courtyard with other neighbourhood kids.

And then nine years ago she'd met these kids, all grown up, and they talked about it for the first time and realised they had *all* spoken Ukrainian at home but never talked about it.

'It was like – holy shit. Holy shit!' she recalled.

'What were your thoughts at the time?'

'Well . . . holy shit,' she said, more thoughtfully. 'I was really amazed, and so infuriated with this system, the regime, the colonial Soviet Union. I didn't know that I could hate it even more.'

But it was *how* they'd discovered this shared secret that says so much about modern Ukraine. The Euromaidan protests that led to the revolution in 2013 and 2014 marked the transformational social shift when conversations like this suddenly became not only possible, but urgent and widespread.

Incredibly, the three childhood friends discovered they were all descendants of what Stalin called 'enemies of the people'. Their grandfathers were all political prisoners.

'We were somehow . . . not *told*, but *taught* not to talk about this outside,' she said. Their parents, dissidents, knew each other, had 'common codes' to speak in, but not with their children. For that generation, there was silence – until Maidan.

Now it was beyond question, for all these people, that they were Ukrainian, that Kharkiv was Ukrainian and that Russian imperialism had been exposed as a crumbling and pathetic edifice.

'People are simply becoming aware of how different they are from Russians,' she said. And those people included 'ethnic Russians', whatever that meant now; they might have Russian family and origins, but in terms of culture and outlook and upbringing, in terms of nationality, they were unequivocally Ukrainian. She listed holidays and traditions unique to Ukraine, such as Sviatyi Vechir on Christmas Eve. These differences in religion had previously been lost under the heavy weight of

Moscow's church. So had a mindset rooted in individual freedom, in openness to the world. The revolution had brought all this to light. Now Ukraine had to fight to keep it.

Nataliya's comment about the flower gardens was something of a Kharkiv motif; people spoke often, with real pride and ownership, of the cleanliness and beauty of their public realm, the neat rows of tulips and well-tended parks. It came up again a few days later when I went to see Lyuba and Kolya again, the retired engineers I'd visited five months earlier, in their flat by the woods. I was happy to see them so well – and so cheery.

'You know Kharkiv has often been rated among the most beautiful cities of Ukraine?' Dima, their son, asked me. 'Gorky Park, Shevchenko Garden, the fountains . . .'

There used to be extravagant illuminations at Christmas time in these public spaces. 'How it shone!' Lyuba said. 'Oh it was so beautiful, everything was just glowing!'

'I remember a lot of comments people from Kyiv made, from Dnipro – *oh, we don't have this!*' Dima laughed. 'Really, they marvelled over it.'

I looked it up later. Kharkiv's festive lights had, indeed, been staggering; for a start, there was a 130-foot Christmas tree.

This dark winter, the only thing to marvel over had been the street lights finally coming back on in early March. But to hear Lyuba you'd think the occasion had been equal to any Christmas-lights extravaganza.

'I peeked out and shouted, "Hurray! There are lights, everywhere!"'

Of course then they'd been plunged into darkness again for more than two days, because as soon as Kharkiv turned the lights on, Russia bombed the power station, turning them off again.

Not everything was working, they agreed. In fact, a lot was still not working. But it was only a question of time and, as Kolya pointed out, of continued supplies from the west. 'We need weapons, weapons, weapons . . .'

'Meantime, here we are, staying put,' Lyuba said, happily.

I was eager to get back to Kramatorsk while I had the car, and while there was still time; my third reporting stint was coming to an end. There was a long list of people I wanted to see in the east, including a Czech soldier I'd met here in Kharkiv, Tomas. Any foreigner volunteering in Ukraine intrigued me, and the Czechs in particular had their own long fight with Moscow. Tomas was deployed near Bakhmut now but said we could easily meet again in Kramatorsk. Lev, the medic from the night train, was there too, and her commander was considering my request to embed with the unit. And then there was Sun, another female medic, her call sign a nod to the positivity and warmth she exuded – even in the thick of the Bakhmut battles. We'd talked in Lviv in November, sitting at a little table on the cobbled street, and I'd known instantly that she'd be an incredible person to follow to the frontlines. But we just kept missing each other.

Saddest of all, I kept missing Victoria, the novelist from Lviv. We'd been planning a trip together for weeks. She was constantly on the move, documenting the havoc and horror wreaked on the places Russia had occupied, and earlier in the year I'd seen a photo of her in Kherson, posing outside the famous city council building which had been the backdrop to the jubilant liberation footage last year.

The selfie had made me laugh out loud. While the Internet was awash with journalists' moody profile pictures, gazing, all serious, in flak jackets, here was Vika taking the piss, her head to one side, steadying her oversized helmet. She was pulling a silly face, eyes comically wide, and grinning, as if to say – 'This is all quite mad, isn't it?' It said so much about her. I'd sent her a quick message to that effect.

'Happy to know you,' I wrote.

'Happy to know you too,' she'd replied, with kisses. 'I'm writing from a sleeping bag in a cold hut in the middle of nowhere, but I hope my hugs will reach you,' she'd added, characteristically sweet.

So when we realised we'd both be in Kharkiv in March and, even better, that I could drive us east, we formed a plan. 'I love Kramatorsk,' she kept saying, so excited.

But we never made it, at least not together. I saw her briefly in Kharkiv, but we both were rushing, and then her plans changed, and the trip fell through. We kept plotting together though; we'd talked of an Ireland trip before, and now I promised to take her around Scotland one day. 'After.' This euphemism was cropping up a lot; for some reason we didn't want to say 'after the war'. That sounded too concrete for something totally unknowable, something quite distant and almost unimaginable. So – 'after'. You could make up the most fantastical plans for this future, because it was, to be honest, a little like never-never land.

Total cacophony, a joyous noise, was being made in the Kharkiv Children's Hospital. Kids bashed enthusiastically on xylophones. One seized upon a wooden shaker: 'Ah! Maraca!' he said, with a glorious rolling *rrr*. I was holding a radio mic to capture it all, and grinning from ear to ear.

I'd been missing the company of children intensely; life with only adults is so inadequate. The morning had started with a concert, a woman playing the big *tsymbaly*, or hammer dulcimer, so fast that her hands with the little beaters were a blur.

Now we were upstairs, and two students from the city's University of the Arts were preparing to run a music-therapy session on the oncology ward. They'd been trained in this by the British composer Nigel Osborne, who has long pioneered the work in war zones around the world. With a violin and a guitar, Lena and Tigran started their musical games, and I was soon as absorbed as the children were.

'What kind of animal is this?' Tigran asked, playing a comical, plinky-plunky song. 'A bear!' shouted little Dima, tripping over himself to add, 'No, no – an elephant!'

He was an absolute character, Dima, pale and small but bubbling over with excitement and imagination. This was the aim: let the kids escape, for a moment, this reality of air-raid sirens and war. Tigran encouraged them to touch the guitar strings, feel the sound waves on their fingertips.

Dima's mum watched through the open door, from a waiting room. She looked tired, her face in a constant pinch of worry, though she smiled at his antics.

This was the first session, and though Dima had taken to it straight away, another child, Sofia, was sitting very quiet and still, looking at the floor. She was a wee thing, no more than two, her blonde hair in pigtails. The hospital's psychologist sat on the floor, close to her, talking to her gently. And after a while, the music brought her out; by the end of the hour Sofia was smiling, banging on some djembe drums and shoogling about in a bum-shuffle dance. It was wonderful to watch.

A professor from the arts university, Julia, was sitting with us all on the stripy carpet, joining in with enthusiasm. We'd talked in the Pakufuda bakery a few days earlier, and she'd invited me to this session. They'd be starting an art therapy course soon and expanding the work to other cities.

The session ended, the kids scampered off, and the musicians began packing up. Lena, the violinist, was beaming. 'It's an amazing feeling, watching children who are shy start to come alive,' she said. Tigran talked about the techniques they'd been taught to use with the kids, helping them to really *feel* the music.

'Yes, we feel the vibrations,' he nodded. 'Feel it in our bodies, that's the connection with music. We get them to understand, feel involved in the process.' It was very different, he added, to the one-way interaction of a concert. As we'd seen earlier, no matter what you play, kids don't sit still for long.

I talked to the psychologist afterwards, Vlada. She didn't talk in jargon but rather about emotions, about society. 'The spiritual component is really important in all this,' she said. 'We come together, united, and that togetherness is what supports us at this time.'

This kind of therapy – whether music or art – worked wonders on children of course, Vlada said, but adults needed it too. It could be hard to make this argument when the focus was understandably on survival, on money for the army, on winning the war. But healing couldn't come 'after'. It had to begin now.

CHAPTER EIGHTEEN

I DROVE TO KRAMATORSK again on April Fools' Day, and the heroic Mitsubishi thought it would be funny to have not only a flat battery but also a tyre bulge. I hadn't even spotted it and would have driven merrily off with a tyre on the brink of explosion. Luckily I was with Steve, a Brit I'd met who worked in the aid sector, and he'd noticed. He also kept me from despair as I rang garage after garage, all of them closed. We finally found a roadside lean-to where they changed the tyre for the equivalent of a fiver.

All my plans in the east – the medics, the Czechs, the jeeps – had fallen through, but it didn't matter. Serendipity (or, a local journalist contact) took Steve and I to the office of Tato Hub, a children's playgroup and aid distribution centre of Kramatorsk.

Two volunteers met us and showed us around. Oleksandr was soft-spoken and slightly bashful, a civic activist. Oleksandra, also born and raised here, spoke quickly as she showed us the books about the ecology of Donetsk Oblast, published by the state department for natural resources, where she worked, having retrained as an ecologist a few years earlier – her lifelong dream, she said, smiling proudly.

Children crashed in noisily and filed into the bigger room to start an art class. Their drawings were all over the walls, and little clay figurines were drying on a table next to us. It was a bright, welcoming, happily chaotic space. With all the schools working online, and outside being too dangerous, this was one of the few physical places children could come and play together.

Many people in Kramatorsk, refugees from further east or those left without work, were reliant on charities like this. The volunteers' tasks were endless, difficult and sometimes dangerous; the group included people who went out to evacuate people from towns like Siversk, and some had been killed. They were distributing ten tons of food every day, with the help of various international charities. 'What do you need most, in the long run?' Steve asked.

'Big organisations give food, but almost no one gives hygiene products,' he said. 'Disinfectant for cleaning, stuff for shaving, showering.'

They badly needed nappies and incontinence pads. A pack of Pampers, Oleksandr told us, cost a staggering 700 hyrvnias in the supermarket. Nearly £15. To put that into context, the state pension payment was around 2,000 hryvnias *per month*.

Remembering the woman I'd met last time in Kramatorsk, I asked if it wouldn't be better to hand out money.

'Mmm. Good, but actually, very difficult to control. And someone could buy alcohol.'

'But technically there's no alcohol here,' I said.

'Oh *yes*,' laughed Oleksandr. 'No alcohol here *at all*.'

His own family were in Lviv now, and he admitted it was difficult; the rents were high, so many people competing for space.

And actually Oleksandra had done her time as a refugee in western Ukraine, living first in a village then with 400 others in an old apartment block in Chernivtsi. And yes they were treated well, yes it was a lovely city. But she couldn't bear it.

'My life had turned into some kind of . . . swamp. I couldn't do anything apart from chase after aid packages.' So she came home and threw herself into this work.

Oleksandra had spoken Ukrainian while in the west – 'to avoid any questions, but also out of respect for these people giving us help' – but now we spoke in Russian, her native tongue. Her grandmother had come from Russia in 1955, at a time when large numbers of Russians were encouraged to resettle in Donbas, taking advantage of the plentiful work in the factories, mines and foundries. It was part of what made it such a complicated place now, in terms of identity. Stalin's deliberate famine-genocide of the 1930s had an appalling impact here, wiping out so much of the village population who were Ukrainian speakers. The elimination of whole populations, the wholesale 'resettlement' and replacements, the rewriting of this story with decades of propaganda and uneasy silence about it all – this dark and difficult history was still alive, and perhaps only now, because of the war, it was all coming to the surface.

I leafed through a smart hardback book entitled *Spadshchyna* – heritage, or inheritance – full of photos and stories about the region's Ukrainian past. Local councillors and businessmen posed in front of city hall in embroidered white shirts with the thick red cloth belt – *krayka*. The shirt, a *vyshyvanka,* is popular these days, but the ones pictured were apparently antiques, on loan from the museum.

The council had funded the project, along with the entrepreneurs' club Oleksandr was part of, and you could see the politics of it – 'Donetsk *is* Ukraine' was, after all, a rallying cry at all those demonstrations in 2014, and I'd heard it shouted in Lviv not so long ago. But this was no propaganda. In part because, quite simply, it was true; these traditions had deep roots here, and the folk songs, beliefs, dishes and festivities most certainly weren't Russian.

One such ancient celebration was Hayivka, to mark the coming of spring. Oleksandra told us how they'd put it on last year, a little festival in the park, bringing people together.

'We don't have a history as old as Lviv or Chernivtsi,' Oleksandr said quietly. 'But we do have old buildings in Kramatorsk.' He flipped the pages. 'See, it's a villa. Very beautiful, very historical, but it could be destroyed, and with this project we're trying to keep all this history.'

It was a counter-narrative, struggling to be heard in modern Ukraine and seldom heard beyond its borders: the idea that this region, this 'difficult' part of Ukraine, all smokestacks and grimy industry and poverty, Russian-speaking and of questionable loyalties, was actually something very different. Here, in fact, there had always been Ukrainian culture. Here, as Oleksandra had described with such feeling, they'd been developing green tourism, they were working hard to conserve nature and undo decades of harm. And here, never mind what language was spoken, they were Ukrainian.

To people in Lviv, Oleksandr shrugged, Donetsk Oblast was famous for the terrible events of 2014 – for the Russian proxies in balaclavas stirring unrest and starting war. A man from western Ukraine had even said to his face the other day, 'You don't love Ukraine because you speak Russian.'

He shook his head sadly. 'The guy thought we in Kramatorsk were all "separatists" or something. Actually I think in Kramatorsk people love Ukraine even more, because we saw it all here.'

'You understand what "Russkiy Mir" looks like,' I suggested.

'Yes. We understand that we don't need it.'

The relentless propaganda about higher pensions and benefits if the region joined Russia had worked on some people once, he said. But it hadn't meant they *liked* Russia. They just wanted to have enough money.

In fact when he visited his wife in Lviv he felt he saw a lot of hypocrisy. 'People speak Ukrainian, but they don't all love Ukraine. They love money, they don't want to pay tax.'

And you only had to visit the cemetery here, he added, to see how much cities like Kramatorsk were sacrificing to the war. All those rows and rows of graves.

These two volunteers had such big ideas for their home town, and for the region as a whole. New parks, culture, reintroducing Ukrainian festivities that had been eroded under Moscow rule. Oleksandra talked of a jarring realisation she'd had while in western Ukraine: there, people took time to relax. They strolled in parks without a destination, were always at the cinema. They went to church together on Sundays. The pace of life was so different.

'Whereas we were accustomed to work, not to live,' she said. 'We got through the Second World War and it was just work, work, work. No time for, you know, some kind of happiness index.'

That, she felt strongly, had to change. After all this hardship, things had to be better. 'We have the people, we have the foundations,' added Oleksandr. 'I think we can rebuild it all.'

From this bubble of hope it was back to reality: a terrible strike in Kostiantynivka, half an hour away, had killed six people. We grabbed our things, and Steve drove while I scoured the chat apps for more information and talked to editors.

The site, when we found it, was the familiar mess of police tape and blood and debris and mud and lives turned upside down. Fresh, deep craters, black earth, and mud spattered high onto the facade of the fourteen-storey blocks of flats. A policeman initially barred the way, but when I said I was foreign press he began taking us on a tour. 'It's very good that you're here,' he said, and marched us over to a patch of grass. 'Here's the pool of blood where an old woman died.'

He pointed at the stain, blue-ish now and fading into the mud. 'Those are her glasses.' He pointed again. I crouched to look. Black frames. Covered in blood.

There was something odd about one of the vehicles parked outside the flats – a minibus, half the windows blown out. I went over and peered at the writing on the side. It was British, from the NHS. 'North East Ambulance Service', I read aloud, giving Steve a quizzical look. All the way from Tyneside . . .

Inside one of the stairways of the block, more blood was streaked down the wall, pooled on the landing. We began knocking on doors. Eventually one opened; it was half off its hinges anyway. The owner showed us around for a few minutes. The place was full of broken glass, broken furniture. His enormous grey cat had been hiding in the cupboard when it happened, so there was no harm done really, he said, remarkably casual about it all. But yes, he added, he might think about leaving now. He had a daughter, after all.

Round the back of one block, in a little play park, I found a group of people, kids rushing around laughing like kids do, the women talking quietly, or sitting in numb shock. I spoke to a woman with bright orange hair and pale blue eyes, and a bloody cut on her chin. Victoria.

'It was terrifying,' she kept saying, 'terrifying, terrifying.' She stooped to pick up her big cat, stroking its rich brown fur as she talked; it seemed to help. They'd been inside, a ceiling had come down, everything was explosions and fire and confusion. Her daughter lived on the first floor, son-in-law on the ground floor, and she, Viktoria, on the second floor.

They'd escaped unharmed, but she couldn't stop thinking about how lucky that was, because only yesterday they'd all been out here in the spring sunshine. It had been her grandson's birthday. All the kids from the block played together. The missiles could have struck then. They could all have been killed. She pressed a shaking hand to her mouth, unable to speak. I thanked her, put a hand on her arm. I looked around and saw the children had gathered up some shrapnel, dull grey twists of rocket casing, and made a little pile of it, right next to their climbing frame.

There was only time, once back in Kharkiv, to write the article and pack. I didn't take everything with me. I couldn't, physically. But it was also a sort of guarantee, that Co-op supermarket bag that I left behind, stuffed with my thick winter coat and scarf, my Celox quick-clotting bandages and tourniquets. It was a promise to come back soon, made as much to myself as to anyone else. Part of me just wanted to stay. I'd been saying to friends, half in jest, that visa-wise this was the only bit of Europe I could live in: the Ukrainian government was allowing accredited journalists to stay. I was really considering it. I had so much to learn, particularly about Donetsk, and the best place to learn was right here.

But people were waiting for me, and I had to go. It was a long journey as usual, via Lviv where I stayed with friends in the suburbs, where I had a glorious evening of cognac and silliness and songs and forgetting, but the next day was sleet-cold hungover reality: eleven hours in a car with six strangers to Krakow.

During the drive, terrible news just kept coming. Anton, a musician known to all my friends in Kharkiv, a talented sculptor, a father of three little girls, had been killed at the front.

Then the next message came, from Tomas, the Czech soldier. He had been wounded, he was in hospital in Kramatorsk; would I come? And I wasn't there. I cursed my timing, cursed the war, cursed everything. To my embarrassment I realised I was crying, caught by a wave of emotion that felt like a body blow, a powerlessness that made me want to scream a year's worth of anger. I tried to cover it with a cough, tried to look out the window and distract myself, but it was dark already, nearly midnight, only a few cars speeding past on the Polish motorway, their headlights running in the rivulets of rain on the glass, and Ukraine already many miles behind me.

In the weeks that followed, rattling around the UK unsettled and uneasy, I kept thinking back to Kyiv, some time in spring 2023, that strange spring, people emerging from the awful dark winter, proud that they'd withstood everything that had been thrown at them, the Shahed drones and the power cuts, the cold and the candles. But there had been a sense of resignation, of facing a long struggle. No giddy hope here. The sea of little flags on Independence Square, a sea which grew with each death at the front, had been surrounded by silent figures, heads bowed, a permanent shifting funeral in the city's heart.

'I believe strongly that this is our last chance,' the judge and army volunteer Oleh Fedorov had said, as we sat opposite each other in a cafe in the centre of the city. When we'd first met, in that bunker in Kharkiv, he'd been in uniform. 'It's our last chance to become really free,' he continued. 'To become really independent from them. If we don't win now, Ukraine will never exist again. It will be destroyed. It will become part of Russia.'

All those years of Russian interference, he went on, had been done behind a mask. Now that mask was gone – so at least the way ahead was clear. Just terribly hard. His son, who'd been with him in Kharkiv when we first met, was nearly eighteen now. He wanted to join the army, too. Fedorov had already lost many, many close friends. He knew the price.

'We understand this is the war for our lives,' he said quietly.

'Our crazy, crazy neighbours want us to be dead, and we want to live; we don't have a choice.'

It had been a bright day, and an intense blue dusk now filled the sky. As I went past one of the entrances to the Teatralna metro station, I caught a strain of music. An accordion. I can't resist an accordion. I skipped down the shallow marble steps, leaving the darkening city behind me, down into the electric light of the underpass. I could hear excited whoops and shouts now, the jangly rhythm of a tambourine, and I rounded the corner to find the most amazing scene. Under the low concrete ceiling, to fast, joyous tunes, a crowd of people was dancing, stamping and cheering. Mums with their young children, young women in office clothes, old ladies in felt berets and quilted coats, old gents in flat caps and fur-lined shapkas. My heart, for some reason, was racing – delight, surprise, I don't know. I hovered at the edge, taking photos as unobtrusively as I could, concentrating hard on getting one couple sharp in focus, the light so low I had the lens wide open, but I captured them: a perfect picture. Their hands are clasped together in a ballroom hold, and they're looking into each other's eyes, waltzing slowly in their own world, as if no one else exists. The single fluorescent light above casts a pool around them, everyone else in darkness. I cannot describe the expression on their faces: perhaps something to do with knowing another person deeply. There is contentment there, and pride, too. It is beautiful.

A woman with long sleek black hair flowing around her threw her hands out, ecstatic, her eyes closed; she too was lost in her world. People watched the woman with admiration; she moved elegantly. I put my bags down against the brick wall, and a man with a neat grey beard and a plaid shirt held his hand out with a little chivalrous bow. We waltzed a little, smiling at each other, then the music changed, faster, a polka, and the underpass filled with happy shouts and cheers. The accordionist, his fingers a blur on the keys, threw back his head, shouting encouragement to the dancers thronging around him.

My partner leaned in to say that I danced well, and I told him that we dance a lot in Shetland, that we start early. 'I'll show you!' I said, a bit intoxicated by the whole thing, and did the backstep, a sort of on-the-spot threading of the feet I'd learned as a child at Fair Isle dances. It met with approval, but it's hard to keep up for long. Short of breath and laughing, I drew back from the giddy crowd, thanking the man, who was, himself, an excellent dancer. The accordionist was trying to bring things to an end, but the crowd wouldn't let him, cheering for more, and it all struck up again as I picked up my bag to leave. This is a weekly occurrence, the man told me, something to keep the spirits up. Make sure you come back, next time you're in Kyiv?

I will, I said, sincerely. Soon.

EPILOGUE

TWO EXTRAORDINARY WOMEN I describe in this book are now dead. One made a deep impression on me despite us barely exchanging a word: Vlada Chernykh, call sign 'Aïda'. Drone pilot, crack shot, medic, and brilliant PhD student, she was 28 when she was killed in artillery fire near Bakhmut, just weeks after I spent the day with her small drone team from the Khartia brigade.

The Ria Lounge pizza restaurant in Kramatorsk, frequented by journalists, aid workers and military personnel, was destroyed in a missile strike at the end of June 2023. I was worried, when I heard the news, that some colleagues could have been inside. But I never thought it would be Victoria Amelina.

We'd planned to go to Kramatorsk together, and it didn't work out, but I'd assumed – oh, such stupid optimism we have about the future – that we'd have ample opportunity for our future trips. That promised tour of Scotland, Ireland perhaps. 'After'. But there would not be an after; she died of her injuries several days after the strike. She was 37. Please – read her novels, her war diary, her beautiful poems, the legacy she left us.

ACKNOWLEDGEMENTS

A GRANT FROM CREATIVE Scotland made it possible for me to write this book, in Shetland, in autumn 2023. In Ukraine, I received support from the Rory Peck Trust, the Committee to Protect Journalists, Women in Journalism Scotland and the Edinburgh Freelance Branch of the NUJ.

The very long absences from home, the long spells of sofa-hopping, and, in general, throwing myself into the unknown only worked out because of the hospitality, advice and kindness of so many people. In Ukraine: Ivanna Skyba-Yakubova, Nataliya Zubar, Alla Shakhova, Maksym Bespalov, Marta Znak, Kateryna Mikhalitsyna, Charles Bonds, Nazar Kuzma, Mykahilo Sharkov, Rostislav Djurinskii, Tetyana Oharkova, Volodymyr Yermolenko, Victoria Amelina, Roman Danilenkov, Olena Ihnatenko, Sofia Cheliak, Natalia Kurdiukova, Dmitriy Kotlyarov and his parents Nikolai and Lyubov, Vlad Maslov, Kristina Berdynskykh, Euan MacDonald, Zarina Zabrisky, Paraic O'Brien, Clara Marchaud, Bennett Murray, Quentin Sommerville.

In Romania: Elena Mera Long, Marian and Mihaela Machedon – and Costi, of course.

In the UK and elsewhere: Rachel Eunson, Isobel Mitchell, Paul Goddard, Miriam Brett, Calum Forbes, Marion and Alan Ockendon, Hannah, Anne and John Bateson, Lesley and Jonathan Wills, Karen Smith, Jean Urquhart, Charlotte Wrigley, Roseanne Watt, Stuart Thomson, Pauline Moncrieff, Charlotte Beattie, Matthew Wright, Suzi Compton, Aurora Adams, Patrick and Isabel Gregory, David Patrikarakos, Daria Plakhova,

Andrew Monaghan, Peter Geoghegan, Matthew Zajac, Neal
Ascherson, Heidi Pett, Amanda Coakley, Torcuil Crichton, Jim
Benstead, all the Ramsdens, Carolyn and Gemma Scott-Bruce,
Marta Giannella, Sharon Staunton, Joseph Ritchie, Matthew
Haughton, Phil Barnard, Cath Ness, Daniel Devoy, Susanna
Macdonald, Peter Vann, Áine Molloy and all the Sandy Bell's
family, Steve Taylor, Inge Thomson and Martin Green, Thomas
Green, Craig Williams, Anna Burnside, Daniel Bennett, Chris
Foote, Kenneth Macdonald, Ewan Gibbs, Mark Fisher, Joyce
McMillan, Martin and Kay Shipton, Christie Williamson, James
Jackson, Sebastien Ash, Chris Stout, Jean and John Ross, Jock
Urquhart, Lesley Riddoch, Mags Binns, Andrew Rossetter,
Lesley and Liam Holmes, Maxwell MacLeod, Paul Casciato,
Angus Bancroft, Richard Freeman, Rebecca Curran, Jonathan
Littell, Shaun Bythell, Dani Garavelli, Colin Hattersley,
Maureen Michie, Michele Berdy, Friedrich Moser, Lidiia
Akryshora, and Nicky Peters. And everyone – past and present
– in Fair Isle, the place that made me.

Thank you to all at Polygon/Birlinn, who welcomed me
so warmly, to Edward Crossan for his diligent work, to my
agent Jenny Brown for her unfailing support. While reporting
in Ukraine I had two editors in particular who deserve huge
thanks: Tim Knowles at the *Sunday Post* and Brian Lindsay at
BBC Radio Scotland. So many former colleagues at Pacific
Quay and Pitt Lane were incredibly supportive throughout; it
meant so much.

To those who read the drafts, putting in so many hours and giving
me such encouragement and brilliant feedback, I don't know how
to thank you enough: Chris Silver, Nik Williams, Aoife Keenan,
Hannah Bateson, Robert Alan Jamieson, Hannah Livingston.

Lastly, thanks to my dad Michael, granny Margaret, brother Magnus, and sister Freya Stout. They have supported me at every turn despite the worry I've caused them by going to cover a war. I wish I could have told Cathy about everything I've seen, the people I've met. Mum, you're such a miss.